S0-AIY-452

SOME OF THE BOOKS BY WALTER B. GIBSON

The Complete Illustrated Book of the Psychic Sciences (with Litzka R. Gibson)
Hoyle's Simplified Guide to the Popular Card Games
Family Games America Plays
How to Win at Solitaire
Hoyle's Reference Crammer
Stories from the Twilight Zone
The Twilight Zone Revisited
The Science of Numerology
First Principles of Astrology
The Magic Square
Guide to Knots
Guide to Papercraft
The Fine Art of Murder
The Fine Art of Spying
The Fine Art of Robbery
The Fine Art of Swindling
The Key to Yoga
Brain Tests
Hypnotism through the Ages
How to Develop an Exceptional Memory
The Book of Secrets
The World's Best Book of Magic
Popular Card Tricks
The Magicians' Manual
Thurston's 200 Tricks You Can Do
Thurston's 200 More Tricks You Can Do
Blackstone's Secrets of Magic
Blackstone's Modern Card Tricks
Blackstone's Tricks Anyone Can Do
Magic Explained
Professional Magic for Amateurs
What's New in Magic
Magic Made Simple
Houdini's Escapes
Houdini's Magic

SOME OF THE BOOKS BY LITZKA R. GIBSON

How to Read Palms
Lessons in Palmistry
Care of the Hair and Hairdos
*Latin American Dances
*Dancing for All Occasions

*Under the pen name of Leona Lehman

The Complete
Illustrated Book
of Divination
and Prophecy

The Complete
Illustrated Book of
Divination
and Prophecy

BY WALTER B. GIBSON

AND LITZKA R. GIBSON

DRAWINGS BY MURRAY KESHNER

DOUBLEDAY & COMPANY, INC.

GARDEN CITY, NEW YORK

1973

ISBN: 0-385-03599-3
Library of Congress Catalog Card Number 71-103748
Copyright © 1973 by Walter B. Gibson
All Rights Reserved
Printed in the United States of America

The Mounts of the Palm through *The Plain of Mars,* pages 277–283 from
The Complete Illustrated Book of the Psychic Sciences, Copyright © 1966 by
Walter B. Gibson

Preface

From time immemorial, people have been gripped by the continued desire to know just what the future holds in store. As a result, they have devised and tested many methods of divination ranging from the absurdly simple to the utterly complex. Today, luck and chance play greater parts than ever, if there are such things as luck and chance. Right now, the stock market may be rising or falling, bringing someone fortune or ruin; thousands of dollars may be riding on the turn of a card or the spin of a wheel; letters now being written may mean anything from a fleeting romance to the fate of nations. Hence it is not surprising that the art of divination is more in vogue than ever before.

There are actually three ways whereby the future can be foretold to an appreciable degree. One is by basing an over-all prognostication on the law of averages. Its immutability can be proven by feeding a limited number of half dollars into slot machines at Las Vegas and continuing the process over and over. Anyone who refuses to quit will lose them all, sooner or later; otherwise, the gambling casinos would go out of business.

Another positive method is through forecasts. Anyone living in New England can predict that there will be snow during the coming winter, because there never has been a New England winter without snow. The questions of how much snow and the exact dates on which it will fall may prove more difficult to forecast; but here, again, there may be contributory factors that, if properly observed and understood, may lead to a sure-fire result.

The newest method is precognition, a form of extrasensory perception. Although ESP itself may still be unproven, it is a factor to consider. If you become aware that something is due to happen and it does, if that happens often enough, you will find yourself believing in ESP whether or not you can prove that there is such a thing.

This has roused new interest in all psychic subjects from astrology to yoga, which the authors covered in their previous work *The Complete Illustrated Book of the Psychic Sciences,* showing how such subjects served as guides to personal traits and actions. In addition, various modes of divination were discussed, particularly cartomancy, where a presumably chance layout of cards could serve as a stimulus for precognition.

The interest thus roused compelled the authors to produce a companion volume covering the divinatory field in full. All the material is new, including cartomancy, which covers interpretations of the tarot and the thirty-two-card pack, neither of which was detailed in the previous work. Also included are newer readings with the fifty-two-card pack.

There is no guarantee as to the efficacy of these methods. They have been chosen solely because they are interesting, intriguing, traditional, and, above all, entertaining. Those that are obviously pastimes should be treated accordingly. If any should encourage the reader to precognitive efforts, they should be worth while, if only for intellectual survey.

A Glossary of Methods of Divination at the conclusion of this volume includes a variety of divinations that did not quite make it but might have.

Contents

The Complete
Illustrated Book
of Divination
and Prophecy

I. Various Forms of Divination

ALECTRYOMANCY

This interesting type of divination has been attributed to the famous philospher Iamblichus, who died about the year 330, after restoring various mystic rites dating back to the times of the ancient oracles. His followers did quite well until Valens became Roman Emperor of the East and began a campaign to stamp out oracles, soothsayers, astrologers, and even philosophers, since their trend was to favor those practitioners of the mystic arts.

As the campaign gathered momentum, the threatened seers met in secret conclave and decided to chart their own course through their divinatory devices. Since all were followers of Iamblichus, they chose his favorite method, alectryomancy, for this purpose. According to reliable accounts, a large circle was traced on the ground and divided into sections bearing the letters of the Greek alphabet. Grains of wheat were sprinkled on the letters and a white rooster was placed in the center of the mystic circle. From then on, the sponsoring seers watched intently while the inspired fowl moved from one letter to another, spelling out a message as it pecked at the grains. That message was interpreted as the answer to the question mutally chosen by the onlooking seers.

The mere conditions of this divinatory process made it all but impossible to obtain results without the aid of some outside influence, whether supernatural or simply human. The rooster, acting on its own, would ordinarily approach a random letter, devour the grain, and then proceed around the circle until it had its fill. If it deviated from that course, going hither and yon about the circle, it could logically be assumed that some psychic factor had come to the fore.

Probably the bird was brought back to the center of the ring after pecking the grain from one letter, so as to be given a fresh start for the next. This would have allowed time for more grain to be placed on the original letter, so that it could be repeated. Otherwise combinations like a double E would have been impossible.

At that, there must have been many false starts where the first few letters failed to make sense. To allow for that, an elaborate preliminary ritual was required to put alectryomancy to the test. Any failure could then be attributed to some flaw in the initial ceremony, so that the only remedy would be to try again. That, of course, could go on and on until the rooster finally pecked out enough letters to make partial sense. That was the way with most oracles; they had a habit of coming through with just enough information to make them right no matter what turned out.

In the case of the Emperor Valens, the savants who resorted to alectryomancy were cautious in their query. They were twenty-four in all, and, suspecting that there might be a spy in their midst, they did not inquire directly about the emperor's fate, but simply asked the name of the person who would succeed Valens on the throne. There is no record of how many trials were made, but there may have been a lot, because the most the rooster could produce were the Greek letters theta, epsilon, omicron, delta, corresponding to TH-E-O-D in the modern English alphabet.

Naturally, the inquiring philosophers had an ulterior motive; namely to curry favor with the future ruler whose name they had divined, so they would be better off when he succeeded Valens. Their plan boomeranged, however, for when Valens learned of the meeting through his spies, he treated the whole thing as a conspiracy to stir up a revolt against him and put someone in his place.

To prevent that, the emperor ordered the immediate execution of the man most likely to be designated by the mystic letters T-H-E-O-D. This happened to be the court favorite, whose name was Theodorus and who was probably the very man that the philosophers hoped to win over to their cause. But Valens did not stop with that; to make sure that he had picked the right man, he went after every Theodorus he could find, then extended the slaughter to other unfortunates whose names began with the fatal letters. That really swelled the list, for such names as Theodore, Theodorite, Theodosite, Theodote, and Theodule were common around Constantinople in the year 375, at least until Valens obliterated them.

Seers and philosophers came in for wholesale persecution too, but the T-H-E-O-D prediction still kept cropping up, until Valens, at his wit's end, decided that he had been after the wrong man all along.

Valens' young nephew, Gratian, had just become Roman Emperor of the West, backed by the efforts of a very capable general named Theodosius. Gripped by the notion that Theodosius was meant by the oracle, Valens trumped up charges of treason against the loyal general and induced Gratian's advisers to have him executed at Carthage, where he had just completed a successful campaign in Gratian's behalf.

With Theodosius out of the way, Valens was confident that any threat to his reign had been eliminated. Two years later, he boldly attacked an invading horde of Visigoths without waiting for Gratian to arrive with reinforcements, which he deemed unnecessary. Valens was killed in the battle, his army was overwhelmed, and only Gratian's arrival saved the Eastern Empire from utter confusion. Immediately, Gratian realized that a strong arm was needed, and he recalled that Theodosius had a son by the same name who had fled to Spain after his father's execution. Summoning the younger Theodosius from exile, Gratian appointed him as Emperor of the East, and he became known to history as Theodosius the Great.

Thus the prophecy gained through alectryomancy was fulfilled, for Valens actually was succeeded by an emperor whose name began with the letters T-H-E-O-D and whose very existence Valens had either overlooked or had regarded as too trifling to cause him any worry. But the Emperor Theodosius showed neither awe nor gratitude toward those who had predicted his rise to power. More probably, he held them responsible for the cruel fate that had overtaken his illustrious father, for he stamped out ancient forms of divination more relentlessly than Valens had.

In later centuries, alectryomancy was revived along with other ancient divinatory arts, and mention is made of it by various writers of the Middle Ages. In the course of time, it underwent many minor changes. Among its most striking offshoots, gyromancy was a standout. Or perhaps it should be termed a dropout, for it utilized a much larger lettered circle about which the soothsayers personally tramped in endless procession.

That is, endless until they began stumbling or falling by the wayside. Then sharp-eyed observers noted the letters where the participants faltered and spelled out words, just as with the rooster and the wheat grains. Instinct was responsible in both cases. With alectryomancy, the rooster was hungry; with gyromancy, the people were giddy. That left them both in the laps of the gods—or did it?

With alectryomancy, the hungry roosters could have taken cues from the soothsayer, who might have turned them toward the proper letters or placed the grain closer, to catch their eyes more quickly. With gyromancy, the human subject could have responded to a gesture calling for a stumble at the right time. Either way, the soothsayers could have kept complete control, even though their system did backfire when they spelled out T-H-E-O-D, and then they decided that it was time to quit.

To give alectryomancy a proper test, we must leave it strictly to chance, in the hope that some unseen power will take over and guide the instrument involved, whether it be a hungry rooster or a staggering human. But once we admit the existence of the unknown factor, any instrument may be employed.

One good method is:

DIVINATION BY ROULETTE

The device used is a miniature roulette wheel; these come in various sizes and are obtainable at novelty stores or hobby shops. They have thirty-eight sections, numbered irregularly from 1 to 36 and with two marked respectively o and oo, situated opposite each other. For divination purposes, an ideal wheel should bear letters of the alphabet instead of numbers, with figures 1 to o, with the two extra "pockets" labeled "Yes" and "No." But any wheel can be used just as well by utilizing the accompanying chart:

1	2	3	4	5	6	7	8	9	10
1	2	2	4	6	6	7	8	9	o

11	12	13	14	15	16	17	18	19	20
A	B	C	D	E	F	G	H	I	J

21	22	23	24	25	26	27	28	29	30
K	L	M	N	O	P	Q	R	S	T

31	32	33	34	35	36
U	V	W	X	Y	Z

o	oo
Yes	No

The procedure is as follows: First, ask a question, preferably the sort that can be answered by a single word, such as the name of a person, place, thing, or action. Then spin the roulette wheel and drop a small ball (supplied with the wheel) on the wheel while it is revolving and check the section in which the ball lies when the wheel stops.

Note the letter, according to the chart, spin the wheel again, and note the next letter, continuing thus until the answer is spelled out. If you are definitely after a word, ignore any figures (1 to o) in which the ball drops and spin again. Do the same with the sections representing "Yes" and "No" unless the question can be answered in the affirmative or the negative.

Some questions can be answered by numbers instead of words; in such cases, you ignore the letters and keep track of the figures instead. Here, again, "Yes" and "No" may sometimes be taken into account. As a good example, one man, testing the divinatory wheel for the first time, put the always popular question: "Which race should I play today?"

It so happened that he was going to the track that afternoon and that ten races were slated, so that the first figure that the wheel delivered could be acceptable (counting 10 as ten, rather than zero). He had already chosen several possible winners but didn't feel sure of any, so he felt that it would be best to bet his modest bundle on a single race. He didn't have to wait long for an answer. With the first spin, the ball dropped into the double zero (oo) registering an emphatic "No." He took that to mean not to bet at all, so he held onto his money, and wisely. Not one of the horses he had picked came through.

In spinning for words instead of numbers, you can hit snags from the very start. A string of letters like P-V-I-W-R-H-C-C would probably have stumped all twenty-four ancient seers who strained so hard to get as far as T-H-E-O-D before giving up, to their later regret. In that case, the best plan is to start all over, concentrating more strongly on the question.

As an example, one questioner asked: "What should I do now?" He'd gotten as far as B-W-Q-Q-G, when he realized that he wasn't giving it proper attention, so he fixed his mind on things he might be doing, such as getting to work, making a phone call to his broker, taking the car to be fixed, and so on. He began a new series, and the first two spins brought the letters T-V. Since that was short for "television," he turned on his set and to his surprise tuned in on a special newscast telling of an important shake-up in a foreign government. The questioner had his answer, then and there. He got on the phone in time to tell his broker to sell certain threatened stocks before the market dropped.

THE DIVINING DIAL

Instead of using a roulette wheel, you can make a simple dial on a square of thick cardboard, mixing the letters of the alphabet in the form of a circle. In this case, figures can be omitted, as well as the words "Yes" and "No," getting back to the original layout recommended by Iamblichus. From the same cardboard, cut a narrow strip, pointed at one end, so it will serve as an arrow. Push a half-inch wire nail up through the center of the dial and then through the arrow, making it loose enough to spin freely.

By simply spinning the arrow and noting the letters to which it points, you can list them exactly as with the wheel. The operation is much faster, since you are dealing with letters only and the spin is much shorter. Again, you can begin over after a false or meaningless start, but by watching for abbreviations or initials, answers may occasionally fall in line.

Adding or eliminating letters is also allowable if the rest make sense as a result. Always, Q can be accepted as "QU," since in regular spelling Q is usually followed by U. The letters T-W-N could be interpreted as "town," or L-N-R for "Eleanor" if the message could logically concern someone of that name.

One casual questioner dialed the letters Z-L-B-I-N-B-F-D—and decided to give up, as the word "BIN" had no special significance. But shortening it to "IN" produced Z-L-B IN B-F-D. The questioner knew nobody with either set of initials but recalled that the town of Bedford was not far away, so the B-F-D might refer to it. But who was Z-L-B? The best thing was to drop the "Z" and decide what "L-B" could signify. It was the abbreviation for "pound," but that didn't help, so the questioner began running through words that started with "L" and contained "B," promptly hitting on the word "library."

That sprang to mind because only recently the questioner had looked for an important book in the local library but found that they didn't have it. Since he was driving over Bedford way, he decided to look for it there, though Bedford was a much smaller town with a very small library. Imagine his surprise when he found that the Bedford Library did have the very book he wanted. He never did find out what the "Z" stood for, but he is still sold on the science of alectryomancy.

ANAGRAMMATIC DIVINATION

This could very well be titled "anagramalectryomancy," for that is exactly what it is, but the shorter term of "anagrammatic divination" is preferable, as it is more understandable. Either way, it adds up the same. Whatever the method of picking letters one by one, the law of averages must be considered. You can't count on the Hand of Fate to be agreeable when it comes to adding a few extra vowels to express a simple thought.

To be agreeable, it might simply pick GRBL, which might be interpreted as "Garble," which would be unfortunate; or better, as

"Grable," which would be agreeable in itself. Yet, even better, the Hand of Fate or the Law of Averages—whichever you believe in, though many people insist that they are one and the same—should have the privilege of spelling it out in full.

To do that, we introduce the table of "letter frequencies," which apparently was utterly unknown to the ancients but which is common knowledge to us moderns. This requires a set of anagram cards or tiles, which manufacturers supply in varying quantities or proportions, the following totals being typical (figures indicate quantity of each letter):

A—15; B—4; C—6; D—8; E—20; F—5; G—4; H—10; I—12; J—2; K—2; L—8; M—5; N—15; O—15; P—4; Q—2; R—15; S—12; T—15; U—8; V—4; W—4; X—2; Y—5; Z—2.

This comprises a set of two hundred letters, which can be written out on slips of paper or squares of cardboard if need be, though the manufactured sets are preferable and easier to handle. Since there are at least two of every letter, it is possible to spell out full words, including double letters; but don't be too optimistic on that score. You may get too many doubles, like three or four E's in a row, or a string of assorted vowels with no consonants to break the monotony. So some weeding out may be needed.

The procedure is to shuffle the cards or mix the tiles face down, then deal or draw them, one by one, turning each face up to form a word in the order drawn. As usual, allowance can be made for missing letters, others can be eliminated, Q can be accepted as QU, and any abbreviations may be acceptable.

Best of all, some letter combinations can be treated as anagrams, being turned into words through simple rearrangement. In one case, a questioner asked: "Whom should I invite to the party?" and the lettered tiles spelled out L-R-A-O-C. That was enough. One of the girls the questioner had in mind was named Carol, which was composed of those very letters.

In another case, a man wanted to recommend someone for a special job, so he tried the anagram method to obtain a suitable name. The letters E-H-B-R-T turned up, and he wondered whether it indicated Herbert or Hubert, as he had a friend by each name. So he tried another letter and it proved to be "O," leaving the answer still in doubt. The next letter that came up was "R," which was in Herbert's favor, since the row now stood:

E-H-B-R-T-O-R

But the "O" still bothered the questioner, and he felt he should turn up another letter on the chance that a "U" would swing the choice back to Hubert. But as he checked the letters again, he noted that if he eliminated the "H," he would have Robert, the name of another friend, completed before he added the second "R." That left him in such a quandary that he felt a further check was due, and he found to his amazement that the letters as they now stood spelled the word "brother."

Now it happened that the questioner had a brother, but he hadn't considered him in connection with the job because he had been running through his list of friends. He contacted his brother, found he would be interested in just such a job, and recommended him accordingly. The brother's name happened to be William, and not one of its letters appeared in the final message.

This simply proves that since alectryomancy has always been enigmatic, it has a right to be anagrammatic as well. But in many cases it may produce mostly gibberish, time after time, until you find a string of letters that lend themselves to some sort of interpretation. When that occurs, the usual rule is to take whichever answer hits the highest percentage of correct letters; as in the case of "brother" over the names involved. But even that is not infallible. You can still go wrong, as the Emperor Valens did.

Perhaps the best way to put it to the test is to use a specific event involving a stated number of names, the more limited the better. One man tried it on the day of a Kentucky Derby, in the presence of a reliable witness, and came up with the following letter sequence:

J E B P C D N C N I P A E R T M S C

Among the horses entered for that particular derby was Rae Jet, whose name looked promising because of the first two letters, J-E. From there on, Rae Jet was a lost cause until the twelfth letter, when suddenly the rest of the letters came up in quick succession, which made Rae Jet look like the winner; but not quite.

The questioner had kept turning up letters because the original pair, J-E, also figured in the name of another horse that was entered in the derby, Majestic Prince. Except for the third letter, "B," and the sixth letter, "D," all those that followed were found in the name "Majestic Prince," which was encouraging indeed, and the fact that P, C, N were all repeated only emphasized them more. Then, when A, E, R, T, M, S put in a rapid appearance, the name Majestic Prince was practically spelled out in full, needing only an extra "I." In all, sixteen of the eighteen letters in the row could be used for the final choice: MAJESTIC PR-NCE.

Naturally, Majestic Prince won the derby. Rae Jet, whose score was only six of the first fifteen letters, finished far behind. At that, Majestic Prince had trouble, barely nosing out a horse named Arts and Letters. If you wonder why, just study the last seven letters in the row and you will find that four of them spell A-R-T-S in regular order, indicating that Arts and Letters would be in there at the finish, which Arts and Letters was.

All of which means to try it for yourself and form your own interpretations, if any. Remember that all oracular divinations may be two-edged; sometimes, instead of telling you which path to choose, they name the one you should avoid. So you should give alectryomancy a few preliminary tests to find out whether you rate as a winner or a loser where that ancient psychic science is concerned. Once you are sure of your rating, you should be able to proceed with sheer abandon.

BUTTON DIVINATION

This is a modern form of an older divinatory process performed with two pearls, one white, the other black; and seven tiny sea shells, which were shaken in a large sieve, seven times, and then studied and interpreted according to their positions and whether or not the shells were inverted.

Since none of the items named are readily available today, buttons can be used instead. Two fairly large buttons—one white, the other black—serve for pearls. Nine small buttons (instead of only seven) are used as shells. These small buttons should be of a common type; slightly hollow on one side, slightly humped on the other, so that when shaken about, they may land either way.

Instead of a sieve, the buttons can be placed in a small cup, shaken about, then poured onto a table. Or they may be held between the cupped hands, which are shaken and then opened, letting the buttons fall and scatter. Positions of the small buttons are noted in relation to the large "marker" buttons. Whichever marker has the majority of small buttons closest to it is used—along with those buttons—for divination purposes.

For example: If five of the nine buttons are closer to the white marker than to the black marker, those five are retained, along with the white marker. The same applies if six, seven, eight, or all nine are closer to the white than the black. The black marker and the buttons closest to it would simply be disregarded. If the black marker should have a majority of buttons within its range, the white marker and its minority would be disregarded.

Next, a study is made of the buttons that have been retained, to see whether the majority have their hollow sides or humped sides upward. Here, again, the majority are retained and the rest rejected. But the majority must consist of four buttons or more; otherwise, all are rejected and the entire lot must be shaken for another trial, or the divination itself regarded as uncertain.

For example: If six buttons fall near the white marker and either four, five, or six have hollows up, they would be interpreted accordingly. If three were hollows up and three were humps up, there would be no interpretation.

If five buttons fall near the black marker, and either four or five have humped sides up, they would be interpreted accordingly. If only three show humps, none count. In a case like this, it might be that the four buttons near the white marker would be all alike (either humps or hollows) but they would still be rejected, because it takes five buttons to make a majority.

The interpretations that follow may be applied in a general way or toward some specific enterprise or desire that a person may express:

Majority nearest the white marker
Four or more with hollow sides up:

Health, wealth, and happiness over a continued and possibly prolonged period. Love, business, friendship all show promise if given due attention.

Four or more with humped sides up:

Interrupted happiness and temporary setbacks. You can win out if you persevere and seek new fields and friends if necessary. Self-confidence will solve your problems.

Majority nearest the black marker:
Four or more with hollow sides up:

Unexpected good fortune may await you, so count on luck if effort fails. Your troubles may be frequent but small. Worry is your one real enemy, so avoid it. Look for a rainbow.

Four or more with humped sides up:

7900

A token of bad luck. If failure confronts you, it may be better to start over, rather than try to patch things up. This relates to business more than love or friendship, but if those are intermingled, matters may be that much worse.

If five or more buttons form a well-defined cross, the following significations may be added:

Nearest the white marker: Four or more with *hollow sides up* mean interrupted happiness; how severe, time alone will tell. Four or more with *humped sides up*, something you have done or planned to do may cause you deep regret, so avoid it if you still can.

Nearest the black marker: Four or more with *hollow sides up* indicate that whatever luck is due you should come very soon. Four or more with *humped sides up* mean that if luck does come your way, don't take it for granted. Something else may nullify it.

If five or more buttons form a well-defined circle, the following significations may be added:

Nearest the white marker: Four or more with *hollow sides up* indicate that you may receive valuable gifts or a sum of money. Four or more with *humped sides up* are travel tokens, signifying a pleasant journey or a welcome visitor.

Nearest the black marker: Four or more with *hollow sides up*, anything that you are counting on may prove disappointing or not worth the trouble involved. Four or more with *humped sides up* mean that a coming trip may be dangerous or unprofitable and therefore something to be avoided.

If eight of the small buttons happen to fall nearest to one marker, there is a chance that four may show hollows and the other four humps. In that case, they cancel each other and the buttons should be shaken again. Otherwise, the majority rules as usual.

This form of divination combines the elements of astragalomancy, in which words were spelled from lettered bones that were tossed at random, along with the rarer practice of margaritomancy, where pearls jumped about magically beneath an inverted pot, thereby delivering a message. No record was left telling just how that was done, so modern seers will have to be content with the method that we have just described.

MYSTIC CABALA
Based on the Rule of Nine

The predictive power of numbers as applied to individuals is evidenced by the events of the Trojan War, which dates back to approximately 1200 B.C. The rule applying to that period was simply that, in any form of contest or dispute, whoever or whichever came up with the name containing the most letters was sure to triumph.

Thus GREEKS versus TROJANS seemingly gave the latter a rather slight edge of 7 letters to 6; but the Greeks called themselves HELLENES and thereby gained an 8-to-7 advantage. Taking the names of the nations, GREECE wins over TROY by 6 to 4; or, using the ancient names of HELLAS and ILION, the score is 6 to 5. In individual names, the Greek leader, AGAMEMNON stood 9 to 5 over PRIAM, the Trojan king, while the victory of ACHILLES over HECTOR was assured by a count of 8 to 6.

The same tradition applies to the founding of ancient Rome; when strife arose between the twin brothers ROMULUS and REMUS, it was Romulus who triumphed by 7 letters to 5, thus fulfilling an omen that he was to become the real founder of the city that still bears his name.

Of course, this was too good to last. It probably reached a peak when ALEXANDER, King of Macedon—later known as Alexander the Great—conquered the world by outlettering every rival who opposed him. But from then on, long names and lengthy titles apparently were adopted in the hope that they would assure supremacy regardless of merit, or lack of it. But Fate couldn't be tempted that simply. ROME, with the shortest name of all, soon became the dominant nation of the era.

That led to the development of a truly cabalistic system, wherein special values were assigned to certain letters and whoever ran up the highest total became the winner. But long names still could help, especially if letters of higher values were purposely included in them. So that system, too, left much to be desired. The upshot was a unique cabala dependent, not on the size of the total, but on the remainder after that total is divided by the number 9, which has always been noted for its mystic qualities.

The advantage in this case is that everybody has an equal chance. While the values of the letters are apparently arbitrary, being attributed to an old manuscript discovered in the late 1700s, they form a balanced result, as experiment will prove. The procedure runs as follows:

First, add up the figures represented by a person's name in accordance with this table:

```
            A—13
B— 3   C—22  D—24  E—22
F— 3   G— 7  H— 6  I—20
J—10   K— 1  L—10  M—33
N—13   O— 8  P—16  Q— 7
R—13   S— 9  T— 1  U— 2
V— 9   W— 9  X— 6  Y— 6
            Z—1
```

Now, take a person's name and add up the figures; divide the total by 9 and note the remainder, as:

```
H— 6        C—22        M—33
E—22        A—13        A—13
N—13        R—13        D—24
R—13        O— 8        G— 7
Y— 6        L—10        E—22
─────       ─────       ─────
60÷9=6      66÷9=7      99÷9=10
Remainder of 6  Remainder of 3  Remainder of 9
```

When the division comes out equally as in the case of Madge, count it one unit less and take the additional 9 as a remainder (99÷9=10 with 9 as remainder, instead of 99÷9=11 with no remainder).

Having thus ascertained the individual numbers of two persons or more, you can prognosticate their chances in a contest according to the following table:

```
1 over 3, 5, 7, 9   4 over 1, 3, 6, 8   7 over 2, 4, 6, 9
2 over 1, 4, 6, 8   5 over 2, 4, 7, 9   8 over 1, 3, 5, 7
3 over 2, 5, 7, 9   6 over 1, 3, 5, 8   9 over 2, 4, 6, 8
```

This means, very obviously, that in any form of contest in which the participants have similar qualifications, Henry, with 6, should win when opposed to Carol, with 3. However, Carol, with 3, should win when opposed to Madge, with 9. Still, Madge, with 9, should win when opposed to Henry, with 6.

If two remainders come out the same, the issue is somewhat doubtful, but since the remainders have canceled each other out, you can revert to the older system of choosing the name with the higher (or highest) total. Since you have already divided it by 9 and have eliminated the remainder, you will be dealing with the quotient rather than the original total, but it amounts to practically the same thing. For example:

If CAROL with 66÷9=7 with a remainder of 3, should be opposed to BERT with 39÷9=4, with a remainder of 3, Carol would gain preference, as Carol's quotient, 7, is 3 points higher than Bert's quotient, 4.

Apply that rule as a tie breaker and you will find that it works out in the long run. But don't expect it to be infallible. Every system of divination is subject to human error. The great object is to reduce the percentage of failure and increase success proportionately. But don't hope to hit 100 per cent all the time. If you did that, there would be nothing to look forward to, and, even worse, that would put an end to all the fun.

THE FLOATING SLIP

In this form of sortilege, questions are written upon slips of paper, all about the same size. These are placed in a large bowl and water is poured into the bowl until it is nearly full. As the papers swirl about, they gradually rise to the surface and float there. The first to do so is removed and read; its message is accepted as the omen for the day.

This procedure is not always as simple as it sounds and therefore is subject to various modifications. The smaller the papers, the better, as they will have less tendency to stick together; therefore, instead of writing out the questions, it is preferable to make a list of them for reference and then number the slips accordingly, checking the floating slip later. The numbering should be done in pencil, as ink is apt to run.

Another problem is the tendency of the slips to rise so soon that it is hard to tell which is first and some may be blocked by others. To offset this, use paper that is somewhat porous, as pages from a cheap pad, or second sheets of typing paper. Immerse these in a small amount of water at the bottom of the bowl and let them soak until they sink.

Later, before filling the bowl with water, separate the slips sufficiently so they will not adhere to one another. Then, when the water is poured in from a pitcher or faucet, its swirl will spread the slips about and they will tend to rise, usually end upward. They should be watched until one finally floats absolutely flat; that slip is then accepted as the one whose prediction will be fulfilled.

As with all forms of divination, due allowance should be made for normal prospects. You just can't team up near impossibilities with almost certain facts and expect positive results. There is a wide margin between such questions as, "Will I make a million dollars?" and "Will I pass my driver's test?"—too wide, in fact, for them to be considered as part of the same sortilege.

One intriguing procedure with the floating slips is to list the horses in a coming race, or the runners in a track event, or the teams in a baseball or football league and see which floats first. This can be used to pick not only a winner, but a runner up as well. But this should be accepted only as an indication, not as an actual prognostication. Often there are races or contests in which certain contestants should never even be considered, as the chances are too much against them at the very start. If one of those slips should be the first to float, it should be accepted as a token that the contestant will probably do better than anticipated; nothing more.

According to some authorities, exactly thirteen slips should be used in the floating test; otherwise the spell will be broken. This, however, does not eliminate events in which there are less than thirteen participants. To conform to that proviso, simply add enough blank slips to bring the total up to thirteen. If a blank is the first to float, the outcome remains doubtful. The same applies to groups of personal questions. List those that have some likelihood of coming true, and add blanks to reach the required thirteen. But do this only if you find that the test has been failing badly when less than thirteen slips are used.

The floating slips may also be used to determine which of several important questions is most apt to come true or be answered in the affirmative. Here you simply write out things you hope for along with others that you may dread, to fill out a full list of thirteen. All should be kept within reasonable bounds, and where an outcome is highly doubtful, two opposing questions can be written out, as: "Will I pass tomorrow's exam?" and "Will I fail in the exam tomorrow?" If one comes up, the answer is "Yes." If some other question is answered, the doubt will still remain, so far as the exam is concerned.

PLUCK A DAISY

Among traditional methods of fortunetelling, the plucking of daisy petals is one of the most popular. Usually, it has a romantic motif: A young man, thinking of his sweetheart, plucks a daisy by chance and then plucks its petals, one by one, reciting, "She loves me—she loves me not—" and so on, the answer coming with the plucking of the final petal. Conversely, a girl can apply the rule to her boy friend, reciting, "He loves me—he loves me not—" until the last pluck tells.

This method can be applied to other matters as well, such as the outcome of a game, a business deal, or whatever question you may want answered, provided that it can be decided with a simple "Yes" or "No," the count being made in that manner. The more personal the subject,

1 and 2) Pluck-a-Daisy. Thirty-two daisies randomly placed on these pages, half of which have an even number of petals.

the better; and also the chances should be nearly equal, so the daisy will really be the deciding factor.

This fits with the theory on which many such auguries are based. The answer to the question may already be buried deep in the person's subconscious mind, but any attempt to rationalize it only turns it into pure guesswork. The plucking of a random daisy, being itself a subconscious act, is therefore attuned to the same circumstance. Whether the plucker gauges the petals as odd or even due to some psychic power of his own, or the hand of fate is the actual guiding force, the one thing that really counts is the result.

That leaves just one problem, the availability of daisies. The fact that they bloom only in the springtime, and then but briefly, is probably why they are usually consulted on the question of love alone, since love is in the air during that same season. Even at that, you generally have to go to the country to find daisies, which limits the field still more.

So to turn this form of divination into a year-round pastime covering any suitable well-balanced question that can be answered with a "Yes" or "No," we have provided a printed daisy patch. It consists of replicas of random daisies, numbered from 1 to 32, half having an even number of petals; the other half odd. All the consultant has to do is pick a daisy on sight, then count its petals and get the right answer, Yes or No.

THE PROPHETIC COIN

The coin used for this divination can be an ordinary penny, but it should be a fairly bright one, so that "heads" and "tails" can be easily distinguished from each other. In addition to the coin, you need nine cards, numbered from 1 to 9. Ordinary playing cards will do, but there are various games, like *rook* or *flinch*, which are played with numbered cards, so if any of those are available, all the better. In a pinch, cards can be cut from thick paper on thin cardboard and numbered on one side. In that case, they can be cut square, measuring about two and a half inches each way.

The divinatory procedure runs as follows:

Mix the nine cards and lay them on the table, numbered side down, so that they form three rows of three each, with the width of a penny between them. Now hold the penny about a foot above the table and drop it edgewise onto the center of the middle card. The penny will bounce and either settle on that card or roll onto another.

Note first whether the coin lies heads or tails. Then turn up the card beneath it, note the number, and refer to the accompanying table, which will supply appropriate advice pertaining to the immediate future.

If the coin should roll clear of the cards, try it again, until it lands on one. By giving the coin a slight spin when dropping it from between thumb and second finger, it may go in any direction and it will be less likely to settle on the middle card. But since the cards are mixed to start, a straight drop does not matter, as nobody knows the number on any card until it is turned up.

TABLE OF FORECASTS

CARD 1   *If Heads:* Whatever you want, now is a time to get it if you act independently and directly.

           If Tails: Don't let anybody talk you into doing something you don't want to do. They may be using you to their advantage.

CARD 2   *If Heads:* Start giving advice instead of taking it. A real opportunity may be awaiting your decision right now.

           If Tails: Curb your urge to help the underdogs. Their bites may be worse than their barks, and you may be blamed for stirring them to action.

CARD 3   *If Heads:* Whatever you are planning right now, try to think of a way to do it better, rather than take a wrong course.

           If Tails: Stop bragging about your big ideas. If they are good, people may appropriate them; if bad, those same people may laugh at you.

CARD 4   *If Heads:* If you have work to do, get it done before starting anything else. Otherwise, you may be giving up a sure thing for something uncertain.

           If Tails: Practical things are best for you. Stay with them. Let other people cook up wild ideas while you turn them into money.

CARD 5   *If Heads:* Don't let the urge to go places divert you from something you should do now. You may regret it before your fun is over.

           If Tails: Avoid all gambling or speculation. Somebody may be looking for an easy mark with your exact qualifications.

CARD 6   *If Heads:* A good time to settle down and enjoy life quietly, particularly if it will make other people happy.

           If Tails: You have been too easygoing. Stop letting people impose upon you before they demand even more than they are demanding now.

CARD 7   *If Heads:* If you have a hunch, follow it. If not, sit tight. It's better to use intuition than to force a situation.

If Tails: Whatever you are planning to do, keep up a cheery front. Any gloom or worry may drive away the very people who can help you most.

CARD 8   *If Heads:* Whatever you are planning, make sure it is practical, then think in bigger terms, especially where money is concerned.

If Tails: Now is a time to save, not just for a rainy tomorrow, but to have money on hand for a business opportunity that may be already coming your way.

CARD 9   *If Heads:* Your power of persuasion can gain you what you want right now. But be sure you are right or the people you convince may turn against you later.

If Tails: Don't let anyone or anything disturb your peace of mind. Face any issue squarely, state your case, and you will win.

This type of oracle can be used almost daily, provided its answers are applied to short-range purposes that reach fulfillment before the same query is proposed again, though actually there is no reason why they should not overlap. Just keep it within bounds and it will provide clean, wholesome fun, not only for yourself, but others. What is more, you may be surprised how well it works out. Keep your own box score and decide for yourself!

III. Divination by Numbers

THE SCIENCE OF ARITHMANCY

Divination by numbers began with ancient methods from which many modern ramifications have been derived. Some of these depend upon cabalistic calculations, but there are others involving numbers only, and these are both practical and popular, particularly when they form a numerological sequence, which goes beyond the limitations of a mere coincidence.

These "predictive progressions," as they are also termed, frequently add up in a most surprising way. They also follow different patterns; with some, a single person may be the focal point, while with others, there may be identical sequences involving two different persons, proving that the old saying "History repeats itself" is not only true but may be applied in a prophetic way.

French history is particularly rich in such predictions, due largely to the influence of the famous Nostradamus, whose prophecies are still reaching fulfillment after four centuries; while Cagliostro is credited with having introduced numerological sequences into some of his predictions, with remarkable results. So to show how far this mode of divination can carry, we shall give a few of earlier and fairly complex examples, then proceed with the later and simpler types that apply more strongly to our world of today.

THE FADIC NUMBER

The term "fadic" applies to any number, or combination of numbers, that can be interpreted as influential in a person's life or career because of its constant recurrence. Such numbers were once called "fatalistic," and in some striking instances—as with historic events—that may still apply. But in general, and particularly with individuals, "fadic" is more apt, as it indicates probabilities rather than positive predictions. However, once a recurrent chain is established, its influence is likely to increase, if only because of the impression it makes upon the person or persons directly concerned.

The simplest way to establish a fadic number is to take the day of the month on which the person was born and reduce it to a single figure. Thus a person born on the third day of the month would have 3 as a fadic number. The same would apply to a person born on the twelfth: $12=1+2=3$. The same with the twenty-first: $21=2+1=3$; and also with the thirtieth: $30=3+0=3$.

Next, you count the letters in a person's given name, as ROY$=3$; MARIE$=5$; RICHARD$=7$; CATHERINE$=9$. The number thus determined may also prove significant. For example, anyone with the number 3, whether determined by date of birth or by name—or by both —should look for things to happen not only on a day that adds up to that number, but in a month attuned to the same vibration, as March, the third month, signifies 3; as does December, the twelfth month, since $12=1+2=3$. Equally important may be the year, as $1983=1+9+8+3=21=2+1=3$.

Just how important a supposedly fadic number may prove to be is a question in itself. Unless something significant occurs during days, months, or years that conform to such a number, it might be disregarded. Still, there is the chance that it might evidence itself in some other way, as with the winning number in a prize drawing, or a friendship formed with someone who has the same fadic number as your own. Combinations may also figure, so that a girl named Marie (5) born on the seventh, 16th, or 25th of the month (each a 7), could regard either 57 or 75 as a potential fadic number.

A fadic number should be considered momentous rather than "lucky" in the popular sense. It represents a change or climax in a person's career and therefore can call for caution as much as optimism. In a sense, fadic numbers may be classed as milestones along life's highway, except that they occur at irregular intervals. Lesser markers should also be considered, in the form of associated numbers. With the nine basic numbers, the groupings are as follows:

With 1, 2, or 7, a person having one of those as a fadic number should watch for a recurrence of either of the other two. With 3, 6, or 9, the same applies, with 9 especially significant, as it is composed of the other two. With 4 and 8, the two are practically interchangeable, since 8 is twice 4; when strongly recurrent, these may be more ominous than favorable. With 5, there is a strong affinity toward persons or events attuned to that same number, while any other number may have fadic implications if it recurs quite frequently.

Numerologists have gone far beyond these simple rules by forming complex calculations based on Pythagorean principles. Hence any number that is strongly recurrent may be regarded as fadic in its own right.

THE FADIC NUMBERS OF KING EDWARD VII

As an example of the recurrence of fadic numbers and their general significance, highlights in the life of King Edward VII of England are of striking interest. He was born on November 9, 1841, establishing 9 as a birthday number, and he was named Albert Edward, each with six letters, setting 6 as a name number. Both add up to 12 (6+6), which reduces to 3 (1+2=3), giving him the third number in the 3, 6, 9 triplicity.

As Prince of Wales, he made a good-will tour to Canada (6 letters) and the United States (each 6 letters, doubling to 12), in the year 1860, which reduces to 1+8+6=15=1+5=6. In the year 1863, which similarly reduces to 9, he was married to Princess Alexandra (9 letters) of Denmark, daughter of King Christian (9 letters), who happened to be King Christian IX, another 9.

In 1869, which reduces to 24=6, the Prince of Wales visited Egypt; during the completion of the Suez Canal, spelled with 9 letters. That was indeed a fateful combination, since England acquired control of the canal exactly six years later. In 1890, which reduces to 1+8 +9=18=1+8=9, he became involved in a gambling trial which threatened his popularity, but weathered it finely, again proving the efficacy of the fadic number 9. In 1899, another 9 year, he was fired at by a would-be assassin named Sipido (6 letters), who very naturally missed.

When Queen Victoria died in 1901, the Prince of Wales succeeded her, but due to the Boer War, which had begun in 1899, his coronation was postponed until its end in 1902, which reduced to the auspicious number 3. Thus the war that had begun in a fadic year (1899), when he was merely a prince, ended in the first fadic year after he became king. It should also be noted that he was in his sixtieth year when he became king and was actually sixty years of age when crowned, thus emphasizing the fadic number 6. As a final touch, instead of being crowned as Albert, he chose the name Edward, thus becoming Edward VII, increasing the 6 letters of his name to the fadic total of 9.

Now comes a most curious phase. The long-delayed coronation was set for late in June, which, being the 6th month, was appropriate, but instead of the highly fadic 27th (2+7=9), the 28th was chosen. That week, the king became so seriously ill that the celebration was postponed and an operation was performed on the fadic 24th (2+4= 6), which proved highly successful. A new coronation day was set for the 9th of August, conforming perfectly to the fadic requirement. With his new name number 9, Edward VII, crowned on the 9th, reigned for 9 years, until 1910, when his death occurred on the 6th of May, which, like the date of his operation, corresponded to the lesser fadic number, 6, which again provided an ominous touch.

Most significant of all was the fact that King Edward VII was in his sixty-ninth year, which combined the two numbers that had shown such fadic tendencies from his birth until his death. According to some reports, he had long felt a strong presentiment that he would not live beyond his sixty-ninth year. How far that may have influenced the outcome is debatable, but it seems apparent that 9 was his Number of Destiny. He had it at birth, it followed him through life, and even after death, the fadic 9 fulfilled its claim, for there were exactly nine kings in his funeral procession.

THE FADIC NUMBERS OF KING HENRY OF NAVARRE

Unique among numerological sequences was that of King Henry of Navarre, who ruled France as King Henry IV from 1589 until 1610. He was known both as Henri de Bourbon and Henri de Navarre, each name being spelled with exactly fourteen letters. He was born on the 14th of December in the year 1553, which adds up 1+5+5+ 3=14. By adding 14 days, *plus 4 more*, we come to the first day of the new year, which forms the radix, or starting point, of Henry's progression; namely, January 1, 1554.

As confirmation of these figures, it should be noted that Henry's first wife, Marguerite de Valois, was born on the 14th of May, also in the year 1553; and that her name contained 14 letters *plus 4 more*. Thus 14 became Henry's fateful, or fadic, number, with 4 bearing further significance, presaging that he would become King Henry IV with Marguerite as his queen. In fact, the prospects of their marriage were discussed by their families at the time of Henry's birth, which adds all the more import to the following tabulations:

Starting from the beginning of the Christian era:

Fourteen centuries (of 100 years each)	1400
Fourteen decades (of 10 years each)	140
Fourteen years (of 1 year each)	14
First year of Henry's life	1554

Taking 1554 as the radix year, Henry had reached the age of 35, twice 14 plus one half of 14, in 1589, when Henry III, then ruling France, was killed by an assassin named Jacques Clément, spelled with 14 letters. Thus Henry of Navarre became King Henry the Fourth, which in French is written Henri Quatre Roi, another example of the fadic number 14, since the title is composed of 14 letters, in conjunction with the number 4.

That combination reached a high point when Henry IV was confronted by immediate rebellion throughout his realm. He took the field against the rebels and in 1590 met them in a decisive battle on the *14th* of March near the town of Ivry, spelled with 4 letters. The result was a decisive victory for Henry IV, which brought ultimate establishment of his rule.

Whether or not Henry IV recognized the importance of those fadic numbers, he had presentiments regarding his death, which became stronger as the years went on and reached a climax as a new progression developed, based directly on the old but incorporating both 14 and 4. It ran as follows:

Starting from the established radix	January 1, 1554
Add: 14 years multiplied by 4=56	January 1, 1610
Add: 14 weeks	April 9, 1610
Add: 4 weeks more	May 14, 1610
Add: 14 hours	2 P.M. May 14, 1610

Not only did the *14th* of May bring up Henry's number; it was the birthday of Queen Marguerite, whose age was also 56—14 times 4— or would be until that date. Henry had divorced Marguerite ten years before and had married Marie de Médicis, whose name, like Henry's, had 14 letters.

After continued stalling, Henry had finally agreed to let Marie be crowned queen, though he had expressed a distinct foreboding that he would be in grave danger the next time he attended an important function. He set the ceremony for May 13, arranging for the new queen to enter Paris on the sixteenth, thus skipping the old queen's birthday, being either tactful, fatalistic, or both. The coronation went off well, and the next day, *May 14*, Henry, although still on tenterhooks, decided to visit one of his ministers, after a midday dinner.

So on this fateful day, Henry's carriage turned into a narrow street called the Rue de la Ferronnière, spelled with 14+4 letters, the extra four being "de la," which are sometimes omitted in street names. However, 14+4=18 was appropriate, this being the birthday of Marguerite de Valois, with her name of 18 letters. According to one account, a decree had been passed on May 14, 1554, ordering the widening of the Rue de la Ferronnière, but it had never been put into effect. So here was Henry IV, with his fadic numbers 14 and 4, tempting fate doubly in going down a street whose name corresponded to the same formula. What happened was exactly what might be expected.

As the king's carriage passed a little shop that bore a sign of a crown above a heart pierced by an arrow, an assassin sprang from the doorway, reached the carriage in a single bound, and stabbed the king twice in the left side. Only the narrowness of the street permitted this; a few steps more and the king's companions could have blocked the attack; in fact, on previous attempts, they had. But this time it seemed fated. According to a detailed report by François de Malherbe, a French author attached to Henry's court, who questioned all the eyewitnesses and summed their statements. He told how the carriage returned to the Louvre and the king was carried upstairs to a couch where he died; and at *two o'clock* was placed upon his bed. If ever a prophecy was pinpointed to the dot, that was it.

There was even a fateful touch in King Henry's choice of François de Malherbe as a member of his retinue, as it would have been difficult indeed to find anyone better qualified to recite the details of the assassination so exactly. When the letters in the name François de Malherbe are counted, they come to the same 14 and 4 that figured so repeatedly in the life and death of King Henry of Navarre.

One student of such sequences has summed this series with the comment: "What coincidences! And also what ingenious calculations." That is, if they are no more than odd coincidences or curious calculations. Quite true, they might be either, or both, but the fact that they fitted with King Henry's premonitions places them somewhat in the category of corroborative evidence.

Anyone inclined to accept them as such will find additional confirmation of the prophetic factor in the further recurrence of the fadic number 14 in the fortunes and misfortunes of the Bourbon monarchs who succeeded Henry IV as rulers of France.

THE FADIC "14" THROUGH FRENCH HISTORY

By one numerological calculation, the predominant "14" in French history can be traced from the coronation of King Henry I, which took place on a *14th* of May, a date that was to prove so fateful. This was a few years before Henry I began his sole reign in 1031, because his father, Robert II, wanted to establish Henry as his successor to offset the jealousy of two younger sons.

Thus the start of the first Henry—Henry I—as future king presaged the end of the reign of the last Henry—Henry IV, who was to die on another *14th* of May, more than five and a half centuries later, as has been detailed under "The Fadic Numbers of King Henry of Navarre."

Supporting this is a very remarkable factor: In 1030, the rebellion against the succession of Henry I broke out in full force, and his father, Robert II, was unable to quell it. So Henry I, then twenty-two years old, actually took up his own kingly cause in 1030. He was fighting the rebels when his father died the next year and continued until he finally defeated them and established his full rule. Thus, taking the year 1030 as the radix and applying the fadic number 14 exactly 4 times to represent Henry IV, we have:

Henry I successfully defeats rebellion beginning in	1030
14 decades (10 years each) added 4 times	140
	140
	140
	140
Year of Battle of Ivry, when Henry IV defeated rebels on the *14th* of March	1590

A very remarkable linkage, as each king's future depended on the fateful year involved. But fadic numbers can work two ways, and Henry IV was unable to escape the ominous 14 that marked the very hour of his death on May 14, 1610. That also linked the first Henry with the last, but it did not end there.

Henry IV was the last king of that name, but not the last King of France. Instead, he was the founder of the Bourbon dynasty, so it was logical to presume that the fadic 14—whether good or bad—would carry its influence into succeeding reigns. That applied directly to his son and heir, Louis XIII, who was born in 1601 and became king on the very day that Henry IV died, warning him against any year or date represented by the fadic 14 and particularly the 14th of May.

With Louis XIII, the fadic 14 formed the following sequence:

Born in 1601, married Anne of Austria in 1615:   *Age* 14 times 1
Risked life in attack on Pass of Susa in 1629:   *Age* 14 times 2
Died on *14th* of *May* in the year 1643:   *Age* 14 times 3
Figures of year 1643. Added 1+6+4+3.   *Total* 14

Note that the fatal *14th* of *May* repeated itself with Louis XIII, who died at *almost the same hour* as his father. Whether or not he knew that number was coming up is a question. When he died, he was quoted as hoping he could live until the next day, because it would be a Friday and Fridays were his lucky days. But the 14th of May took precedence, regardless.

The recurrence of the fadic 14 reached its zenith under the rule of Louis XIV, known as the "Grand Monarch" whose reign was one of the longest of all time. Born in 1638, he succeeded to the throne on the fatal *14th* of May, but his very title, Louis the *14th,* offset that baleful influence, though it became ominous in his later years. The Louis XIV sequence runs:

Became king at age of five, in 1643   1+6+4+3=14
Life endangered at Bléneau in 1652   1+6+5+2=14
After death of Cardinal Mazarin, his
  adviser, he took full power in 1661   1+6+6+1=14
Planning to attack Holland, he signed
  secret treaties with England in 1670   1+6+7+0=14
Driven from Holland and Italy in 1706   1+7+0+6=14
Died in the year 1715   1+7+1+5=14
Age at time of death, 77 years   7+7=14

The fadic 14 continued through the reign of Louis XV, who ascended the throne in 1715. Significant events occurred in other fadic years whose figures added up to 14, but plots and counterplots were so rife during this reign that it is difficult to set definitive dates, with the exception of 1733 (1+7+3+3=14) which marked the beginning of the War of the Polish Succession. Highly significant in the light of the distant future was the year 1760 (1+7+6+0=14) in which all Canada was taken over by the British. As for Louis XV himself, he died in 1774, completing a reign of 59 years, with figures conforming to the fadic formula: 5+9=14.

King Louis XVI, born in 1754, was unlucky enough to become heir to the throne when his father, the Dauphin of France, died in 1765.

He succeeded his grandfather, Louis XV, in 1774. Using that as a radix, we find:

Louis XVI became King of France in the year   1774
Add fadic number   14

Issued edict convoking the States General,
which triggered the French Revolution   1788

Result: Storming of the Bastille on the *14th* of July,   1789
Acceptance of Constitution on the *14th* of September,   1791
Taking the unfortunate year of 1765 as a radix:
The future Louis XVI became Dauphin of France in   1765
Add fadic number twice   14
14
Execution of King Louis XVI   1793

It might be added that the trial of Queen Marie Antoinette began on the *14th* of October and was followed, as was to be expected, by her execution. This concluded the misfortunes of the Bourbon dynasty, as indicated by the fadic number 14, but the disposal of the individuals shifted the fatalistic burden onto France itself. How the fadic 14 figured from then on is another sequence in itself.

VERTICAL SEQUENCE PREDICTIONS

In contrast to predictions based upon an arbitrary or self-established fadic number, there are those which stem from the radix itself, wherein the figures of a given year provide its own fatal period. Those figures are simply added to the date to determine the year of attainment, and this can be repeated to form a continuous chain. With individuals, the year of a person's birth is usually taken as the primary radix. For example:

Napoleon I was born in   1769
Add (1+7+6+9=23)   1
7
6
9
Napoleon commissioned a captain,   1792
French Republic established

January

What a world of difference there was between those two events at the time they occurred! Yet how interrelated they were to be in the years immediately to come! That is why this stands out as a striking example, because from here on, we have two types of vertical sequences: the recurrent and the progressive.

With the Recurrent Vertical, the same total is repeated, becoming a fadic number in its own right. With the Progressive Vertical, a new total is established by adding the figures of the new date. We have taken Napoleon's sequence as an example, because it illustrates how both can work out.

On the left, the recurrent; on the right, the progressive:

Napoleon I born in	1769	Napoleon I born in	1769
$1+7+6+9=$	23	$1+7+6+9=$	23
Republic founded	1792	Commissioned captain	1792
Add fadic number $23=$	23	Add $1+7+9+2=$	19
Battle of Waterloo	1815	Birth of Napoleon II	1811

Note how each sequence reached a fulfillment in a year of vital importance. Unless the republic had been formed, Napoleon could never have risen to emperor; and unless he had become emperor, he would never have met his Waterloo. That covers the recurrent phase.

As for the progressive sequence, only by becoming an army officer could Napoleon have displayed the military genius that made him emperor; and, as emperor, he held the great hope to establish a dynasty, which became possible with the birth of a son and heir.

Due to Napoleon's death in 1821, neither sequence reached another year of attainment. The progressive sequence fell just one year short, for by adding the figures produced by 1811 to the year itself, the result would be $1811+1+8+1+1=1822$. That might indeed have been a very eventful year for Napoleon, had he lived, for it has long been claimed that plans were under way to rescue him from the island of St. Helena and bring him to America, but he died shortly before their completion.

Dates other than the year of a person's birth may be taken as a radix, then added in vertical form to determine an event of equal importance. Here are two more from French history:

Louis XVI ascended throne	1774	Son of Louis XVI died	1789
Add $1+7+7+4=$	19	Add $1+7+8+9=$	25
Death of Louis XVI	1793	Ascension of Louis XVIII	1814

Those, of course, were single tabulations, in which the fadic number was neither recurrent nor progressive. Naturally, this reduces their significance, as the result might be regarded simply as coincidence. But when vertical predictions form identical combinations, their prognostications become proportionately stronger.

Thus if Louis Philippe, the last King of France, had studied his fadic number, as represented by three separate sequences stemming from the same radix, the year of his sudden elevation to the throne, he might have suspected approaching disaster. Here they are:

Louis Philippe became King of the French in	1830
He was born in 1773, with vertical figures.	1
	7
	7
	3
Added, these give the year he was deposed.	1848

Louis Philippe became King of the French in	1830
Queen Maria Amelia was born in 1782.	1
	7
	8
	2
Again, the year Louis Philippe was deposed.	1848

Louis Philippe became King of the French in	1830
He married Maria Amelia in 1809.	1
	8
	0
	9
Again, the year Louis Philippe was deposed.	1848

Remarkable indeed, except that it too could be charged to coincidence on the ground that it would have to happen more than once to prove that it meant something more. So that was just what it did do, with Napoleon III, the last emperor of France, who should have profited by the earlier example, for his own ran:

Napoleon III was fully recognized as Emperor of the French in	1853
He was born in 1808, with vertical figures.	1
	8
	0
	8
Added, these give the year he was deposed.	1870

Napoleon III was fully recognized as Emperor of the French in   1853
The Empress Eugénie was born in 1826   1
8

2
6

Again, the year Napoleon III was deposed.   1870

Napoleon III was fully recognized as Emperor of the French in   1853
He married Eugénie in 1853.   1
8

5
3

Again, the year Napoleon III was deposed.   1870

Remarkable, indeed, the duplication of two such sequences. They were cited often through the years, but they had all but faded into oblivion until in the year 1926, when both pretenders to the French throne—royal and imperial—died within a few days of each other. That brought up recollections of the identical sequences back in the previous century.

It also raised the question: Why aren't such prophetic sequences operating right now, in one form or another? Actually, they were in operation right then, along even simpler terms, except that nobody took time to notice it. Going back to fundamentals, we have mentioned two forms of vertical sequence predictions, the Recurrent Vertical and the Progressive Vertical, both long established and well proven. So let us see how they added up in the concurrent careers of two would-be Napoleons of the twentieth century:

Benito Mussolini *Recurrent Vertical Sequence*		*Adolf Hitler* *Progressive Vertical Sequence*	
Year of birth	1883	Year of birth	1889
Add figures 1+8+8+3=	20	Add figures 1+8+8+9=	26
In Switzerland, avoiding military service	1903	Corporal in World War I	1915
Add fadic number 20	20	Add figures 1+9+1+5=	16
Italy's Supreme Dictator	1923	Nazi party established	1931
Add fadic number 20	20	Add figures 1+9+3+1=	14
Mussolini overthrown	1943	Hitler overthrown	1945

During the opening months of World War II, London newsstands used blackboards instead of placards to advertise their wares thus:

Mussolini, we know, is an old So and So—
To Hitler, the Beast, he has pandered.
So read how we'll win, from those partners in sin,
In the *Times* and the *News* and the *Standard!*

How right they were! But instead of spelling it out poetically, they could have added it numerologically to come up with the exact dates that marked disaster for the scheming pair. The gift of prophecy is still with us, for those who know how to interpret it. There are certain variables, but those also conform to numerological laws and are therefore further definable in specific terms of their own.

The comparison just cited proves this quite clearly. The first inkling that Mussolini was sufficiently important to warrant prophetic study came with his sudden surge to power in 1923. Taking his birth date, 1883, as the radix, with its fadic number 20, it became obvious that his vertical sequence would be the recurrent type, with $1883+20=1903+20=1923$. Hence the next step would be $1923+20=1943$.

But when Hitler emerged as a threat to Germany's stability in 1931, acceptance of his birth date, 1889, as the initial radix, showed that his vertical sequence would have to be the progressive type to hit 1931 as a fateful year, as the tabulation shows. Hence taking 1915 as a new radix $(1915+1+9+1+5=1931)$ and 1931 as another radix $(1931+1+9+3+1=1945)$, we hit 1945 squarely on the button.

Thus at the outbreak of World War II, and definitely after Mussolini joined forces with Hitler, any student of numerology could have traced the two sequences up to that time and predicted the fall of the two dictators, each to the exact year, with the prophecy gathering momentum as the tide of war turned against them. However, this remarkable prognostication still cannot be accepted as infallible.

Suppose that having established Mussolini's sequence as recurrent because he attained such full power in 1923, Hitler's sequence also had been listed as recurrent, on the assumption that 1931 represented his emergence and not the attainment of the power he really sought. In that case, taking his birth date, 1889, as the only radix, with fadic number 26, the sequence would have run $1889+26=1915+26=1941$. That happened to be the very year in which his power hit its high point, with his attack on Russia and Japan's entry into World War II as his ally.

So one sequence is as good as the other, which makes them both significant and therefore doubly prophetic. The fact that the recurrent sequence ends in 1941 does not matter, because anything may happen to a person between two fateful years. In Hitler's case, it would have been a long stretch on a recurrent basis: 1941+26=1967. But oddly, that is significant too. During the 1960s, a rumor grew that Hitler, like other notorious Nazis, was still alive and in hiding somewhere. Perhaps he did live until 1967 and then died in obscurity to fulfill a recurrent sequence!

INDIVIDUAL APPLICATION OF PROGRESSIVE VERTICAL SEQUENCES

Since the affairs of nations are often cyclic, they are apt to follow a recurrent pattern, whereas those of individuals are far more likely to be progressive. Or in other terms, recurrent sequences may cover general events; progressive sequences, those of a specific nature.

As a result, progressive sequences, with their irregular periods, are far more common than the recurrent type. They apply particularly to people in everyday life and sometimes to a surprising degree. You will probably find that a progressive sequence has played an important part in your own life, as well as the lives of many of your friends; or better still, if you are young enough, its fulfillment may yet be in the future.

But don't expect miracles. Once in a lifetime is often enough for a fadic indication to come through powerfully. Also, the term "indication" is well chosen. Rather than marking an actual event in a person's career, it denotes a change from one numerological period to another, bringing the individual under a new and sometimes totally different influence that often has a permanent or at least an indelible effect upon his future motivations.

Hence the more important a person is, the greater or more complex his connections, the more striking the result may be. But the result itself may well be the cumulation of a period rather than an isolated achievement. Similarly, it does not have to represent the pinnacle of a person's career, but may be simply the fulfillment of a purpose that in itself presages greater things ahead.

Thus an engagement in the terminal year of a fadic period may be the forerunner of a happy marriage; a graduation with high honors may bring a worth-while business offer a few years later; the striking up of a chance friendship may be the nucleus of important social connections. In some cases, an off year, representing a transition or preparatory period, may be of high significance, although unrecognized at the time.

Look back into your own experience, or that of your friends, and see how remarkable some of these indications can be. The general procedure, as already given, is to take a person's year of birth, form a progressive vertical sequence and check each year of attainment for its significance, using it as a radix for the next. The first such year often occurs in childhood and therefore may not be too significant a date in itself, hence the second, third, or even later dates may represent some greater fulfillment. Yet all are important, in as much as anything occurring in one of those years may set the pattern for the period to follow.

As a good contrasting illustration, take the cases of two friends, Clyde Burke and Harry Vincent, who were born only two years apart and whose progressive vertical sequences run:

	Clyde Burke			*Harry Vincent*	
Born in year	1929		Born in year	1931
Add 1+9+2+9=	21		Add 1+9+3+1=	14
	1950			1945
Add 1+9+5+0=	15		Add 1+9+4+5=	19
	1965			1964
Add 1+9+6+5=	21		Add 1+9+6+4=	20
	1986			1984

Clyde Burke was a junior in college when he reached the age of twenty-one in 1950, so following the trend of those times, he married a co-ed in the same class. Many such marriages have broken up, but not theirs, for Burke and his wife were the same age and the year conformed to the fadic number (21) governing their first period. That would have been an excellent sign, even if the number had been Burke's alone, but as they both had it, it became doubly favorable.

As a result, the Burkes celebrated all their wedding anniversaries happily and particularly their crystal wedding, or fifteenth anniversary, in 1965, when Clyde was promoted to sales manager of his company and good luck seemed rampant. The reason, of course, was that he'd reached the year of attainment marking the end of his second fadic period, represented by the number 15.

According to numerological forecasts, the Burkes should be due for a great year in 1986, since it represents the culmination of another fadic period. Of course, changes of circumstances, accidents, various fortunes or misfortunes may intervene. Numerology does not allow for those, as it deals in indications only. So, assuming that the unpredictable has not asserted itself, we can picture the Burkes attending their thirty-fifth college reunion and being acclaimed as the pride of the Class of 1951, never realizing that their marital bliss really dated back to the year before, the fateful year of 1950.

So now, let's see what happened with Harry Vincent.

At fourteen, he won prizes for scholarship, fitting his first fadic period of fourteen years, but he did not appreciate it, as the envy of his schoolmates forced him deeper into studies that he might otherwise have foregone. After college, he went through law school, opened a law office, and was married—unhappily, as it turned out—and was wishing he had taken up some other profession until, at the age of thirty-three, he was offered a junior partnership in an important law firm.

That was in 1964, and the offer stipulated that, at the end of twenty years, the head of the firm would retire, making Harry the senior member. Harry himself was somewhat amazed by the quickness with which he accepted the terms, and he often wondered why twenty years had seemed such a logical stipulation. That was because he had studied law instead of numerology. Harry simply didn't realize that 1964 was the year of attainment of his second fadic period of nineteen years, and that 1984 would mark the end of the next, a twenty-year period.

Some persons' lives are so uneventful that it would seem difficult to pick out a standout year and check it against the fadic figures. But usually some significant result is forthcoming if you probe deeply enough. Conversely, in dealing with the life of a celebrity, there are so many eventful years that you might be almost sure to make a hit. That, however, should not be taken for granted except in very special cases.

With a movie star, appearing in a new picture every few years, it could be true; similarly, anyone constantly seeking publicity would fall in the same category. But there are many persons who have risen into sudden or startling prominence from a routine career that might have continued almost unnoticed, or at least have been just one of many, rather than become something remarkable or unique.

Compare the parallel careers of Dwight D. Eisenhower and Charles de Gaulle, who were both born in the same year, 1890. Their progressive vertical sequences, gained by adding the figures of each sucessive date, ran:

$$1890+1+8+9+0=1908+1+9+0+8=1926+1+9+2+6=1944$$

Through the first two periods ending in the 1908 and 1926, both became officers in the armies of their respective countries, but met with disappointment during World War I. While Eisenhower was commanding a training camp in Gettysburg, Pennsylvania, and hoping to get overseas, which he never did, De Gaulle was serving time in a German prison camp and feeling even more frustrated. That was not surprising, for they were both midway in a fadic period—1917–18 being the halfway mark between 1908 and 1926—without realizing it.

From 1926, both proceeded along their paths of duty, oblivious to the fact that they were Men of Destiny. It took World War II to prove their worth. Due to America's forced entry into the conflict and France's earlier capitulation, the timing was such that Eisenhower, as Supreme Commander of the Allied Forces in 1944, gained the rank of general of the army in that same year; while De Gaulle, as commander of the Free French forces, returned to Paris to head the new French Government, also in 1944.

Each went on to become president of his country and to gain additional fame and honor, but there is no need to trace their mutual progression further. As military men, by training and profession, each had attained the apex of a soldier's ambition, and whatever followed represented a deserved recognition of that achievement.

There is a very special reason why this dual sequence came through as it did. Study its figures and you will see that it is not just a progressive sequence, in which each new year of potential achievement becomes a new radix, producing a fadic number of its own. It is a recurrent sequence as well, for just as the figures of the primary radix, 1890, add up to 18, so do those appearing subsequently in the series 1908, 1926, 1944—and from there on, as 1962—and 1980—had they been needed to reach fulfillment.

Thus according to the rule of vertical sequences, this dual result was doubly destined to occur, so it would not have required a gift of prophecy to surmise what was in store for General Eisenhower and General de Gaulle as they neared the fadic year of 1944. Our search for truth shows that numerology could have supplied the answer on its own.

FAMOUS EXAMPLES OF VERTICAL SEQUENCES

The vast territorial expansion of the United States of America was remarkably presaged by a periodic prediction of the vertical sequence type, beginning appropriately with the year 1776, in which, by the course of human events, the thirteen American colonies declared their independence and took over all available territory as their own. Here is how the course of empire followed, as shown by vertical tabulation:

United States of America declared independent   1776
(Add: $1+7+7+6=21$)   1
   7
   7
Break with France leading to naval conflicts and   6
later the acquisition of Louisiana by U.S.   1797

$$\text{(Add: } 1+7+9+7=24)\qquad \begin{array}{r}1\\7\\9\\7\\\hline\end{array}$$

Florida officially acquired from Spain by U.S. $\overline{1821}$
$$\text{(Add: } 1+8+2+1=12)\qquad \begin{array}{r}1\\8\\2\\\hline\end{array}$$

Texas takes first step toward independence from $\begin{array}{r}1\\\end{array}$
Mexico, later becoming state of U.S. $\overline{1833}$
$$\text{(Add: } 1+8+3+3=15)\qquad \begin{array}{r}1\\8\\3\\3\\\hline\end{array}$$

End of war with Mexico. Arizona, California, $\begin{array}{r}3\\\end{array}$
New Mexico, and Utah added to U.S. $\overline{1848}$
$$\text{(Add: } 1+8+4+8=21)\qquad \begin{array}{r}1\\8\\4\\8\\\hline\end{array}$$

Full establishment of U.S. government in Alaska $\overline{1869}$
$$\text{(Add: } 1+8+6+9=24)\qquad \begin{array}{r}1\\8\\6\\\hline\end{array}$$

U.S. protectorate established in Hawaii, followed $\begin{array}{r}9\\\end{array}$
by a republic later annexed by U.S. $\overline{1893}$
$$\text{(Add: } 1+8+9+3=21)\qquad \begin{array}{r}1\\8\\9\\3\\\hline\end{array}$$

First ship through Panama Canal $\overline{1914}$

While periods of expansion allow some flexibility as to exact dates, those composing the sequence are highly significant throughout. In 1797, France was at war with England and molested all neutral shipping, directly threatening the expansion of the United States. The challenge was met with naval warfare, resulting in various treaties that culminated in the Louisiana Purchase, six years later.

When President Andrew Jackson began his second term in 1833, support of the United States was practically guaranteed for Texan independence and the later entry of Texas into the Union. The Convention of San Felipe, in 1833, demanded recognition of Texas as a separate Mexican state; when that was refused, revolution and complete separation followed.

Though Alaska was purchased in 1867, the payment was not made until the next year, and 1869 marked the full establishment of military posts that represented American authority. The opening of the Panama Canal, linking the Atlantic and Pacific Oceans, represented the final attainment in 1914, and led directly to the purchase of the Virgin Islands, three years later, as a defense measure for the canal.

Perhaps the most remarkable and certainly the most publicized of periodic predictions was the vertical sequence that foretold the rise and fall of the German Empire. According to one well-established account, this was made in the year 1829 by a psychic named Katherine Speesman, who had recently arrived in Berlin. She was asked by Prince William, the second son of King Frederick William III of Prussia, to predict the future of that kingdom and of Germany as well.

The seeress took 1829 as the radix for a vertical sequence, not just because it was the current year, but because it marked the starting point of Prince William's own ambition toward the expansion of Prussia. That was the year of his marriage to Augusta, the daughter of Grand Duke Charles Frederick, of Saxe-Weimar, which automatically brought that state into the Prussian fold.

The tabulation and its prognostications ran:

Marriage of Prince William	1829
(Add: 1+8+2+9=20)	1
	8
	2
	9
Foundation laid for future German Empire	1849
(Add 1+8+4+9=22)	1
	8
	4
	9
Prince William crowned Emperor of Germany	1871
(Add 1+8+7+1=17)	1
	8
	7
	1
Death of Emperor William I	1888
(Add 1+8+8+8=25)	1
	8
	8
	8
Final year of the expanded empire	1913

Whether or not these events were foretold in precise detail, the figures stand on their own merits, for they represent the most vital years in Germany's course of empire. King Frederick William III was succeeded by his eldest son, Frederick William IV, who pursued such a liberal course in Prussia that a parliament composed of lesser states offered him the imperial crown of Germany in 1849, the exact year of attainment represented by the first step in the predicted sequence.

Though the king rejected the offer, the seeds of imperialism were sown and Prussian prestige was established by his brother, Prince William, who put down revolts in surrounding territories during that same key year of 1849. Within a dozen years, William succeeded his hesitant brother and all vacillation ended. As King William I of Prussia, he relied on Bismarck as his chief adviser, and following successful wars against Austria and France, he was crowned Emperor of Germany in 1871, fulfilling the second stage of the periodic prediction.

Adding up to the next brings a double stroke, probably the most fateful year in German history, whether or not the seeress realized it, though probably she did, because it would take a seeress to call the turn. That fateful year, 1888, marked not only the death of Kaiser William I, but also that of his son and successor, Frederick III, the most talented and liberal of all the Hohenzollerns, known to his subjects as "Unser Fritz" and esteemed internationally as the husband of Princess Victoria, oldest daughter of Queen Victoria of England, a happy marriage that should have brought perpetual good relations between those two nations.

But no. The death of two German emperors in the same year gave a negative aspect to the Speesman prediction. The seeress had scored a double hit, whether she foresaw it or not, but the chances are that she did, because from then on the periodic progression took a baleful turn. Unser Fritz, the beloved emperor, died after a reign of a mere three months, leaving the empire—which already had acquired vast African possessions—to his eldest son, who became Kaiser William II. Under his regime, thousands of Pacific islands came under German control and the empire reached its peak in the predicted year of 1913.

Whether or not this periodic prophecy was well known before the year 1888 is a question, but it was cited frequently prior to 1913, sometimes as a "warning" for the sword-shaking Kaiser William II, who may have felt that the baleful influence was past when he unleashed his war hordes in August 1914. Before that year was ended, Allied forces had taken over all of Germany's Pacific possessions and the African colonies were under a persistent attack that eventually led to their dismemberment.

The Speesman prediction roused still more comment following

World War I. Some students of prophecies decided that it had reached
fulfillment in 1913 and that any further prognostications regarding
Germany would need a new radix starting from some eventful year.
Others questioned the finality of 1913 on the ground that the defeat of
Germany and the abdication of the Kaiser did not occur until five
years later. All agreed, however, that its continuance would be worth
watching, according to the following progression:

$$
\begin{array}{lr}
\text{Final year of the German Empire} & 1913 \\
\quad (\text{Add } 1+9+1+3=14) & 1 \\
& 9 \\
& 1 \\
& \underline{3} \\
\text{Another fateful year in German history} & 1927
\end{array}
$$

That particular year, 1927, proved so uneventful that almost everyone
conceded that the prophecy had been completed back in 1913. In 1927,
Germany had become a member of the League of Nations and President von Hindenburg celebrated his eightieth birthday, but those could
hardly be called momentous events. Still less important were the antics
of a political crackpot named Adolf Hitler, who in 1927 established an
official organ for his insignificant Nazi party and urged his principal
lieutenants, Goering and Goebbels, to run for election to the Reichstag,
which they successfully did.

As events were to prove, that year, 1927, actually marked the rise of a
new German imperialism that threatened to regain all the lost German
colonies and temporarily took over most of Europe in addition. Hence
by the time of World War II, followers of periodic predictions had
given new heed to the old Speesman prophecy and had added still another progression:

$$
\begin{array}{lr}
\text{Resurgence of German imperialism under Nazi guise} & 1927 \\
\quad (\text{Add } 1+9+2+7=19) & 1 \\
& 9 \\
& 2 \\
& \underline{7} \\
\text{Climax of German imperial progression} & 1946
\end{array}
$$

That final date, 1946, was indeed appropriate, for it marked the sen-
tencing and execution of the surviving war criminals responsible for the
resurgent progression just given, and the year 1946 also found Germany partitioned into East and West, with Prussia itself divided, apparently ending the imperialistic threat for all time.

If carried further, the progression would produce 1946+1+9+4+6=1966, a year of no outward change in German affairs. Whether or not 1966 happened to be another "sleeper" with some hidden ferment seething dangerously, deep beneath the unruffled surface of the *status quo* is a question that should be fully decided by a further application of the progressive formula: 1966+1+9+6+6=1988.

That year will mark the hundredth anniversary of the accession of Kaiser William II, whose urge for power stirred still deadlier ambitions that were not finally extinguished until 1946. So if nothing happens in the centennial year of 1988, the prophetic progression will stand as stated with its climax in 1946.

The remarkable sequence of the Speesman prediction raises the logical question: Since the periodic progression proved so exact in the case of Germany, why can't the same system be applied just as effectively toward determining the key years and ultimate destinies of other modern nations and their ruling dynasties?

The answer is a double affirmative. The same system can be so applied, and it has been so applied, with the same impressive results. A striking example is that of modern Italy, which is the precise parallel of the German progression, with the dominating strength of a single kingdom gaining the support that turned it into an imperial power, with resultant disaster.

The year 1849 forms an ideal radix for the Italian progression. In that year, the dream of a united Italy became a hopelessly lost cause that only some fantastic prognostication could raise from the bottomless depths of utter despair. In 1849, King Charles Albert of Sardinia, or Piedmont, struggling to shake off the yoke of Austrian oppression, was so overwhelmingly defeated at the Battle of Novara that he immediately abdicated and his son, Victor Emmanuel II, became head of the ruling House of Savoy.

The new regime gained sufficient concessions from the Austrians to maintain a substantial degree of independence, until the time arrived to strike for further freedom. A united Italy was realized as the first step in a vertical sequence, and further tabulations, as given below, carry this remarkable progression through the key years of imperial expansion to its highly prophetic conclusion:

Victor Emmanuel II ascended the throne in	1849
(Add: 1+8+4+9=22)	1
	8
	4
Victor Emmanuel II made his entry into Rome, establishing	9
it as the capital of united Italy	1871

(Add: 1+8+7+1=17)	1
	8
	7
Establishment of Italian colonial possessions	1
on the Red Sea, as foundation of empire	1888
(Add: 1+8+8+8=25)	1
	8
	8
Italy occupied Libya, vast African province	8
gained from war with Turkey	1913
(Add: 1+9+1+3=14)	1
	9
	1
Full establishment of Fascist regime, leading	3
to further imperial ambitions	1927
(Add: 1+9+2+7=19)	1
	9
	2
Following conquest of Ethiopia and debacle of	7
World War II, Victor Emmanuel III abdicated in	1946

The importance of the progressively predicted dates cannot be over-stressed. The first Italian Parliament was held in 1871. It was in 1888 that Italy concluded a series of treaties with local sultans that led to the formation of the colony of Eritrea on the Red Sea; and in that same year, 1888, France and England defined their boundaries in Somaliland, leaving the rest open for Italian occupation. In 1913, Italy took over Libya and in 1927 Mussolini took over Italy, with the demand that all opposing political parties be outlawed, which duly followed.

The final year, 1946, gains special emphasis, as not only did Victor Emmanuel III abdicate, but his son and successor, Humbert II, lost the crown a month later when the Italian people voted in favor of a republic. Thus Italy lost two kings in the key year 1946, as Germany did in the key year 1888.

Modern Japanese history provides a well-defined periodic prediction dating from 1867 when Emperor Mutsuhito ascended the throne and Keiki, the shogun, or military ruler, resigned, ending the feudal rule that he and his predecessors had held for nearly seven centuries. That, according to good authority, "must be ranked among the signal events of the world's history," which is very true, because of the following sequence:

End of the shogunate, and the beginning of Japan's 1867
trade with the Western World 1
8
6
7
___

Promulgation of a new constitution 1889
1
8
8
9
___

Completed takeover of Germany's Pacific 1915
possessions during World War I 1
9
1
5
___

Invasion of Manchuria, resulting in setting up 1931
of puppet state of Manchukuo 1
9
3
1
___

Surrender of Japan, ending World War II 1945
1
9
4
5
___

Establishment of Eisaku Sato as new premier 1964
1
9
6
4
___
Possible highly eventful year in Japanese history 1984

Here, again, there is a strong chance that we are dealing with a completed sequence, stemming from 1867 as the radix and ending with the fadic year of 1945, which actually marked the end of the imperial regime. In that case, some new event may serve as radix for another sequence, but in the meantime, we can look forward to 1984 as a year of potential significance.

Another remarkable vertical sequence is found in the career of Earl Kitchener, famous British field marshal:

Year of Kitchener's birth   1850
Add figures of date: $1+8+5+0=$ 14
Schooling toward a military career   1864
Add figures of date: $1+8+6+4=$ 19
Assigned to Egypt, where he eventually
took full command   1883
Add figures of date: $1+8+8+3=$ 20
Assigned to India, where he built up
an army for World War I   1903
Add figures of date: $1+9+0+3=$ 13
Assigned to Russia, to organize an army
that would win World War I   1916

Every key year in Kitchener's career marked an important date in English history. Always, his efforts were crowned by success, as they probably would have been if he had reached Russia in that fatal year of 1916. Instead, the cruiser *Hampshire*, on which Kitchener sailed, was torpedoed, and he went down with it, so that the climax of the vertical sequence proved to be the year of his death.

The life of Mark Twain provides a remarkable vertical sequence, which is not only worthy of close study in its own right, but is substantiated by other forms of divinatory science. He was born on November 30, 1835, so taking that year as a radix, his sequence can be tabulated thus:

Year of Mark Twain's birth   1835
Add figures of date: $1+8+3+5=$ 17
Took his first job on a newspaper   1852
Add figures of date: $1+8+5+2=$ 16
Completion of his first book,
The Innocents Abroad   1868
Add figures of date: $1+8+6+8=$ 23
Went abroad to begin new writing career   1891
Add figures of date: $1+8+9+1=$ 19
Year of Mark Twain's death   1910

Between the key years of 1868 and 1891, Mark Twain made a fortune and then proceeded to lose it; between 1891 and 1910, he went still deeper into debt but regained all that he had lost. In 1890, when he was bankrupt and heavily in debt, Cheiro, the famous palmist, studied his hand and told him that in 1903, his sixty-eighth year, he would become suddenly rich. Cheiro made a similar prediction two years later and Mark Twain made a skeptical entry in his notebook in regard to it.

On October 22, 1903, with only a month and nine days to go, Cheiro's prediction was fulfilled. Mark Twain noted that his income from the previous year amounted to over $100,000, and on that date, he signed a contract that guaranteed him a minimum of $25,000 a year for the next five years, a fortune in those days. Whether Cheiro included a numerological calculation in making the prediction was not stated, but he was good at that, too, so it could have figured. However:

Astromancy, or its counterpart, aeromancy, confirmed the over-all calculation from radix to climax, where Mark Twain was concerned. He was born in 1835, in the same month when Halley's comet reached perihelion, and he took that as a personal omen, saying that "I came in with the comet and I expect to go out with it." He died in 1910, in the same month when the same comet reached perihelion. He was too young to see it when he was born, too ill to see it when he died, yet he was one of the few persons in whose lifetime the comet appeared twice.

How far Mark Twain may have shaped his own destiny by anticipating the comet's return is worthy of consideration by all sincere students of divinatory processes.

The year 1876 forms the logical radix for a periodic prediction involving modern Spanish rulers, and the fate of the nation as well. It was in that year, 1876, that the restored monarchy gained full hold under King Alfonso XII, whose army drove the rival Carlists from the country and established him as the descendant of the Bourbon line. Taking it from there, the vertical sequence runs:

Establishment of Alfonso XII, with new Spanish constitution   1876
(Add: 1+8+7+6=22)   1
   8
   7
   6

Loss of colonies following Spanish-American War   1898
(Add: 1+8+9+8=26)   1
   8
   9
   8

First full year of dictatorship under Primo de Rivera   1924

(Add: 1+9+2+4=16)   1
    9
    2
    4

First full year of dictatorship under Francisco Franco   1940
(Add: 1+9+4+0=14)   1
    9
    4
    0

Establishment of U.S. military bases in Spain   1954
(Add: 1+9+5+4=19)   1
    9
    5
    4

Important year in modern Spanish history   1973*

Of all periodic progressions, that of modern Russia truly cast a baleful shadow before, if only it had been noted soon enough to realize the full import of its fantastic prognostications. If ever the saying "If man shed blood, by man shall his blood be shed" was due for prophetic realization, it applied to the Romanoff dynasty, as the following vertical tabulations will clearly show. For a starting point, we take the birth year of Russia's hand-picked "Man of Destiny," Alexander I, who was much better fitted to rule Russia than his father, Paul. The progression runs:

Birth of Alexander I, future Czar of Russia   1777
(Add: 1+7+7+7=22)   1
    7
    7

Paul sold out to Napoleon and a noble cabal plotted
to murder him, and put Alexander on the throne   7
    1799
(Add 1+7+9+9=26)   1
    7
    9
    9

Death of Alexander I; accession of Nicholas I   1825
(Add: 1+8+2+5=16)   1
    8
    2
    5

The great Anglo-Russian Alliance, controlling Turkey   1841

* This sequence was compiled in 1972, hence 1973 was still in the future. As we go to press in 1973, Franco has resigned as Premier of Spain, thus verifying the prediction.

$$\begin{array}{ll}
\text{(Add: } 1+8+4+1=14) & 1 \\
& 8 \\
& 4 \\
& \underline{1}
\end{array}$$

Collapse of the alliance, start of the Crimean War
death of Nicholas I, and succession of Alexander II   1855

$$\begin{array}{ll}
\text{(Add: } 1+8+5+5=19) & 1 \\
& 8 \\
& 5 \\
& \underline{5}
\end{array}$$

Russian occupation of Khiva and Kokan   1874

$$\begin{array}{ll}
\text{(Add: } 1+8+7+4=20) & 1 \\
& 8 \\
& 7 \\
& \underline{4}
\end{array}$$

Death of Alexander III; accession of Nicholas II   1894

$$\begin{array}{ll}
\text{(Add: } 1+8+9+4=22) & 1 \\
& 8 \\
& 9 \\
& \underline{4}
\end{array}$$

Murder of Rasputin; last year of Czarist rule   1916

Almost uncannily, this vertical sequence predicted the death of every Russian czar and the end of each monarch's rule over a period of more than a century, with one exception, the assassination of Alexander II in 1881. That was due to the accidental success of one of many attempts made on the czar's life by highly active anarchists of the period, hence none of its political reverberations were anticipated or planned, as with the other events listed.

Historians generally concede that Alexander I was party to the murder of his father Czar Paul, the "Mad Emperor," which was plotted in 1799 but postponed until early in 1801, due to the death of one of the chief instigators. The murder of Rasputin in 1916 was the result of a similar plot, this time to rid Russia of a "Mad Monk" who was the real power behind the throne, which tottered within a few months.

Hence the abdication, imprisonment, and murder of Nicholas II were simply a matter of course, stemming from that date, 1916. Along with the czar, the entire royal family was massacred by the Bolshevists in 1918, including the czar's only son, Alexis, the direct heir to the Russian throne. In his case, there is striking confirmation of the power of periodic prediction. Just as the birth year of Alexander I, 1777, furnished a two-step vertical sequence marking the year of his death, 1825; so did the year 1904, in which Alexis was born, form the radix of a single vertical prediction that marked the end of the Romanoff line:

Birth of the Czarevitch Alexis, son of Nicholas II	1904
(Add: 1+9+0+4=14)	1
	9
	0
	4
Fated death of Alexis and end of dynasty	1918

Great though the changes wrought in Russia since the Revolution, absolute rule has still held sway, with new policies following the death of one leader and the succession of another. The liquidation of troublesome individuals is still part of the Russian scene, and far from escaping the toils of a periodic prediction, as in the imperial days, the present regime has simply produced a potent progression of its own, as witness:

Year of Russian Revolution and start of Bolshevist rule	1917
(Add: 1+9+1+7=18)	1
	9
	1
	7
Start of drastic party purges under Stalin	1935
(Add: 1+9+3+5=18)	1
	9
	3
	5
Death of Stalin, marking great change in Russian policy	1953
(Add: 1+9+5+3=18)	1
	9
	5
Death of Khrushchev, who succeeded Stalin and reversed	3
many of his policies	1971
(Add: 1+9+7+1=18)	1
	9
	7
	1
Another highly important event in Russian history	1989

It should be noted that these years, while representing vertical tabulations, also show a regular periodic progression of 18 years, a type of prediction that is frequently of high importance in the affairs of nations. Hence it is quite likely that the year 2007 will mark some vital point in Russian history, but whether or not it should occur, the vertical prediction will still stand, with the figures of 1989+1+9+8+9=2016, bringing the progression to the centennial of the Russian Revolution, 2017, which is sure to be an eventful year.

A classic example of a progressive vertical sequence is that of the four Georges, the British monarchs representing the House of Hanover, who ruled for more than a century in uninterrupted succession. Each year of attainment in the progression marked either the accession of the next in line or an event of utmost importance or significance in the survival of the monarchy itself.

Here is the tabulated progression:

George I became King of England in	1714
	1
	7
	1
	4
George II became king (on death of George I)	1727
	1
	7
	2
	7
Start of Stuart rebellion against House of Hanover	1744
	1
	7
	4
	4
George III became king (on death of George II)	1760
	1
	7
	6
Meeting of first Continental Congress as	0
prelude to the American Revolution	1774
	1
	7
	7
Execution of King Louis XVI during French	4
Revolution, as a threat to all monarchs	1793

                                                  1
                                                  7
Allied victory over Napoleon, ending   9
threat of French invasion of England   3

                                                1813

The abrupt end of this sequence, with no date for the accession of King George IV, has a remarkable significance of its own. By 1813, George III was still king in name only, having gone so hopelessly insane late in 1810 that he was utterly unable to rule and the government was in the hands of his ministry.

Taking the last year of rule by George III as a radix   1810
                                                            1
                                                            8
                                                            1
                                                            o
                                                          -----
George IV became king (on death of George III)   1820

That raises the question whether the career of George IV could have been projected by a similar process. Yes, if during the early stages of the madness of George III a new progression had been started from the birth of George IV, thus:

King George IV was born in the year   1762
          Add 1+7+6+2   1778
          Add 1+7+7+8   1801
          Add 1+8+o+1   1811

In the year 1811, Parliament bestowed the title of regent on the future King George IV, giving him monarchial powers. By a curious circumstance, he was also named regent of the German state of Brunswick, until its youthful ruler came of age. Continue the progression:

First year of George IV as Regent of England   1811
                                                   1
                                                   8
                                                   1
                                                   1

Last year of George IV as Regent of Brunswick   1822

The reign of King William IV (who succeeded George IV) was brief indeed, lasting only seven years, but his accession to the throne in 1830 marked the start of a progressive vertical sequence that increased in significance as it proceeded and therefore can be cited as an outstanding example of numerological prediction, as it accurately pinpointed the wars and conflicts that offered the greatest threats to the British Empire over the next century; namely:

$$
\begin{array}{rl}
\text{William IV became King of England in} & 1830 \\
\text{Add } 1+8+3+0=12 & \\
\text{Beginning of War with Sind, in India} & 1842 \\
\text{Add } 1+8+4+2=15 & \\
\text{Outbreak of the great Sepoy Mutiny in India} & 1857 \\
\text{Add } 1+8+5+7=21 & \\
\text{War with Afghanistan} & 1878 \\
\text{Add } 1+8+7+8=24 & \\
\text{End of South African War with Boers} & 1902 \\
\text{Add } 1+9+0+2=12 & \\
\text{Beginning of World War I} & 1914
\end{array}
$$

As a result of World War I, the British Empire reached its period of greatest expansion, so 1914 can be accepted as the culmination of that particular progression. Baleful predictions of conflict in 1929 $(1914+1+9+1+4=1929)$ did not materialize, for by then the principal British dominions had acquired an independent status as members of the League of Nations. Events of the future where Britain was concerned will be covered in the next progression.

If ever the coming course of empire was foreshadowed by a periodic sequence, that rule held true with Queen Victoria of England. The progression that began with the year of her birth, in 1819, has carried on through five more reigns, over a century and a half, into that of another queen, Elizabeth II. Not only that, starting from the radix of 1819, every step in the progression has had to do either directly with the throne and its impending prospects or with the ministry. Every date in the progression has literally been of major consequence, as follows:

$$
\begin{array}{rr}
\text{Victoria was born in the year} & 1819 \\
& 1 \\
& 8 \\
& 1 \\
\text{Succeeded to the throne in 1837 and was} & 9 \\
\text{crowned queen the next year; namely} & \overline{1838}
\end{array}
$$

<pre>
                                                          1
                                                          8
                                                          3
    Her daughter, Victoria, married Prince Frederick   8
     of Prussia, cementing Anglo-Germanic friendship   1858
                                                          1
                                                          8
                                                          5
                                                          8
    Retirement of Lord Beaconsfield as prime minister   1880
                                                          1
                                                          8
                                                          8
          Year of the Golden Jubilee, celebrating the   0
              sixtieth year of Victoria's reign   1897
                                                          1
                                                          8
                                                          9
     End of the prime ministry of David Lloyd George,   7
              great leader in World War I   1922
                                                          1
                                                          9
                                                          2
    Accession and abdication of Edward VIII, with   2
              George VI as successor   1936
                                                          1
                                                          9
                                                          3
      Retirement of Sir Winston Churchill, great   6
         prime minister of World War II   1955
                                                          1
                                                          9
                                                          5
                                                          5
       An important year in modern British history   1975
</pre>

Though this almost fantastic progression hit every high spot in British political history, it was overlooked until after the death of Queen Victoria and even then was regarded simply as a personal progression. The fact that her birth year added up to her coronation and finally to her jubilee was significant, but the in-between links of the chain did not apply directly to Queen Victoria herself.

Considered in terms of the English throne, however, those dates take on great importance. By 1871, the King of Prussia had become the Emperor of Germany, so that Victoria's daughter, due to her marriage in 1858, later became Empress of Germany. Her son was the notorious Kaiser Wilhelm II. He was later blamed for provoking World War I, with England as his prime target. If ever coming events were foreshadowed, this was an outstanding case.

Meanwhile, Benjamin Disraeli had become British prime minister again in 1874 and promptly pressed a foreign policy fitting the demands of British prestige and interest. By gaining control of the Suez Canal, Disraeli paved the way to proclaiming Queen Victoria as Empress of India. Disraeli himself was elevated to the peerage as Lord Beaconsfield; hence the end of his ministry, in the key year of 1880, marked the limit of British imperial policy.

Just as Disraeli had established the empire, so did Lloyd George uphold it when he became prime minister during the trying years of World War I and guided England through to victory. The resignation of his cabinet, in 1922, another year of the progression, marked a further decline in international affairs, leading to the appeasement policy that brought on World War II. But before that, the progression reached a fadic year that confronted the English crown with the greatest crisis in its history, even threatening the throne itself.

That was in 1936, when England had three monarchs: George V, who died early in the year, to be succeeded by his son, Edward VIII, who in turn abdicated in favor of his brother, George VI. Only then was the prophetic power of the Victorian progression recognized in full; yet there was more to follow. When the British Empire was hard pressed in World War II, another great prime minister, Winston Churchill, arose to preserve it and the British crown as well. His retirement in 1955, the next year in the fateful progression, terminated the greatest ministry of all, with a new queen, Elizabeth II, on the throne of England, another remarkable link in the progressive chain.

The history of the House of Hapsburg, the ruling family of Austria, provides a long succession of ill-luck that increased to unprecedented proportions during the last years of the dynasty. The chief target of the jinx was the Emperor Francis Joseph I, who was said to have regarded himself as unlucky, despite the fact that his reign of sixty-eight years was one of the longest in modern history. During it, Austria and Hungary were established as a dual monarchy, with Francis Joseph as ruler of both, and very significantly, his career was foreshadowed by a dual period sequence, each with its own radix but both culminating in a common climax, which in itself marked a double tragedy and ultimate disaster.

Francis Joseph was born in the year 1830, marking one radix of the twin progression. In the year 1848, he was practically precipitated to the Austrian throne through no direct effort of his own, due to the abdication of his predecessor, the Emperor Ferdinand I; hence that forms a proper radix for a sequence of its own. From those beginnings, the progressions run concurrently, as follows:

Year of Birth 1830	
Add 1+8+3+0=1842	
Add 1+8+4+2=1857	*Year of Accession* 1848
Add 1+8+5+7=1878	Add 1+8+4+8=1869
Add 1+8+7+8=1902	Add 1+8+6+9=1893
Add 1+9+0+2=1914	Add 1+8+9+3=1914

That year, 1914, marked the assassination of Archduke Francis Ferdinand, the emperor's nephew and heir to the throne, with his wife the Princess Sophia, at Sarajevo, in Bosnia. That double murder triggered World War I, which brought ruin to the Austrian Empire and the House of Hapsburg.

Any numerologist could have readily forecast some startling result from such a double climax, even though it turned out to be more stupendous than anyone might have even imagined. Possibly it was overlooked because none of the intervening dates seemed particularly important at the time; and probably no one thought in terms of a dual progression, hence each could have been discounted separately. However, in retrospect, two years of attainment stand out sharply in the longer progression, as they have a direct bearing on the climax, as represented by 1914.

The first of those key years is 1857, which marked the birth of the Crown Prince Rudolph, the only son of Francis Joseph I and the original heir to the Austrian throne. At the age of thirty-one, Rudolph was found dead with the Baroness Marie Vetsera, in his hunting lodge at Mayerling, outside Vienna, under mysterious circumstances that were never fully explained, although the case was officially declared to be a suicide pact.

This double tragedy strangely foreshadowed the double assassination that was to occur at Sarajevo, many years later. Its importance lies in the fact that had the Crown Prince Rudolph lived, the Sarajevo affair would never have occurred, and the whole course of history would have been changed, for Rudolph would have been the target for assassination; not Francis Ferdinand.

Even more significant in the first progression is the year 1878, for that was when Austria-Hungary occupied the provinces of Bosnia and

Herzegovina, which were eventually annexed to the empire. It was the indignation roused among the predominant Serbian population of Bosnia that led to the assassination of Francis Ferdinand when he made his ill-fated visit to the Bosnian capital of Sarajevo.

So the dual progressions of the Emperor Francis Joseph were as ill-fated as the tragedy they predicted, and the war into which the emperor promptly plunged his nation proved to be his own undoing and brought about the destruction of his dynasty.

Singularly, another periodic progression found its climax in another assassination that marred the reign of Francis Joseph. It involved his wife, the Empress Elizabeth and mother of the ill-starred Prince Rudolph. It ran as follows:

$$Empress\ Elizabeth,\ born\ in\ \ \ 1837$$
$$Add\ 1+8+3+7=1856$$
$$Add\ 1+8+5+6=1876$$
$$Add\ 1+8+7+6=1898$$

In September of that year, 1898, which also marked the fiftieth year of the reign of Francis Joseph I, the Empress Elizabeth was attacked and slain by a crazed assassin while on a visit to Geneva, Switzerland.

That is not all.

When Francis Ferdinand and Sophia were married in the year 1900, the marriage met with disapproval from Emperor Francis Joseph, and the Princess Sophia was forced to renounce any claim to the throne where her children were concerned. She had a son born in the fadic year of 1902, which added vertically, 1+9+0+2, produces the fatal year of 1914, when he would have become heir to the throne following his father's assassination, except for the renunciation. Striking enough, but even more remarkable is the following:

$$Marriage\ of\ Francis\ Ferdinand\ and\ Sophia\ \ \ 1900$$
$$Add\ 1+9+0+0=1910$$
$$Add\ 1+9+1+0=1921$$

In that year, 1921, the Emperor Charles I, who did succeed Francis Joseph I, was exiled to Madeira, where he died in 1922. He had gained the throne on the death of the old emperor in 1916, lost it as a result of

World War I, and failed in an abortive effort to regain it. Thus the marriage year of Francis Ferdinand and Sophia presaged the end of the glory that neither they nor their children were ever to gain.

When a numerical sequence is applied to a person's career, age becomes the principal factor. A child is said to be in its first year until its first birthday anniversary; after that, it is one year old and remains so until its second anniversary. However, during that latter period, the child would also be in its second year, becoming two years old on its second anniversary; and so on.

As a simple illustration, take a man who was born on April 10, 1950. By using the year 1950 as a radix, its figures add as follows: 1+9+5+0=15. Hence April 10, 1965, would have marked his fifteenth birthday anniversary, not his "fifteenth birthday," as popular parlance puts it. So from April 10, 1964, when he entered his fifteenth year, until April 10, 1966, when he was still fifteen years old, he came under that fadic influence. This allows a "spread" of two years instead of only one, but April 10, 1965, would have been regarded as the focal point. Hence the proximity of an event to that date might have added to its significance, though not necessarily so.

To show the extent to which this can be tabulated and traced, we can take the historic case of three men who were all born in the same year, within a span of a little more than three months, and whose affairs were to become strangely interwoven. The year of their birth was 1769, so in each case, it is the radix of the sequence that followed. The three men were Napoleon, born August 15, 1769; the Duke of Wellington, his great adversary, born May 1, 1769; and Lord Castlereagh, born June 18, 1769, who, as Britain's Minister of War, dictated an aggressive policy against Napoleon and picked Wellington as the man to implement it.

By taking 1769 as the radix for all three, the results are quite surprising, as follows:

1769	Wellington (born)	Castlereagh (born)	Napoleon (born)
1			
7			
6			
9			
1792	Decided upon a military career	Established as a member of Parliament	Banished from Corsica

1			
7			
9			
2			
1811	Victorious in	Headed British	Birth of son,
1	Spain and elevated	Government following	establishing
8	to an earldom	assassination of the	the imperial
1		Prime Minister*	dynasty
1			
1822	Represented British	Death by suicide	Dead on St.
1	Government at		Helena†
8	Congress of Verona		
2			
2			
1835	Refused offer of		
1	the prime ministry		
8			
3			
5			
1852	Death		

THE PRESIDENTIAL SEQUENCE

Unique among periodic predictions is the presidential sequence that has occurred regularly at intervals of twenty years. Beginning with the election of William H. Harrison as President of the United States, in 1840, every president elected in a year divisible by 20 has died before completing his term of office. The list runs as follows:

William H. Harrison, elected in   1840
Abraham Lincoln, elected in   1860
James A. Garfield, elected in   1880
William McKinley, elected in   1900
Warren G. Harding, elected in   1920
Franklin D. Roosevelt, elected in   1940
John F. Kennedy, elected in   1960

* Spencer Perceval, born in November $1762+1+7+6+2=1778+1+7+7+8=$ 1801. In that year, he became Attorney General. Adding $1801+1+8+0+1=$ 1811. The assassination occurred prior to June 1812, bringing it within the fadic year.

† Napoleon died on May 5, 1821, a few months prior to the start of his fateful fifty-third year, but it is probable that his death was hastened by adverse conditions.

It should be noted that Lincoln died after being elected to a second term in 1864; and that McKinley was first elected in 1896, then again in 1900. Roosevelt had already served two terms when he was elected for a third term in 1940, and died after being elected for a fourth term in 1944. However, the "key" years and their prognostication still apply.

Whether or not this progression was noted prior to Harding's election in 1920, it was definitely discussed at the time of his death in 1923, and the progression appeared in a book on numerology published in 1927. A national magazine made a feature of it, prior to the election of 1940, speculating on the possibility that it would continue and apply to the successful candidate, which it did, in the case of Franklin D. Roosevelt.

By then, the singular sequence was forgotten by the general public. But it was probably remembered by various persons who claimed prophetic vision, for some of them came up with ambiguous prognostications of disappointment and danger confronting the presidential candidates in the 1960 election. These were later interpreted as full-fledged predictions of the death of President Kennedy, presumably obtained through the psychic powers of the individual prognosticators through their own favorite methods.

But it is an equally foregone conclusion that, if the vague prophecies had failed to materialize and the gifted seers had been called to account, they could very readily have blamed it all on the failure of the presidential periodicity. But the presidential periodicity has never failed since its inception. Perhaps it never will. Whoever runs for president in 1980 will be assuming a calculated risk, as every twentieth-year president has, and will, until the sequence comes to a logical completion, as all such progressions do.

For example: This is logic, more than prophecy. What significance can be attached to the "20-year jinx," as the presidential progression may properly be termed? One logical conclusion is that the "20" interval refers to the "20th century." Bluntly put, whoever becomes president in 1980 might not survive his (or her) term (or terms). But whoever wins the election in the year 2000 should be in to stay. That is, by one mode of calculation. But there are others.

It could very well be that the turning point will be reached before 1980 and that year will mark a striking departure that will explain the whole purpose of the progression. Indeed, as the world stands today, who knows if there will even be a presidential election in 1980? The bogging down of current conceptions, by 1980, 2000, or even further on, may someday be traced back to the radix year of 1840, or even further back, as we shall show, for the simple reason that no one has ever explored the preliminary possibilities.

At least no one until now.

Let us go back to the radix of 1840 and carry on from there. According to *The Science of Numerology*, the book published in 1927, there were *two* progressions, not just one, stemming from Harrison's election in 1840. One, already discussed, was the "twenty-year sequence." The other was the "fourth president progression," which ran as follows:

Zachary Taylor, elected president in 1848, died in office.
Abraham Lincoln, fourth president after Taylor, died in office.
James A. Garfield, fourth president after Lincoln, died in office.
William McKinley, fourth president after Garfield, died in office.
Warren G. Harding, fourth president after McKinley, died in office.

There the sequence stops. The twentieth year and the fourth president, a dual prediction, truly unstoppable, was to meet the test for this simple reason. Following Harding, there had been three presidents: Coolidge, Hoover, and Roosevelt. A new man as the *fourth president* to be elected in the *twentieth year*, would be doubly doomed, according to a progressive prophecy already known and well publicized.

Would anyone dare that challenge?

One man did: Wendell Willkie, an energetic forty-eight-year-old campaigner, who polled more votes than any other defeated candidate up to that date. But Franklin D. Roosevelt defied tradition and ran for a third term, which he gained, thus saving Willkie from the sure doom that would strike anyone who challenged that double chain of disaster.

But fate deemed otherwise.

Before the completion of the four-year term that he never served, Wendell Wilkie was dead. If Franklin D. Roosevelt had accepted tradition and refused a third term, it simply wouldn't have mattered. The double jinx was something that no one could beat.

That really should have marked the end of it, but it didn't. If F.D.R. had retired at the end of his third term, the "twenty-year jinx" would have been cracked along with the "fourth president" hoodoo. But when F.D.R. ran for a fourth term and made it, the "twenty-year" chain remained in force and was fulfilled. That kept the soothsayers in business for another twenty years, and the death of John F. Kennedy, who was elected in 1960, added twenty more.

That raises the question: How did it all begin? Oddly, theories have been scant on that score. The prophets generally have begged the question, or, as mentioned earlier, they may have studiously avoided it, to take personal credit for their predictions yet have an alibi if they go wrong. One astrologer is said to have attributed the fatal sequence to the baleful influence of the planet Saturn, claiming that it becomes especially virulent every twenty years. But no parallel cases were cited, and why this should apply so strongly to the American presidency and not to the affairs of other nations is as much a puzzle as the sequence itself.

However, since the chain is definitely cyclic, the proper course is to backtrack to the year 1800, the first of the "twenty-year," election periods and see what might have been fated there. At that time, presidential electors voted for two candidates; the one receiving the most votes became president; the next best became vice-president. The 1800 election resulted in a tie, with Thomas Jefferson and Aaron Burr polling 73 votes each. That put the choice up to Congress, who named Jefferson as president and Burr as vice-president.

This was largely due to the influence of Alexander Hamilton, who strongly opposed Burr, and later Burr provoked a duel with Hamilton and shot him. Burr was indicted for murder and his political career was ended. By the time of the next election, the mode of choosing president and vice-president was changed, each being voted on separately. Not only that, the office of vice-president itself was jinxed for years to come, as though Burr's action had given it a sinister blotch.

The next two vice-presidents, George Clinton and Elbridge Gerry, each died while in office. The next man, Daniel Tompkins, was elected in 1816 and again in 1820, the second stage of the "twenty-year" cycle. Tompkins completed that second term but died a few months later. His successor, John C. Calhoun, served one term and was re-elected, but resigned before completing the next. Apparently, nobody was getting anywhere by being vice-president, any more than Aaron Burr had.

Things changed when Martin Van Buren was elected vice-president in 1832 and went on to win the presidency in November 1836, which happened to be less than two months after the death of Aaron Burr, who had cherished that same ambition. But apparently the hoodoo didn't die with Burr, for Van Buren was defeated when he tried for a second presidential term in 1840 and from then on failed in every effort to regain the presidency.

That same year, 1840, marked the switch of the jinx from the vice-presidency to the presidency with the sudden death of President William H. Harrison a month after his inauguration and the unexpected assumption of presidential powers by the vice-president, John Tyler, who had been strictly a compromise candidate. From then on, the jinx followed the new pattern.

Significant though the Burr sequence may be, there is a question whether it would be strong enough to carry into further generations, or even trigger any cyclic action. Nor is Burr's cruel spite toward

Hamilton indicative of an urge to frustrate future claimants to an ambition that Burr himself could not attain. Again, in looking for the origin of a cyclic curse, we must find someone with the power to project it, as well as a long-range target.

So we take the year 1810, when William Henry Harrison was governor of the Territory of Indiana, where he received Tecumseh, chief of the Shawnees, and his twin brother Tenskwatawa, more commonly known as "the Prophet," though to a great degree he was merely Tecumseh's spokesman, for the famed chief had his own visions of the future and was emphatic in expressing them.

Just as the United States had become a nation, so did Tecumseh plan to establish a great Indian confederation that would rival it in the Midwest. As chief of those tribes, Tecumseh announced that if the Americans encroached further into Indian territory, war would result. After delivering that ultimatum, Tecumseh went south to rally other Indian tribes to his banner. When some of the Creeks refused to join him, he predicted that when the time came he would stamp his foot and shake down all their villages. With that grim prophecy, Tecumseh headed north.

Meanwhile, Harrison, expecting trouble, moved toward the town of Tippecanoe, where the Prophet had been assembling warriors while awaiting Tecumseh's return. Adding his own exaggerations to Tecumseh's predictions, the Prophet assured the warriors that they would be immune from American bullets, so they followed him in a surprise attack on Harrison's troops. The immunity proved nonexistent, the Indians were routed, Tippecanoe was destroyed, Tecumseh's power was shaken, and Harrison held Indiana.

With the advent of the War of 1812, Tecumseh rallied his former followers and joined the British in Canada. About that time, the Creek nation was horrified when their villages were demolished by a tremendous upheaval. The cry went out, "Tecumseh has stamped his foot!" and many tribes were ready to join his cause. Actually, it was a tremendous earthquake, the biggest that the United States has known before or since, that shook the entire Mississippi Valley and frightened settlers as well as Indians.

When the British retreated from Detroit in 1813, Tecumseh demanded that they make a stand, even predicting that he himself would be killed, but that it would be worth the sacrifice to halt the American advance. The British commander, General Proctor, finally agreed and met the Americans in the Battle of the Thames. The American army was commanded by none other than General Harrison, who had blasted Tecumseh's grandiose plans at Tippecanoe and now ruined them forever. Harrison's cavalry, headed by Colonel Richard M. Johnson, routed the British forces, and Tecumseh was slain as he had predicted, shot down in hand-to-hand conflict by Colonel Johnson.

That defeat caused many tribes to desert the British, and without Tecumseh to rally them the dream of a united Indian nation was gone. Whether Tecumseh heaped dying curses on both Harrison and Johnson, his twin brother Tenskwatawa most certainly voiced such maledictions during the twenty years that followed. The Prophet went West and lived with the Indians beyond the Mississippi until his death in 1834. That was when both Harrison and Johnson began to have grandiose plans of their own, involving a nation much bigger and more powerful than any that Tecumseh had hoped to found.

In the 1836 election, William Harrison ran for President of the United States on the Whig ticket, while Richard Johnson ran for vice-president on the Democratic ticket, basing his campaign slogan on the proud boast that he had killed Tecumseh. Both ran into complications: Harrison lost to the Democratic candidate, Martin Van Buren, partly because the Whigs failed to give him full support, some voting for "favorite sons" instead; while Johnson lost so many Democratic votes for the same reason that for the first and only time, the vice-presidency had to be decided by the U. S. Senate, which sustained Johnson, although he lacked a majority of electoral votes.

All this could have resulted from some powerful "whammy" laid by Tecumseh or Tenskwatawa or both, but nobody gave it much thought until after the next presidential election, in 1840. Then Harrison ran against Van Buren again, this time with full support of the Whigs, who nominated John Tyler, a Democrat, for vice-president, hoping to gain votes by the compromise. Now, Harrison took credit for settling the Techumseh menace, with the slogan, "Tippecanoe and Tyler too." Meanwhile, Johnson went campaigning in his own behalf, still trying to retain the vice-presidency as the hero who had ridden along with Harrison at the Battle of the Thames.

It would have been remarkable indeed if Harrison and Johnson had wound up as heads of the United States Government, just as Tecumseh and Tenskwatawa had planned to control a great Indian confederation. But the individual hopes of William Henry Harrison and Richard Mentor Johnson were so utterly wrecked that it indeed seemed that the Indian brothers must have laid a curse upon them. Harrison and Tyler won handily, while Van Buren went down to defeat, taking Johnson with him. But Harrison died a month after his inauguration and Tyler became president, leaving Johnson to bemoan the fact that he had won the vice-presidency in the wrong year, with the wrong party, and with the wrong running mate.

Many Indian prophecies were of a recurrent nature, particularly the baleful type, so if we grant that Harrison and Johnson were the victims of Tecumseh's curse, it can logically be accepted as periodic, which would account for the twenty-year jinx that continued from 1840 onward. The twenty-year interval itself is highly significant, when we note that long after Tecumseh's time an Indian prophet named Wodziwob instituted a ceremony called the Ghost Dance, which was to bring back the spirits of many warriors, including such chiefs as Tecumseh, who would win back the West for the tribes still living there.

Wodziwob's visions failed to materialize, but just *twenty years* later, the Ghost Dance was revived by another prophet, Wokova, and spread like wildfire among the Western tribes. This was exactly *eighty years*—four times the significant number twenty—after Tecumseh had delivered his ultimatum to William Henry Harrison, then Governor of Indiana.

Back then, Tenskwatawa had performed a ritual with a magic bowl, a sacred torch, and a string of mystic beads to give Tecumseh's followers supposed immunity to bullets, resulting in their defeat at Tippecanoe. Now, eighty years later, Wokova's prophecies roused a similar belief. Stirred by visions of their own, the Ghost Dancers painted dream symbols on their shirts, confident that they would counteract enemy gunfire. When the charms failed to work, many of them were massacred at the Battle of Wounded Knee.

We have cited these cases simply to prove that the Indian prophecies should not be misjudged because they occasionally backfired. The fact that they aroused such fanaticism proves that their cyclic prophecies usually worked, but that they ebbed and flowed; and that their followers—not the prophets—occasionally went the wrong way. But they may have been right most of the time.

So today, it may be our land, and therefore your land, but once it was their land, and it may still be tomorrow, which was the day they continually looked for, and perhaps may eventually find. So let us apply their cyclic rule to the presidential progression, which may—or may not—have been started by Tecumseh but was fated to go on and may continue to do so, until it finally dwindles into oblivion, as such things generally do.

But even as it diminishes, it may be subject to rise and fall, so let us see how—or how not—it may have operated since the year 1840. Just twenty years after that fateful date, the United States was faced by the greatest crisis in its history.

That was the presidential election of 1860, wherein:

The man who should have been elected president was Stephen A. Douglas, the Democratic candidate, except that the Southern Demo-

crats wouldn't go along and put up their own man, John C. Breckin-
ridge. That split brought about the election of Abraham Lincoln, the
Republican candidate, who polled only about one third of the popular
vote. That raises the question: What would have happened if Douglas
had been elected? The answer is one of the most overlooked enigmas in
American history, because:

Stephen Douglas, first in line for the twenty-year presidential jinx,
died within *three months* after he would have been inaugurated on
March 4, 1861, which would have made his tenure of office the shortest on record, next to William H. Harrison, the original target of Tecumseh's wrath. Naturally, Douglas would have been succeeded by his
vice-president, whose name, like his career, has been still more thoroughly overlooked. He was Herschel V. Johnson, of Georgia, who fa-
vored the Union but had such strong Southern sympathies that, if he
had become president at that crucial time, it might have helped to
avert the Civil War.

Thus, like Richard M. Johnson, Herschel V. became another candidate for vice-president who failed to make it and thereby lost out on the
presidency as well. The fact that they were not related makes it all
the more logical that Tecumseh had a hand in it, since neither he nor
Tenskwatawa could have known the wide prevalence of a family name
like Johnson, and therefore might have wished bad luck for all John-
sons who aspired to high office.

Proof of this came when Abraham Lincoln, already under the baleful influence of the twenty-year cycle, ran for his second term in 1864
and dropped Hannibal Hamlin, his vice-president, taking on Andrew
Johnson instead. A little more than a month after his new term began,
Lincoln was assassinated and Andrew Johnson became president, only
to run into worse luck than either of his namesakes. Impeachment
proceedings were brought against him, and the U. S. Senate came just
one vote short of removing him from office, which all but ended his political career.

In 1896, William McKinley was elected president on the Republican
ticket, with Garret Hobart as vice-president. Among the defeated candidates was Joshua Levering of the Prohibition Party, whose running
mate was named Hale Johnson. Whether or not that was a bad omen,
Garret Hobart, the man who was elected vice-president, died before
finishing his four-year-term, while President McKinley went on to re-
election in 1900, only to encounter the fatal twenty-year cycle and die
in office.

Until then, the jinx had applied to the vice-presidency as well, for
all the men who had succeeded to the presidency had simply finished
that term and then failed to gain renomination. But that spell was

broken by McKinley's successor, Theodore Roosevelt, who ran for president in 1904 and was elected. But "Teddy" also tempted fate once too often. In 1912, he sought the presidential nomination again and when the Republicans refused to go along, he formed the Progressive Party and ran as its presidential candidate.

Though the Progressives polled a larger vote than the Republicans, the split enabled the Democrats to pile up a still higher total. So T.R. was defeated in his final drive, proving that the twenty-year hoodoo was still at work, since he had been elected with McKinley during the cyclic year of 1900. As if that were not enough, Teddy took as his running mate on the Progressive ticket a senator from California named Hiram Johnson, another significant link to the constantly recurring jinx.

In 1920, the Republican nomination was wide open for almost anybody. Republicans and Progressives had reunited, and Teddy Roosevelt had been regarded as a prime candidate, which would have made him the first man to run for election in two fateful years, for vice-president in 1900 and president in 1920. But T.R. died suddenly in 1919, a year before the impending election, so Hiram Johnson went after the presidential nomination on his own.

Instead, the Republican Party nominated Warren G. Harding as a "dark horse" presidential candidate and promptly offered Hiram Johnson the vice-presidential place on the ticket. But he refused it, having his mind set on the presidency and nothing less. He thereby lost the presidency, because when Harding won the presidency and later died in office, Hiram wasn't there to take over. So again, the twenty-year cycle and the Johnson legend were linked in a surprising fashion.

One remarkable factor in the presidential sequence was that its periodic blight took effect, not only upon winning candidates, but upon losers as well. This has been touched upon in the preceding pages, and a full list of some two dozen persons could be cited, showing how the jinx years paved the way to political obscurity up until Teddy Roosevelt ran for the presidency in 1904 and won it, though his luck faded later, as has been described.

With Harding's death, Calvin Coolidge became president, and in 1924 he ran for the presidency and won it, thus emulating T.R.'s success of twenty years before. But in 1928 he voluntarily returned to private life, announcing that he did not "choose to run" for another term. By then, the "twenty-year jinx" had become known, and possibly it was too uncanny for canny Cal. In any case, his political career was ended, as with all who figured in the cyclic years.

Then, in 1932, a man arose to defy all such traditions and more. That was Franklin D. Roosevelt, who had run for vice-president on the losing Democratic ticket in 1920. Along with the twenty-year jinx, F.D.R. faced the fact that no defeated candidate for the vice-presidency had even been nominated for the presidency. But F.D.R. won both the presidential nomination and the election in 1932 and in 1936 as well, bringing him to the cyclic year of 1940. He won then, too, becoming the first man to run in two such years—1920 and 1940—and he shattered the third-term precedent in addition, going on to win a fourth term in 1944, only to die while still in office.

F.D.R.'s successor, Harry Truman, went on to win the next election in 1948 and then retire, at the end of that term, as Coolidge had. So all was serene until 1960, when John F. Kennedy was elected and became a victim of the fatal chain two years later. There was just a hundred years between the elections of Lincoln and Kennedy, and by a remarkable coincidence, J.F.K. was succeeded by Lyndon B. Johnson, another link to the prophetic past. However, L.B.J. did not merely finish out the unexpired term, he ran for president in 1964 and won an overwhelming victory, then announced his retirement in 1968, following the pattern set by Presidents Coolidge and Truman.

Some analysts of the presidential progression feel that it began with Abraham Lincoln and ended with John F. Kennedy, pointing out, among other factors, that their assassins, John Wilkes Booth and Lee Harvey Oswald, each spelled his name with the same number of letters, fifteen. Pursuing that analogy further, we find that Garfield's assassin, Charles J. Guiteau, also had a name with fifteen letters.

That failed to hold, however, with McKinley's assassin, Leon F. Czolgosz, whose name was two letters short. But many persons have forgotten that, a few months after Franklin D. Roosevelt became president-elect in 1932, an assassin fired six shots at him in Miami, but wounded other persons instead, including Mayor Cermak of Chicago, who died as a result. The name of that assassin was Giuseppe Zangara, whose name is spelled with fifteen letters. So the coincidence may still be significant. But by the same token, it could go back to Richard M. Johnson, who also had fifteen letters in his name, and he was the man who killed Tecumseh.

FATAL THIRTEEN
(Spelled with 13 Letters)

In the annals of the AMERICAN PRESIDENCY, the THIRTEENTH MAN (13 letters) to be elected to that office was JAMES BUCHANAN, whose name is spelled with 13 letters. He was the only

PENNSYLVANIAN (spelled with 13 letters) to become president. During his term, SOUTH CAROLINA (13 letters) seceded from the Union and Buchanan was surrounded by SECESSIONISTS, spelled with 13 letters. These included important members of the WAR DE-PARTMENT (13 letters) and JACOB THOMPSON, spelled with 13 letters, the Secretary of the Interior, who was born and raised in NORTH CAROLINA, spelled with 13 letters and then became a MISSISSIPPIAN, which is also spelled with 13 letters. On the advice of JEREMIAH BLACK (13 letters), the Secretary of State, and WIN-FIELD SCOTT (13 letters), commanding general of the U. S. Army, the President dispatched MAJOR ANDERSON, spelled with 13 letters, popularly known as BOBBY ANDERSON, another 13 letters, to hold the CAROLINA FORTS (13 letters) which commanded the harbor of Charleston. Some were abandoned and PALMETTO FLAGS (13 letters) were raised over them, but Anderson still flew the STARS & STRIPES (13 letters) above one, which thereby became FORT SUMTER, U.S.A., spelled with 13 letters. To relieve the fort, the SLOOP BROOKLYN, also spelled with 13 letters, a warship armed with TWENTY-TWO GUNS (13 letters) and captained by DAVID FARRAGUT, spelled with 13 letters, was sent south but was recalled. Instead, a merchant steamer STAR OF THE WEST (13 letters) took a company of soldiers commanded by CHARLES R. WOODS (13 letters), but it was fired upon when it crossed the CHARLESTON BAR (13 letters) and was forced to retire. When Fort Sumter refused to surrender, a bombardment was ordered by P. T. G. BEAUREGARD (13 letters), the general of the Confederate forces. The first shots were fired from CUMMING'S POINT, spelled with 13 letters, where ROS-WELL RIPLEY (13 letters) was the colonel commanding the batteries. Later, LOUIS T. WIGFALL (13 letters) went to Anderson with terms of surrender and Fort Sumter lowered its flag on the THIRTEENTH of April, 1861.

IV. What Today Can Mean
to You

HOW TO ATTUNE THE VIBRATORY
POWER OF YOUR BIRTH NUMBER
TO ANY DATE IN ANY YEAR

According to numerology, every date can be added up, figure by figure, and then reduced to a single number that represents the vibratory influence of that day. Applied to a person's date of birth, this produces a birth number, which represents his or her predominating vibration throughout life.

As an example, a person born on June 28, 1947, would start with the figure 6, representing the sixth month, June, and continue with the remaining figures, thus: $6+2+8+1+9+4+7=37$, which is composed of figures $3+7=10$, which becomes $1+0=1$. That is the individual's birth number.

Another example: December 4, 1970, would start with the figures 1 and 2 for the twelfth month, December, and the figures of the entire date add up to $1+2+4+1+9+7+0=24$, which is broken into $2+4=6$. That would be the birth number of anyone born on that particular date.

Here, however, another factor enters, one that hitherto has seldom been developed to its full degree. Taking a person with the birth number 1, as in the first example of June 28, 1947, how would that person's affairs be governed on a day like December 4, 1970 (which has as its vibratory influence 6)? The answer is, the traits or motives indicated by

Number 1 would have to be checked against the vibratory conditions governing the number 6 to learn how well they harmonized or what conflicts might be anticipated.

The important thing is that, where dates are concerned, the day rules the person rather than the other way about. A birth number is similar to an astrological calculation, or the sign under which a person was born. The only notable difference is that there are nine vibratory numbers as opposed to twelve signs of the zodiac. No two persons are exactly alike, but those with the same birth number are apt to have the same natural trends or underlying characteristics, according to numerology.

Similarly, days have their differences, even though their vibratory numbers may be identical. Here we have another analogy between numerology and astrology. The days of the week, beginning with Sunday, can be enumerated from 1 to 7 inclusive, just as they are named after the seven original planets used in astrological calculations. So by applying this to the day in question, we find 63 (9×7) possible interpretations that may apply to any day throughout the year and thus serve as a daily numerological guide. These, in turn, are dependent upon the birth number of the individual, making 567 interpretations in all.

To utilize these, proceed as follows:

First, establish your birth number by adding the figures of your birthday, month, day and year, as already described.

Next, find today's number by the same process.

Finally, note the day of the week, without bothering about figuring it numerically, since the weekdays already are in sequence.

Assume that your birth number is 1 and that today's number is 6 and that it happens to be Saturday. You go through the pages that say "When birth number is 1" until the column at the left declares "And today's number is 6." You run down that to the notation "If Saturday—" and there you have it, your numerological indication for that day and those to follow.

Try it and prove it to your own satisfaction. But do not limit yourself to today. You can pick any date, past or future, as well as present, and see if it would have worked out or is going to work out. Not only that, you do not have to confine it to your own experiences. You can check it against those of other people—past, present or future—and see how well it tallies, by using their numbers as bases. These should be treated strictly as indications; never as actual predictions, for these good reasons:

If you follow some of the advice given for a certain day, it may offset any undesirable factors mentioned; hence the actual outcome depends to a great degree upon yourself.

Many of the indications, whether good or bad, may carry over to the next few days, or even longer; hence any daily reading may have to be modified by circumstances that are now beyond control.

Also, other numerological factors or other psychic influences may be involved, thereby tempering the usual indications.

Finally, when other persons are directly concerned, their vibratory indications must also be checked for the date in question, to see if there are any points of harmony or conflict, so you can plan accordingly.

WHEN BIRTH NUMBER IS 1

AND DAY'S NUMBER IS 1

If Sunday: Immediate prospects are fine, but don't be stubborn if you meet with arguments. Switch tactics and get around them.

If Monday: A time to attend to minor matters, routine work, or correspondence, thus laying the groundwork for something bigger.

If Tuesday: Nothing ventured, nothing gained. Go after anything you really want, but move fast before someone else snatches it.

If Wednesday: Take steps to improve business and social contacts. Inspire confidence in others, without demanding an immediate return.

If Thursday: Act now if you have well-laid plans; otherwise, plan carefully before you act. Avoid any decisions depending on emotions.

If Friday: Whatever you start today may grow in big ways. If you have a worth-while project, don't neglect it. Push it now.

If Saturday: A good day to further personal ambitions, but don't act too self-important. Let people appraise you for your true worth.

DAY'S NUMBER IS 2

If Sunday: Any hesitation on your part may spoil your coming plans. Get things off the ground now, or you may find your efforts wasted.

If Monday: Don't listen to wild rumors or be influenced by other people's ideas. Rely on your own judgment and act accordingly.

If Tuesday: Seek advice from friends or family before making any rash decision. A time to return favors and make other people happy.

If Wednesday: Avoid changing plans or taking sides in any argument, as people are apt to misunderstand you and misquote you.

If Thursday: You may have to seek new friends or places to get what you want, but now is the time, provided your plans are worth it.

If Friday: Don't count on gaining your ambitions just now. Bolster your future by helping others gain theirs. Be a good loser.

If Saturday: Big results may hinge on an immediate decision. Seek good advice before going all out on whatever you choose to do.

DAY'S NUMBER IS 3

If Sunday: Try something new and see it through. A trip, whether for business or pleasure, may clear your mind for rapid action.

If Monday: Remember your friends by giving them presents or offering them any help they need. They will show lasting appreciation.

If Tuesday: A time to work with others who are as anxious for results as you are. An exchange of ideas may open new opportunities.

If Wednesday: Even if you are badly frustrated, stay with your present aims. Someone is sure to recognize your abilities and lend a helping hand.

If Thursday: If you think that you are going somewhere, make sure it is in the right direction. An aim too easily gained may spoil something better.

If Friday: Whatever your talent, now is the time to develop and display it. Pick work and surroundings best suited to your capability.

If Saturday: The more you try to figure what to do, the more undecided you may become. If this is not your day, let matters go until later.

DAY'S NUMBER IS 4

If Sunday: Work for harmony in the week to come, avoiding any friction or argument with family or associates. Watch how much better things will go!

If Monday: Don't brood over trifles. Each day you fritter away puts its burden on the next. Take routine work cheerfully and it will be easier.

If Tuesday: Whatever you do today may have big consequences. So do it well. Don't let anything divert you from your purpose.

If Wednesday: Diversify your interests without neglecting present work or projects, and your advancement should be certain.

If Thursday: Any new opportunity in a familiar field may prove to your advantage. A change of scene may give you new energy.

If Friday: Don't let present worries wear you down. It's better to put up with them than to let wishful thinking guide you to a futile future.

If Saturday: If you are planning something important, put it into action before you talk about it. Otherwise, someone may beat you to it.

DAY'S NUMBER IS 5

If Sunday: An active or exciting life is your best tonic against gloom or depression. If you are feeling moody now, go out and find fun!

If Monday: The more enterprising you become, the greater your chance of success. For the present, rely on your own judgment about taking up anything new.

If Tuesday: Any new experience may be a step toward your ambition. A good day to take chances or demand whatever is due you.

If Wednesday: A time to face issues. If you have been avoiding any friends or obligations, it may be to your advantage to square them now.

If Thursday: Whatever you do or start today, you're apt to regret it and wish you'd done something else. So avoid anything that may bring worry.

If Friday: Your present interests may be causing you to neglect someone who cares greatly for you. Give time to romance or friendship.

If Saturday: Any speculative project may prove profitable, provided you give full time to it. Make sure you get your share for the work involved.

DAY'S NUMBER IS 6

If Sunday: A real day to win friends and influence people, particularly the kind who can help you. Be optimistic but act conservatively.

If Monday: Contact friends whom you haven't seen in a long time. They may have news that will surprise you. This can lead to something bigger.

If Tuesday: Don't let friends or social functions interfere with your immediate purposes. Be cordial but noncommittal and keep your ideas to yourself.

If Wednesday: Events beyond your control may upset your present plans. Avoid conflicting interests until you are sure which is best, then go along with it.

If Thursday: Watch out for false or fickle friends. They may be hoping to block your plans and turn them to their own advantage.

If Friday: The more things you propose, the more your friends or associates will demand that you produce. Go your own way if you can.

If Saturday: Go along with people who have new ideas and like to enjoy life, provided you are free from financial risk. Otherwise, stay on your own.

DAY'S NUMBER IS 7

If Sunday: Set yourself a course of intensive study and stay with it. This could be a step to a great future. Watch for such indications.

If Monday: Don't let any immediate setbacks worry you. Shake off any despondency and follow your present inclinations. A smoother path is ahead.

If Tuesday: Ease the day's drive by seeking refinement and culture. Weigh decisions in terms of balancing work with relaxation.

If Wednesday: Bring yourself up to date on anything you plan. You may be depending too much on your own limited opinions or observations.

If Thursday: Whatever your present problems, hard work should cure them. Think ahead and forget the past. Watch results pile up!

If Friday: Watch out for clever schemers who are eager to defraud you. By living too much to yourself, you may become prey to such persons.

If Saturday: Gear yourself for immediate results on the intellectual plane! Business, friendship, even romance may hinge upon a meeting of the minds.

DAY'S NUMBER IS 8

If Sunday: Whatever you are planning now should bring big financial returns. But don't let anybody talk you out of it. Keep it for yourself!

If Monday: The bigger your hopes, the more they may be blasted. If somebody turns you down, forget it and start all over.

If Tuesday: Anything developing today may prove disappointing, as too many people may be involved. Be glad to get whatever comes your way.

If Wednesday: Competition may prove too strong for you to overcome. But don't be discouraged. The experience may prove profitable.

If Thursday: Luck, rather than hard work, may soon bring you financial return or business advancement. Something you own may gain added value.

If Friday: Watch your expenditures closely. You may be wasting money cultivating friends or business contacts who mean little and care less.

If Saturday: No matter how good your judgment, you may be trusting too much in other persons. Sign nothing now, and before you invest, be sure to investigate.

DAY'S NUMBER IS 9

If Sunday: A time for self-appraisal. Find out quietly what you have been doing wrong and correct it. A good step toward gaining popularity.

If Monday: Climb out of your shell! If you have artistic urges, make the most of them. The more you are seen and heard, the happier you may become.

If Tuesday: Don't do favors just to gain popularity or people will turn you into a work horse. Be blunt in your refusals. Friends who count will understand.

If Wednesday: Pass up any project or offer unless it is fully guaranteed. Travel may be to your advantage, but don't go chasing rainbows.

If Thursday: Don't be critical of persons in authority. Their plans may be better than you think, so go along with them. They may have a place for you.

If Friday: Banish your own gloom by cheering up your friends. Once you have shown them how small their problems are, they may help you solve bigger worries.

If Saturday: Popularity may be your quickest path to profit or achievement. Capitalize on past efforts by stressing them to the right people.

WHEN BIRTH NUMBER IS 2

AND DAY'S NUMBER IS 1

If Sunday: Whatever you plan may mean hard work, so don't waste time getting started. Once started, be persistent. The farther ahead you get, the better.

If Monday: Don't let present problems worry you. A letter, a phone call, even a chance meeting may provide the answer to your dilemma.

If Tuesday: You may need help from friends in the course that you are taking, so make sure of their approval now, rather than risk a turndown later.

If Wednesday: You might be mistaken regarding matters that concern you most. Check them carefully before taking your next step.

If Thursday: You have been putting off too many things. Drop all that are unimportant and concentrate on the rest, particularly those involving money.

If Friday: Offer advice freely to friends who need it, but don't insist that they follow it. That way, you'll still be right, regardless of what happens.

If Saturday: Don't worry about making decisions today or over the weekend. Matters may decide themselves, due to a sudden change in circumstances.

DAY'S NUMBER IS 2

If Sunday: A heart-to-heart talk with someone close to you may produce long-lasting happiness through mutual understanding, even if others are involved.

If Monday: If you are uncertain about anything, don't mention it to others. They may exaggerate your worries to hide their own and blame everything on you.

If Tuesday: Look for the bright side of things or dismiss them as unimportant. A glum outlook will spoil your immediate happiness.

If Wednesday: A good day for a decision regarding business or financial matters. Don't spend money on impulse. Try before you buy.

If Thursday: Don't make up your mind about anything. Other people are making decisions for you. Find out what they want and be ready with good answers.

If Friday: You can make people very happy by telling them what they hope to hear. But don't demand a quick answer. They may be even more appreciative later.

If Saturday: Arguments are in the air, so avoid them. Disputes among your friends or associates may produce a situation that only an outsider can settle.

DAY'S NUMBER IS 3

If Sunday: Harmonize your talents and put them all to good use. Be yourself and other people will like you. Happy days are here for you.

If Monday: Shake off discouragement by concentrating on whatever lies immediately ahead. Take time out to study any needed facts with which you are unfamiliar.

If Tuesday: Balance your talents along with your budget, so that you can turn all your efforts into money or more profitable fields.

If Wednesday: Good judgment, capability, willingness to work are potentially yours. Combine them and you may gain prompt results.

If Thursday: The time is ripe to choose between several courses, all attractive, yet at sharp variance. Take whichever offers most to you.

If Friday: Don't be careless about your obligations, even if you have to break off an association that is causing you to forget old friends.

If Saturday: Be tactful! A conflict of interests threatens your welfare both romantically and financially. A final decision will soon be due.

DAY'S NUMBER IS 4

If Sunday: You have been putting off important things too long. Get ready to do them now, or increasing difficulties may cause you great despair.

If Monday: A bad time to risk new ventures or romances. Work hard at whatever is closest at hand and watch for opportunities in the same line.

If Tuesday: Check the immediate past to learn why your present efforts may seem futile. You still can reverse a bad decision and regain needed confidence.

If Wednesday: If desires are unfulfilled, work harder and you may find an immediate answer to a pressing problem. Give first thought to your own welfare.

If Thursday: Any doubts you now have are apt to be doubled, the more you let them keep you from immediate tasks. Let someone else handle trifling problems.

If Friday: Be careful about giving advice to others or taking on new responsibilities, or you may find yourself struggling to get back where you were.

If Saturday: Someone may be plotting to turn your efforts to their own advantage, so don't delay your present projects even if you must work harder.

DAY'S NUMBER IS 5

If Sunday: A good day to shake off restraint and take chances on anything unusual, even an outright gamble. Luck more than effort is apt to pay off.

If Monday: Trying times ahead. If you run out on a bad situation, it may become worse. Keep poised, meet issues, and you may salvage some lost hopes.

If Tuesday: Keep friendship and finance well apart, but don't neglect either. Take chances with your own money or your own plans, but nobody else's.

If Wednesday: Avoid opinionated people and don't let anyone impose on you today, as you are apt to make bad mistakes. Any trip may prove disappointing.

If Thursday: The deeper you are involved in anything, particularly speculation or romance, don't be fainthearted. Going still deeper may see you through.

If Friday: If you've been daydreaming too much, today is the time to drop it. Any wild notions of an adventurous weekend may prove disastrous.

If Saturday: This may be your opportunity to pyramid one bizarre adventure into another, First, plan well, then let yourself go-go.

DAY'S NUMBER IS 6

If Sunday: Choose a definite course, seek the support and company of reliable friends, then see it through. Results may surprise you.

If Monday: If drawn into other people's problems, be smart. Helping those who need it is nice, but it's nicer to help those who may help you.

If Tuesday: Look back into your past experience and follow whatever course seemed worth while then. But don't let other people sway you from it!

If Wednesday: Finish whatever you have started, particularly where other people are concerned. They want you to come through, so prove you can!

If Thursday: If you want to be popular, you'll have to work for it. People who like you will ask you to do things for them. So be forewarned.

If Friday: You may be due for a big surprise. If your friends thrust an unexpected honor or duty upon you, take it eagerly. It may open a new vista.

If Saturday: Play social contacts to the limit. Anything nice you do for people, they'll do something nicer. This should be a wonderful weekend.

DAY'S NUMBER IS 7

If Sunday: Lack of recognition may make you moody and dissatisfied. Better drop outside interests and concentrate on whatever you do best.

If Monday: Indecision is in the air, so avoid starting anything today. Time devoted to study or self-improvement may help you to meet coming problems.

If Tuesday: Treat everything lightly today, varying your interests so your friends will be responsive. Postpone decisions where romance is involved.

If *Wednesday:* Whatever you have undertaken may prove much more difficult than expected, so work hard at it.

If Thursday: When trouble threatens, don't go away mad. Just go away quickly, before you get involved, and stay away until it blows over.

If Friday: Try to square any misunderstandings that hinder business, friendship, or love. You may find that mountains can be reduced to mere molehills.

If Saturday: A day for summing up your hopes and ambitions. Avoid anything that depresses you, including people, but accept advice from those who can help.

DAY'S NUMBER IS 8

If Sunday: Don't buck other interests in your coming project. Go along with them and hope to get your share, or switch to something entirely different.

If Monday: Personal gain may await you if you make a firm decision and follow through with it. Whatever you do, good timing is important.

If Tuesday: No matter how big present opportunities may look, they may prove small in the long run. Pass them up if too much work is involved.

If Wednesday: Swap something old for something new, in belongings, associations, or just ideas, and you may be due for a profitable surprise.

If Thursday: By careful planning, you can turn current problems into profit or advancement, provided you take advice from the right people.

If Friday: Unless you are prepared for complications and capable of meeting them, plans that you think are solid will vanish like castles in the air.

If Saturday: Completion of an immediate purpose can lead to something much bigger if your act wisely and avoid legal entanglements or doubtful promises.

DAY'S NUMBER IS 9

If Sunday: Concentrate on a big ambition, but go after it only if you feel that even partial success will cause people to recognize your capabilities.

If Monday: Whatever you try to do may bring you right back where you started. Any honor or appreciation may not be worth the effort. Think it over.

If Tuesday: Big promises may mean nothing, false friends may deceive you, obligations may nearly sink you, but luck is apt to pull you through.

If Wednesday: Social events may prove of great value. Attend all you can, even if they seem trivial. Make new friends, but count on old ones.

If Thursday: Don't be restless or impatient to get things done. People may think that you want to take advantage of them. Be calm and let them seek you.

If Friday: Help your neighbors and your community. Give your services freely and build up good will. A substantial return may result.

If Saturday: Make sure you are prepared to assume an important office or duty before you accept it. Any failure may give you a bad setback.

WHEN BIRTH NUMBER IS 3

AND DAY'S NUMBER IS 1

If Sunday: Concentrating on one interest may be causing you to neglect better opportunities. Expand your activities and watch results.

If Monday: Don't accept favors from friends unless you are willing to return them in greater measure, but be polite or you will lose popularity.

If Tuesday: Friction over minor matters can ruin your immediate hopes. Go along with other people's ideas, but reserve your final opinion.

If Wednesday: If you suspect that people are plotting against you, don't say so. Chances are you will be right if big plans are at stake.

If Thursday: Don't talk too much or you may spoil things. Set your mind on what you really want and it will come your way.

If Friday: Look back on the past week or more and note what opportunities you missed. The coming weekend is the time to catch up with a few.

If Saturday: Put all your eggs in one basket, then watch the basket! Be cheery, active, sociable, but don't let anyone take what is rightfully yours.

DAY'S NUMBER IS 2

If Sunday: You can get what you want by following established rules, but don't impose your ideas on other people. Humor them as you go along.

If Monday: Avoid any compromise caused by conflicts of opinion. Go one way or the other without committing yourself to unexpected offers.

If Tuesday: Your intentions may be doubted or challenged by someone whose urge is as strong as yours. If you can't lick them, join them.

If Wednesday: Don't look for short cuts to fame or fortune. Develop whatever you have started. A budding romance may flare to great heights.

If Thursday: Present plans can prove profitable if you rely on your own efforts. Unless new friends prove their worth, break off any entanglements.

If Friday: Think twice before proceeding with new plans. Your suggestions may be resented, so keep calm if you are criticized or misunderstood.

If Saturday: A time to turn dreams into reality. Go where the need is greatest and gear your work or capabilities to meet popular demand.

DAY'S NUMBER IS 3

If Sunday: Going to extremes may prove your undoing. If you can't concentrate on one thing, at least eliminate those that cause you the most worry.

If Monday: Give full attention to any big deal coming up, as scattered shots or trifling savings may ruin a real opportunity.

If Tuesday: A time for careful planning, itemizing all aims and seeing each through to a conclusion, as any neglect may mean failure.

If Wednesday: Somebody is trying to use your brains and efforts to further their own aims. A switch of plans may balk them.

If Thursday: Don't try to force your ideas on others. Follow your own inclinations and ask their opinions later, when they can't back out.

If Friday: Anything you start today should bring good results, so if you are full of vim and vigor, make the most of it!

If Saturday: Stop wasting time on things you like to do but that aren't worth the effort. You can gain much more in other fields.

DAY'S NUMBER IS 4

If Sunday: You may be trying to get places too quickly. Slow down, work hard at whatever promises the most, and watch the results!

If Monday: Don't let routine work annoy you. Once your friends and associates recognize your efforts, bigger things will come your way.

If Tuesday: Don't talk too much about your present plans. Get them completed before somebody moves in ahead of you. Jealousy is in the air.

If Wednesday: A time to show your independence. Go where the action is and count on friends to back you if you meet with arguments.

If Thursday: New friends may help toward quick success with hunches coming through. Enjoy yourself but don't neglect important work.

If Friday: Utmost caution needed in any new ventures. Someone may be trying to outdo you, so work hard, and if one method fails, try another.

If Saturday: Be careful not to antagonize anyone this weekend. A trip, either for business or pleasure, may forestall a difficult decision.

DAY'S NUMBER IS 5

If Sunday: A fine day for going places and making new friends. Bold, decisive action may bring you sudden popularity. Make the most of it.

If Monday: A time to expand activities and try out new ideas, but don't leave the job to other people. Exert your initiative to the full.

If Tuesday: Travel may mean profit and pleasure, but make sure you're not missing bigger things at home. Someone may be taking advantage of you.

If Wednesday: Don't let flattering offers draw you from present prospects. Seek advice from friends. They may appreciate you more than you realize.

If Thursday: Whatever you plan today, do it on your own, or someone else will take the glory. Otherwise switch to something else.

If Friday: Plan to expand your viewpoint through travel or personal contacts. This could lead to success in new or untried fields.

If Saturday: If you take a trip or plan a holiday, include friends or family. Avoid impulsive action and make sure that all are happy.

DAY'S NUMBER IS 6

If Sunday: A time to end financial worry by eliminating unnecessary social functions from your budget. Make economy your hobby.

If Monday: Overemphasis on personal desires may prove disastrous to home or business life. Try to allocate sufficient time to each.

If Tuesday: Work in harmony with those around you, complimenting them for extra effort. Ask advice instead of giving it.

If Wednesday: Give thought to small ideas as well as big ones, particularly around the home. Try to set a pattern for further improvement.

If Thursday: Hold back on any rash urge to try something new. Ask the advice of sincere friends before dropping your established work.

If Friday: Don't let self-assurance throw you. If you are too contented, you may be missing opportunities. Look for them.

If Saturday: A time to repay social obligations and pave the way to new. Treat matters seriously, but be optimistic, never gloomy.

DAY'S NUMBER IS 7

If Sunday: Take time out to be yourself and analyze what lies ahead. Postpone any decisions and ignore advice until you see what develops.

If Monday: Don't let worries drag you down. If anything has gone wrong, tackle it again but with a new approach. It should work.

If Tuesday: You have been thinking clearly and may have good ideas that need development. Get busy on that now, even if it means hard work.

If Wednesday: A time to expand your efforts, find new fields, and turn inspiration into reality. But don't waste time on the wrong people.

If Thursday: Don't criticize what other people have to say; just listen. The more you hear, the more ideas you will gain for your own use.

If Friday: You're spending too much time planning and too little doing. Think back to something practical and take off from there.

If Saturday: Keep your mind on creative purposes over the coming weekend. You have ability and know-how. Don't waste them.

DAY'S NUMBER IS 8

If Sunday: Don't talk too much or soon your friends will be spreading your ideas and calling them their own. A good way to lose friends.

If Monday: Original ideas in business matters can pay off big if you work them out in detail. Accept helpful suggestions.

If Tuesday: Don't be impatient with people who try but fall short. Any help you give them will win their loyalty, and you may need it!

If Wednesday: Don't let any outsiders disturb your home life. Ignore glib salesmen and gossipy neighbors. Somebody may be trying to take you.

If Thursday: If things are going smoothly, you may be the object of much envy. Confide only in friends of long standing.

If Friday: A time to pyramid business gains. Diversify your interests so as to follow through on whatever pans out best. Act, then watch!

If Saturday: If you're doing well in any field, start building your name and reputation. Bring people to you, rather than go after them.

DAY'S NUMBER IS 9

If Sunday: Don't let people flatter you with honors that mean more work than prestige. Pass them to someone else and wait for something bigger.

If Monday: Don't try to start a lot of things going before you finish the task at hand. By then, you can make a better choice of something new.

If Tuesday: Things close at hand may need attention. Think in terms of family welfare and community projects. A time to gain real prestige.

If Wednesday: Don't let minor problems distract you from a real goal. The bigger you think, the smaller such obstacles will become.

If Thursday: Ability combined with popularity can bring you prompt profit if you let other persons share. A good time to merge interests.

If Friday: Overambition may start you toward a futile goal. Sound out persons who oppose you, rather than fair-weather friends, then decide.

If Saturday: Whatever you are after, don't be too assertive or demanding. Quiet persistence will win others to your opinions.

WHEN BIRTH NUMBER IS 4

AND DAY'S NUMBER IS 1

If Sunday: Plan a methodical routine of work and study for the days that follow. Do not expect immediate results but depend upon co-operation from others.

If Monday: By establishing confidence with those around you, follow through with your aims. Forget your worries.

If Tuesday: Although you may prefer to act slowly, you may face a quick decision that will prove of great moment.

If Wednesday: Stay with your basic problems and recognition then will go far beyond your present hopes.

If Thursday: If you have been working too much for others, try doing something on your own. Calling upon others will tell you who are your true friends.

If Friday: Making up your mind what to do can prove your own undoing. Stop weighing matters and get busy.

If Saturday: A time to choose a goal. New fields may open as fast as you find them. Confidence in your own ability is all you need.

DAY'S NUMBER IS 2

If Sunday: Bright plans for today may fade through lack of initiative or disinterest. Better to consider future problems and prepare to meet them.

If Monday: A very good time to follow natural inclinations and take advantage of any opportunities that come your way. If others set the pace, go along with them.

If Tuesday: Count on friends or associates to give you what you want, but be agreeable, and if they lack response, do not press them. Avoid any arguments or antagonizing actions.

If Wednesday: Concentrate on purposes rather than results, such as proposed business expansion or long-range promotions. Avoid rash business decisions.

If Thursday: Avoid the urge to do big things or you may wear yourself out and meet with opposition and disappointment. Excellent time for detail work.

If Friday: A good period to discuss contracts, developments, anything that will improve conditions or relations. This day indicates cooperative effort.

If Saturday: Time to catch up on neglected correspondence and to renew old acquaintances, as some future opportunity may develop.

DAY'S NUMBER IS 3

If Sunday: A good day to pick up on details, get obligations and piled-up data out of the way. Correspondence, questions of long standing may be helped here.

If Monday: This should begin an active period with plenty of contacts, following inclinations, and, above all, playing hunches, as they may pay off.

If Tuesday: Avoid rash business decisions and do not pressure other people to make them. Any worry or annoyance will wreck your plans.

If Wednesday: Good time to talk about new projects or proper handling of old. Check on things like legal matters, contracts, if you find other people co-operative.

If Thursday: Count on friends today. They may give you just what you want. Sound them out carefully, however, and drop them if there is any lack of response.

If Friday: Time for a careful survey of minor problems and to do preliminary work on new projects with other persons equally concerned in them.

If Saturday: Get started early, as this is a day of many changes, and you should take advantage of everything that promises results.

DAY'S NUMBER IS 4

If Sunday: Excellent day to embark upon humane or charitable projects. Make harmony the keynote of all discussions and activities. Inspiration often will follow.

If Monday: Good workday. Apply your knowledge to increased production. Look for an increase in money-making funds. Guard your health.

If Tuesday: Do not waste time on unprofitable tasks. Do not let others waste your time either. A good day for concentrated, productive work.

If Wednesday: Devote your time to matters of interest, especially social or public events that may bring you cash for your efforts.

If Thursday: Work with those who show momentum as a carry-over from some previous drive in which you can share. Start early, work late.

If Friday: Avoid immediate issues to plan future events, combining social and business interests.

If Saturday: Strictly a social day, so business or serious matters should be dismissed as soon as possible.

DAY'S NUMBER IS 5

If Sunday: Exert you own initiative and avoid advice from others. Big opportunities should follow in due time.

If Monday: Watch out for trickery and deception by persons who might use your efforts for their own gain.

If Tuesday: Whatever your social talents, develop and use them, as popularity may gain you more than hard work.

If Wednesday: To get things done, do them yourself. Relying on promises can only bring disappointment, even disaster.

If Thursday: Luck should be coming your way in surprising fashion, provided you keep at what you are doing now.

If Friday: Friendship is today's keynote. If need be, put aside chores in order to enjoy and further it, as results may be great.

If Saturday: A time for retrospect. Look back on your accomplishments and consider ways of improving them with less effort.

DAY'S NUMBER IS 6

If Sunday: Let no obstacle stand in the way of your ambitions. Security and peace of mind will be your reward.

If Monday: Your family circle and friends can help you accomplish your secret wish. It is a day for renewal of an old acquaintance.

If Tuesday: The day may be trying but keep a level, cool balance of temperament. Flare-ups are not for you today, lest they hurt later.

If Wednesday: A bad time for getting things done. Try another angle at a later date. Indecision is not the answer.

If Thursday: Seek people who are interested in educational fields. Reach for philosophical trends such as theirs. Try to attend public gatherings where you can be an interested promoter.

If Friday: Everybody has problems. Be of good cheer; yours will pass in due course. No time for instability.

If Saturday: Improve your lot by activating and pushing your ability. Talents must be used and developed if success is to be gained.

DAY'S NUMBER IS 7

If Sunday: Enjoy your friends and activities with others, especially gatherings that place you in better surroundings, but do not neglect family ties.

If Monday: Think before you leap. Weigh every step carefully rather than make a wrong decision. There may be much work ahead.

If Tuesday: Initiative is the keynote of your success, no matter what your intent may be. Choose carefully, then motivate the necessary channels toward your aim.

If Wednesday: Your plans, even if vague, can be activated by social contacts if you employ sound judgment. Money, if need be, can also be raised through the same channels, but presentation is of utmost importance.

If Thursday: Your responsibilities will seem lighter if you can maintain a happy, receptive state of mind. Let others be gloomy, not you.

If Friday: Be careful of sharp practice if making a business contract or purchase. Look into every detail before making a final deal.

If Saturday: A time for action where money is concerned. Do not be afraid to try a new venture, especially if it is a step upward and beyond your expectations.

DAY'S NUMBER IS 8

If Sunday: Do not be hasty to make a change that involves your financial status. Better to stay with your present condition rather than lose money on a gamble.

If Monday: Brace yourself for the unexpected. Look for a different undertaking that may benefit you socially and financially. Nothing is impossible.

If Tuesday: Try to maintain a cheerful mood from morning till night just to keep others happy. It will pay off in time and money.

If Wednesday: Criticism and malcontent could cost you plenty if you resort to such behavior. Try to keep an even balance and work harder to maintain your position.

If Thursday: Make a new plan for future ambitions. Protect yourself and cherished properties against any sort of loss.

If Friday: Do not rely on anyone at present to share your secret desires. Follow your own ideas but study each step carefully.

If Saturday: Try something creative, using your enduring ability for research and study. Do not be impatient.

DAY'S NUMBER IS 9

If Sunday: An ideal day to plan or establish a long-range project based on work already done, or qualifications you are sure you have; but only if you can give it full attention.

If Monday: A time to weigh your coming plans and reserve decisions. Stay with what you are doing and problems may resolve themselves.

If Tuesday: Whatever you do today, you may wish you had done something better. But don't let that discourage you. Chances are that you will find that you could have done worse.

If Wednesday: Be careful about whatever you undertake. Overambition, or an urge to get results too fast could trigger setbacks that might nullify past efforts.

If Thursday: You can go all out for any big project, provided other people propose it or strongly favor it. Sound them out before trying to force your ideas on them.

If Friday: A time to establish yourself with family and friends. Try to improve your home life or your present surroundings.

If Saturday: Relax and review your past efforts; then concentrate on ways to get more out of work and life. Think of yourself for a change.

WHEN BIRTH NUMBER IS 5

AND DAY'S NUMBER IS 1

If Sunday: All your drive and originality should harmonize with those in power even though you may not like to conform.

If Monday: Start the month with all the drive of your initiative and ability. Weigh carefully all the knowledge you have acquired.

If Tuesday: Make the most of your opportunities but do not neglect the work at hand. Do not shun advice from superiors.

If Wednesday: Do not let your enthusiasm become too aggressive. You are important and wanted, so work hard and with confidence.

If Thursday: Look for immediate possibilities. Study everything carefully. Do not try to jump too far ahead. Good prospects ahead.

If Friday: Take care of all correspondence. Dependability will bring you cumulative results if you so choose. Do not be radical.

If Saturday: Go along with those in power. Do not let moodiness retard your ambitious nature. Be forceful, analyze carefully.

DAY'S NUMBER IS 2

If Sunday: Proceed with your personal goal but do not let your interests conflict with those of other people close to you.

If Monday: Balance your budget to meet the requirements of any new scheme you may plan for the future. Stay calm but determined.

If Tuesday: Concentrate on your own talents. Best to select a single personal slant that reflects one side of your versatility.

If Wednesday: Avoid impulsive buying or activities. Either would be costly. Constant effort will pay off. Look into science projects.

If Thursday: Check into the needs for security benefits. Chances are not for you. Avoid extremes. Guard against unnecessary debts.

If Friday: Others may waste your time on chitchat; this is not for you. Create confidence in people and you will achieve success.

If Saturday: Apply your studious ability to your interest in practical things and you will be able to increase your finances.

DAY'S NUMBER IS 3

If Sunday: Check your financial status today. Make sure your future is safe and sound. Enjoy yourself but provide for your needs.

If Monday: Whatever may be your working problems or situation, it is best to maintain harmony with those around you.

If Tuesday: Use your own good counsel to help those near you. Your personality can do much to keep harmony among your friends.

If Wednesday: Do not overlook your opportunities because of restlessness or boredom. Routine duties require patience and application.

If Thursday: You may need advice and counsel regarding money matters. Do not hesitate to seek new methods of advancement.

If Friday: New surroundings may be what you want, but be sure you hold onto work or present means of maintenance and security.

If Saturday: This should be a very happy day. One for the enjoyment of love, friendship, or family ties.

DAY'S NUMBER IS 4

If Sunday: This may be a trying day. Exert your most diplomatic ability to avoid friction. Leave complications to others.

If Monday: Again this may be another day of altercations with people near you. If you can't help, do not interfere.

If Tuesday: A good time to consider a new venture or employment, but do not be hasty. Weigh every aspect carefully.

If Wednesday: A propitious day to try something new with your occupation. Consult someone else about fresh ideas.

If Thursday: Accept the love and affection of one who is close to you. Happiness that is shared makes everything look brighter.

If Friday: If you travel today be very careful. The unexpected can happen if you do something impulsive.

If Saturday: Do a good turn for yourself. Study your personal needs and make a quiet resolution to be kind to yourself.

DAY'S NUMBER IS 5

If Sunday: Contemplate on friendship today. Phone, write, or visit one of them if you are able to do so. Friends are valuable.

If Monday: Increase your efforts. Try to work harder even if your project is a hobby. You will be the benefactor.

If Tuesday: A decision may face you, so take your time. Give due consideration to every phase, but try to maintain your own viewpoint.

If Wednesday: Plan ahead for a month or more. Include recreation with work. Try to find a new interest that will add to your income.

If Thursday: Change your tactics for a while. You will find more happiness and less friction around you if you avoid certain people.

If Friday: Chat with a friend or two. Enjoy yourself. Your affection is needed to build morale in others. Love helps the lonely.

If Saturday: Do not depend upon gossip. Learn the truth about people before you formulate an opinion that may be harmful.

DAY'S NUMBER IS 6

If Sunday: Do not let the jealousy of another person upset you. Slanderous remarks can be halted and are often retroactive.

If Monday: If you feel you are obligated to loan money to a friend or relative, be sure you have ample and proper security.

If Tuesday: Refrain from quick decisions. Your impartiality may make you hypocritical, so take it easy and act with deliberation.

If Wednesday: Your days can be brightened with social activities if you so desire. An excellent time to move around with new groups.

If Thursday: Clear up all loose ends. Finish tasks that remain undone. Prepare for new interests; at least try one new project.

If Friday: Let people know what you want or need. Do not hesitate to ask for assistance or financial co-operation.

If Saturday: Stay within your own circle at this period. Study and contemplation will add to your progressive nature and ability.

DAY'S NUMBER IS 7

If Sunday: Start early if you want to get ahead. Be careful not to spend more than you can afford. Keep a cheerful attitude.

If Monday: Be co-operative. Do not hesitate to consult with others. Save your money for later days. Thrift is far better than extravagance.

If Tuesday: Visit with your family or close friends if your hours will permit. Help your community in some way.

If Wednesday: Although you may want to get away from present conditions, your best bet is to stay where you are. Good news soon.

If Thursday: Take care of personal business or interests. Do not let any dissension deter you from your course of action.

If Friday: A wonderful time to pursue love or recreational activities. Something vital to you should be given your attention.

If Saturday: Time to take care of finances and plan for years to come. Savings must be protected. Do not tolerate interference.

DAY'S NUMBER IS 8

If Sunday: Try to enjoy whatever activities present themselves today, no matter what problems annoy you. Family comes first.

If Monday: Best to maintain a conservative attitude. Refrain from any arguments. Digression of any sort can harm you.

If Tuesday: Some entanglement may upset you, but try to get something constructive out of it. Be careful of your health. Eat wisely.

If Wednesday: You should be nearing a very good financial period. There may be tempting offers, but be alert to sharp dealing.

If Thursday: Be patient during this time of the month. A change of place or an old relationship may alter your circumstances.

If Friday: Clever thinking on your part may place you in line for better living standards and give you the necessary impetus to push ahead.

If Saturday: It is best to co-ordinate your ideas with those of other people. It would be mutually profitable. Relaxation will help you to decide.

DAY'S NUMBER IS 9

If Sunday: Be self-reliant. It will pay off. Avoid any friction with your associates or even your family. It is too distracting.

If Monday: Keep your opinions to yourself today. Be alert to those around you lest someone betrays your trust and confidence.

If Tuesday: Stay with your creative ability, work hard, but this is a good day too for gaiety and fun. Avoid drudgery but pursue your goal.

If Wednesday: Leave arrogance to others and use your excellent personality to interest other persons around you. Good day for new ideas.

If Thursday: Use your enthusiasm to forge ahead. Get credit if you need it. Experience will bring real opportunities.

If Friday: Your dependability will offset any criticism that may be hurled at you. Let nothing disturb your efficiency.

If Saturday: Stay with routine chores and any private business that is on hand. You are capable of solving your intricate problems.

WHEN BIRTH NUMBER IS 6

AND DAY'S NUMBER IS 1

If Sunday: You may have been neglecting opportunities very close to home. Give them due attention and results may surprise you.

If Monday: A time to go along with others even if you disagree on minor points. Chances are they will accept your way of thinking.

If Tuesday: Someone else may be seeking a reward or honor that is rightfully yours. Don't dismiss such talk as rumor. Check it out.

If Wednesday: If opposing parties are trying to woo your opinion, don't give it too soon. Things may already be turning about.

If Thursday: No need to travel to find romance or opportunity. It may be just around the corner. Which corner? That's for you to discover!

If Friday: People who should appreciate you more are depending on your good nature to accept too many burdens. Better drop them.

If Saturday: If family or friends suggest a trip or a party, crawl out of your shell and go along with them. They'll like you better.

DAY'S NUMBER IS 2

If Sunday: Don't let your sympathies waver during the coming week, or you may lose prestige that you have already gained.

If Monday: Plan for a brief but complete change, according to your capacity. If you've been idling, get to work; if pressed by problems, go have fun.

If Tuesday: Stop crossing mental bridges before you reach them. Most of your problems are imaginary; the rest can cancel each other out.

If Wednesday: A time to start playing cat and mouse, but don't be the mouse! Catlike, watch what other people do, and act to suit.

If Thursday: Well-intentioned persons may either offer good advice or ask for it, but if you have a job to do, ignore them. Put work first.

If Friday: You may be wasting time trying to convince people that you can put across new ideas. Get busy on those ideas and prove it.

If Saturday: Keep the slogan "There's no place like home" constantly in mind when weighing inducements to go elsewhere.

DAY'S NUMBER IS 3

If Sunday: Any new and attractive project should prove to your advantage if it involves your past experience and present capability.

If Monday: You may be sacrificing your talents through fear of insecurity. Seek friendly advice on how to adjust to more profitable circumstances.

If Tuesday: Excellent indications if you make the most of them. Artistic, literary, inventive ability should pay off if you contact the right people.

If Wednesday: Put aside social contacts or interests in hobbies until your present project is finished, or until you are sure of a better job.

If Thursday: Any chance to appear on a TV show, win some honor, or gain election or appointment to office may disrupt well-set plans, so don't be too eager.

If Friday: Complacency and self-sufficiency are your two worst faults. Cultivate friends who will shake you out of them.

If Saturday: Desire for improved position can be gained through home study or by turning your hobby or hobbies to profitable use.

DAY'S NUMBER IS 4

If Sunday: Stop wasting time on endless detail and decide which details are essential for the coming week. Results may amaze you.

If Monday: Give more attention to home life. Put things in place, invite visitors, indulge in instructive reading. All will add up.

If Tuesday: Your present purposes can be gained immediately by putting your existing plans into action instead of talking about them.

If Wednesday: You are apt to be overgenerous, letting others benefit from your efforts. Think of yourself and see what happens.

If Thursday: You may be traveling in a circle so large that you don't realize it. Make it smaller and get back to earth.

If Friday: Between the work you like to do and the work you have to do, you are running yourself ragged. Slow up and wait for people to appreciate you before resuming speed.

If Saturday: Gain from your own efforts will be increased by family funds or business ventures. Keep thinking big and get bigger!

DAY'S NUMBER IS 5

If Sunday: Personal problems may be causing business worries. Unless you promptly choose between them, you may lose out on both.

If Monday: Better put your affairs in order before taking on new projects or going on a long trip. Either can prove grueling.

If Tuesday: Time to take a vacation and visit old friends. Mutual exchange of reminiscences will inspire you. Make it soon.

If Wednesday: Whatever you are doing now, stop yearning to be doing something else. Keep the home fires burning, or you may come back and find them gone.

If Thursday: You are due for recognition of a sort you do not expect. How great it may be depends upon the factors involved.

If Friday: Don't let anyone hinder your drive for success. Once you reach the top, you will find it easier to solve their problems for them.

If Saturday: If you are troubled by past regrets, dismiss them. New contacts, new projects may promise rapid success if you use past experience to advantage.

DAY'S NUMBER IS 6

If Sunday: Home-building, homemaking, handiwork, or handy work should bring you both pleasure and profit if you can keep steadily at them. It's worth trying for a time.

If Monday: New experiences promise gain and recognition, particularly if travel is involved. A time to follow social inclinations and use linguistic ability.

If Tuesday: Expect important invitation or offer in the near future. If accepted, it may prove a steppingstone to something bigger.

If Wednesday: Concentration, study, or special training may open new opportunities, but consider offers carefully and make sure of contracts or legal matters.

If Thursday: Facts learned from relatives or friends may give you a new outlook toward business or profession. Act on advice but don't bank on promises.

If Friday: A combination denoting great intuition. Hunches may pay off in quick succession, both for you and your friends, but don't overdo it.

If Saturday: Long-laid plan or cherished hope is ready for fulfillment, so be alert. A phone call, letter, or a news item may be of vital value.

DAY'S NUMBER IS 7

If Sunday: Old friend or family adviser may snap you from a state of intellectual coma with an exciting project. Take it!

If Monday: If happy where you are, stay there; if happy with what you are doing, keep doing it. With anything else, you may wind up back where you were.

If Tuesday: Responsibilities may be hindering your artistic or intellectual attainments. Decide which is more important and act accordingly, but soon!

If Wednesday: Work with people who appreciate your ability and success is sure. Just make sure you get your share of it.

If Thursday: Whatever you do, somebody else will be involved, either actively or passively. Study your associates right now.

If Friday: A day to take over. Settle family problems. Finish business deals. Have a good weekend. Be yourself on Monday.

If Saturday: Watch out for legal problems. Avoid attractive business deals. Be polite but not obliging to family and friends. You are this weekend's target.

DAY'S NUMBER IS 8

If Sunday: Happiness should be your lot right now. So try to keep that attitude throughout the coming week. If other people swing your way, you're right. If they don't, they're wrong.

If Monday: Some friend or relative is hoping for success and may soon ask your advice. Give it, even though you think that later they will forget you gave it. What can you lose?

If Tuesday: Whatever you plan today should be sure to succeed if you follow it through. Success today should bring success tomorrow. Nothing succeeds like success!

If Wednesday: Everything is coming your way. Word from an old friend; an offer from a new acquaintance; an end to family worry.

If Thursday: Look out for Number One—and that means you! Go through with your own plans for today, tomorrow, the day after—and longer if need be.

If Friday: Domestic and business matters are in the balance. Better let someone else tip the scales before you decide which way to go.

If Saturday: From small beginnings, present operations may branch out to wider fields. It may be wise to remember friends who were with you at the start. They may be helpful later.

DAY'S NUMBER IS 9

If Sunday: People who did you small favors may now be asking large return. Avoid letting sentiment govern generosity.

If Monday: If big ambitions are slow coming through, you may be expecting too much too soon. Try new tactics and take your time.

If Tuesday: Inspiring confidence in those about you may bring you popularity elsewhere. Broaden activities and make new friends.

If Wednesday: If friends ask favors, grant them, but specify a fair and prompt return when needed. It may help a coming project.

If Thursday: Divided interests may be thwarting the popularity that you deserve. Try bringing groups of friends together.

If Friday: You may be wasting time on things you like most rather than those which are more valuable now. Diversify your activities.

If Saturday: The more attractive your present prospects, the more hard work you may expect later. Better study all eventualities before deciding upon your coming goal.

WHEN BIRTH NUMBER IS 7

AND DAY'S NUMBER IS 1

If Sunday: Introspection at this time may start you toward an important goal, provided your constant thought is how to gear your actions to your aim.

If Monday: Turn present knowledge into immediate use. Any reluctance to assert yourself may result in others getting what you should have.

If Tuesday: Balance any gloom or forebodings against a fresh outlook. Cheery companions can help you banish blues.

If Wednesday: Now is a time to put your thoughts on paper, whether creatively, by catching up on correspondence, or keeping a diary or day log.

If Thursday: Putting off an unpleasant or difficult task can be cause of increasing anxiety for yourself and others. Get it done soon or it will be too late.

If Friday: Chance for new and exciting experience may demand sacrificing existing plans. Don't pass up a fantastic future for a prosaic past without due consideration.

If Saturday: Everything in which you are actively concerned points to established, harmonious surroundings as the sure-fire symbol of success. Make the most of it.

DAY'S NUMBER IS 2

If Sunday: You may be holding back on a big opportunity. Whatever you have in mind, go after it. Push your plans with people who can help.

If Monday: Indecision over some important purpose may put you in a hopeless mood. Let others decide and follow their advice.

If Tuesday: Time to diversify your interests. Assert your individuality. A surprise is coming from an unexpected quarter.

If Wednesday: Start thinking of things that other people can do under your direction. You can ease your job or improve your business thereby.

If Thursday: Fun with friends should supplant troublesome tasks. Too much study can cause you to lose interest in subjects.

If Friday: Conference with important people can shape your future beyond all expectations. Seek such opportunity.

If Saturday: Consider turning present experience to broader and more productive fields. A short trip, meeting with an old friend will help.

DAY'S NUMBER IS 3

If Sunday: This is an aggressive period when troublesome situations may upset you emotionally. Avoid complications. Get plenty of rest.

If Monday: Now is the time to help solve difficult problems for other people. Your own interests are due to improve in a surprising way.

If Tuesday: Limit your social activities to a minimum. Take care of tasks that need your complete attention. Lend a helping hand to a neighbor.

If Wednesday: This is a formative and changeable period when you will most likely change your opinions about many things. Attend meetings, broaden your outlook.

If Thursday: Overwork may demand that you rest a little; however, concentrate on your occupation because it will pay better dividends.

If Friday: Conserve your energy. Do not let your associates intrude upon your time or work. Follow your intuition socially.

If Saturday: Use your own judgment and proceed with your aims and ambition. This is a good period to seek advancement.

DAY'S NUMBER IS 4

If Sunday: Use your knowledge to improve your present situation. Your friends will support your cause. Curb unnecessary extravagance.

If Monday: Get an early start today. The morning hours have luck for you if you persevere. Important tasks await you.

If Tuesday: Try to help those who need you, but do not get involved with their personal upsets. However, your own needs come first.

If Wednesday: Let others know your plans so that they can help you if need be. Business outlook is very favorable.

If Thursday: Don't be afraid to venture into a new interest where your talents can expand. Use your own initiative to get results.

If Friday: Exercise patience with any who may be disturbing you. Look for ways to increase your financial gains.

If Saturday: Mutual money matters should take a turn upward. Have all the fun you want but stay close to home.

DAY'S NUMBER IS 5

If Sunday: Unexpected opportunity to travel or broaden your activities may result in hard, intensive work. Weigh prospects carefully.

If Monday: Varied surprises may be coming your way in quick succession. Don't let them worry you. All should be well.

If Tuesday: Be cautious in any business dealings at this time. Somebody may be planning to use your ideas to their advantage.

If Wednesday: Some change is due in your affairs or those of your associates. Be ready to adjust to any new circumstance.

If Thursday: Changing your opinion about certain matters or specific persons may bring you definite benefits in the near future.

If Friday: If you have personal problems, count on their quick solution through the help of trusted friends, if you use their aid.

If Saturday: Any purpose that you have neglected should be pushed now. With special effort, results will tell.

DAY'S NUMBER IS 6

If Sunday: Time to give your mental efforts practical application. Look for ways to turn knowledge into cash.

If Monday: Home life may demand more attention. Give it the same thought that other interests demand, and watch results.

If Tuesday: A day when problems may be magnified in your own mind. Eliminate them until only one remains, then settle that one.

If Wednesday: The bigger your ideas, the greater their chances of success. Test them on little people and watch their reactions. If good, go. If not, no.

If Thursday: You may be so far ahead of your time that you must wait for others to catch up. So stay with what you are doing.

If Friday: Be direct in everything today. Ask favors from friends. In work, aim for something bigger or better or both. Let them answer.

If Saturday: Whatever people want, let them ask you for it. They will give you what you want in return.

DAY'S NUMBER IS 7

If Sunday: Quiet and harmony are needed for your progress. Work out ideas alone without interruption. Tell no one until all is completed.

If Monday: You may be planning too far ahead, on too big a scale. Look for a practical partner or sponsor.

If Tuesday: Discount any worries or obstacles that you encounter. They may be proof that you are on the verge of big success.

If Wednesday: Time devoted to intellectual pursuits will prove well worth while. Read important books, attend lectures, or try playing chess.

If Thursday: Before embarking on a new project, check your knowledge of the subject. Special preparation may be needed to meet changing conditions.

If Friday: If friends seek your help on serious matters, weigh all factors carefully before giving advice. Snap judgment or set opinions may cause them to blame you if things go wrong.

If Saturday: Use new approaches toward solving your problems or improving your position. If one avenue fails, try another. Don't give up!

DAY'S NUMBER IS 8

If Sunday: A day to forget self and gloomy aspects. Shower your affection on your loved ones. The whole day will be brighter.

If Monday: Curb any urge to be temperamental and above all do not be impulsive. Concentrate on your ambitions and any business interest.

If Tuesday: This is a period that needs your understanding. There may be a change in the near future when you will have to make decisions.

If Wednesday: No time to be emotional over occupational duties or conditions at home. Use common sense. Protect any property that you may have or supervise.

If Thursday: Conserve your energy for problems that are likely to arise. Do not let your assets be immobilized. Keep secrets to yourself.

If Friday: Do not let misunderstandings confuse the issues before you. Important decisions will require calmness and good judgment.

If Saturday: Good time to mix with congenial people, perhaps develop new ideas or plan for a different kind of holiday.

DAY'S NUMBER IS 9

If Sunday: Be sure to co-ordinate your social and business activities. Time is the essence today. Exert every effort to increase your exchequer.

If Monday: Better follow the dictates of your associates for a while. Finances need bolstering, so keep your ambitious schemes under control.

If Tuesday: Time to collect whatever may be due you. Do not hesitate to accept hospitality offered by your debtors or antagonists.

If Wednesday: This may be a very trying period, so it is wise to keep an even temperament. Do not let others know that you are worried.

If Thursday: Your responsibilities may weigh heavily upon you, but they must be taken care of. Your reward will come later.

If Friday: Service should be your motto and deliberate aim even though it gives you a feeling of inferiority. You will be the winner.

If Saturday: Your own intuition or an unforeseen cycle of events will cause you to change your ideas. Make new plans if necessary.

WHEN BIRTH NUMBER IS 8

AND DAY'S NUMBER IS 1

If Sunday: You should be in a position to help those around you. Do not let their depression affect you. Take time out for fun.

If Monday: Your generosity is fine, but do not go to extremes with it. Domestic irritation may irk you, but do not show your own whims lest you get into a real problem.

If Tuesday: If you are considering the purchase of securities, bonds, and such, check the veracity of the salesmen before investing. This holds good on small purchases, too. Stay close to home for a while.

If Wednesday: Expedite all your working needs. Be sure your accounts are in order. Talk with other people to improve your interests.

If Thursday: Relax and seek enjoyment in the company of others. Any problems, true or imaginary, will emerge with a good solution.

If Friday: Solve your problems and reconcile your accounts in the morning. Reserve the rest of the day for congenial friends.

If Saturday: A little solitude can bring you excellent results. Study and the perusal of important matters will evolve with ease.

DAY'S NUMBER IS 2

If Sunday: If friends or acquaintances disturb you, dismiss any dejected thoughts. Demonstrate your own initiative and ability.

If Monday: Avoid any parental or domestic boredom. Maintain silence and patience. Look to your career or a personal interest.

If Tuesday: Be sure of your basic security, then do nothing to upset it. Lend a hand to someone needy. Take good care of your health.

If Wednesday: Your loved one may not understand your management of financial arrangements, but you must continue good judgment.

If Thursday: You are likely to have emotional or moody periods at this time due to friction or gossip, but do not let this deter you from your work or activities.

If Friday: Do not waver in your faith or decisions regarding your work or personal matters. Accept changes whenever possible.

If Saturday: This is a day of personal achievement, socially or in business. Dodge grumblers or troublemakers all day.

DAY'S NUMBER IS 3

If Sunday: You may have to face a challenge to help someone whom you do not know or particularly care for. Take time to rest and study.

If Monday: Check over any property or possessions. Be tactful with those around you wherever you go today. Budget yourself now.

If Tuesday: Listen to friends and associates today. You can learn much. Talk only when they have finished. Do not digress from your objective.

If Wednesday: This is a time for news. Be alert; it may be to your advantage. Keep a good perspective on your plans.

If Thursday: Irritability will only make matters worse for you. Best to avoid people or at least not become involved in arguments.

If Friday: Lock up your cash and small properties. Be tactful with your family or those near you. Do not force a showdown.

If Saturday: You should have a new trend of events that will affect your occupation. Help others to better their lot.

DAY'S NUMBER IS 4

If Sunday: Be calm and firm because you may face a crisis that demands cool thinking. Check everything carefully.

If Monday: Avoid emotional reactions with your family or friends. Complications may arise but be firm in your convictions.

If Tuesday: A good time to look into new opportunities. Don't let the day slip away from you. It is of prime importance that everything you undertake is right for you.

If Wednesday: Be cheerful even though you may not feel like smiling. Try to spend less and save more. A surprise is due in the near future.

If Thursday: Progress and advancement are due for those in business. For the homemakers, something new. This is a time for change.

If Friday: You may be unhappy or worried over complications evolving from past years. Be confident and you will eliminate these issues permanently.

If Saturday: You may have to change your plans due to those who surround you; however, your optimism will enable you to gain what you need most.

DAY'S NUMBER IS 5

If Sunday: This is a time for activation. Plan ahead with new work, new ideas. You may be able to achieve much more with the co-operation of friends.

If Monday: This is not a day to seek help from those around you. Do not worry. Concentrate on your immediate responsibilities.

If Tuesday: A good day to start capitalizing on your abilities. Be sure, however, not to offend anyone. Luck should be with you.

If Wednesday: This is a day for raising funds for yourself or for an organization. Check your own assets if the financing is for yourself. Accuracy is important.

If Thursday: Your tact and diplomacy will be your secret aid today. Start early in the day to accomplish your work. Deal only with enterprises that are safe and sound.

If Friday: Get some fun. Try something new. Get away from your present surroundings for a while. Love is important to you.

If Saturday: For the young this is a day for romance and pleasure. For the older folk, get recreation through your favorite form of entertainment.

DAY'S NUMBER IS 6

If Sunday: This is a time to relax, but allot plenty of thought in meditation. Relatives can add to your enjoyment even if in-laws.

If Monday: Cultivate newly made acquaintances. Increase your social activities to balance any changes in your working program.

If Tuesday: Do whatever you can to improve your prestige. Be dignified in all that you do. Keep your witticisms for the evening hours.

If Wednesday: You may find a new impetus for action in the afternoon. Save your money, let others pay now. Good day for sports and entertainment.

If Thursday: Check your health, do not strain or overwork. Avoid any discussions over other people's personal problems. Be receptive but evasive.

If Friday: If you need advice, seek it from friends, but use your own sound judgment. Travel and investments should be considered.

If Saturday: A little solitude is good for you. Do not get into family disputes. Devote your time to real opportunities.

DAY'S NUMBER IS 7

If Sunday: Look to the debit side of your exchequer. This period stresses the word "economy" even though you may not deem it essential. Lunar influences indicate a change for the better.

If Monday: Stay with your old reliable associates and interests. No need to argue with hypersensitive associates. Refer to reliable banking or law firms.

If Tuesday: Your dependents may irritate you whether old or young, but your patience will reward you. This is a very favorable period for you. Stay with it.

If Wednesday: Follow your desires in the morning hours no matter if they pertain to the arts, sports, study of any kind; let it be recreation for you as well as study. It will make your day happy despite any obstacles.

If Thursday: Regardless how high or to what ends your mind may soar, eventually you must meet certain obligations that exist.

If Friday: Make your plans early in the day. Each minute should bring you pleasant satisfaction especially if you include a friend.

If Saturday: Your days should be filled with surprises, not all good, but mostly happy. Plan a few excursions into something different.

DAY'S NUMBER IS 8

If Sunday: Keep your mind on immediate projects. Do not be distracted. Do not let anything pile up, not even debts. Pay them promptly.

If Monday: It will pay to stay with your old reliable friends, but be careful not to offend the sensitive ones. Be cautious of deals.

If Tuesday: Use your analytical ability and patience to ward off small complications with family or associates. New events will bring you unexpected happiness.

If Wednesday: Utilize your morning hours to best advantage; however, do not exceed your physical capacity. Relaxation is as important as drive.

If Thursday: Aim all your forceful nature toward success. Be sure to balance all angles so that you can override obstacles or opposition.

If Friday: Put your plans to work especially where executive ability is needed. You can inspire loyalty by your understanding of people.

If Saturday: Do not resort to ruthless force. Study people and problems at hand. Any mysterious cloud of indecision will pass. Co-operation will help you personally.

DAY'S NUMBER IS 9

If Sunday: Do not waste your efforts. Be above petty jealousies. Use your drive for advancement either in business or social circles.

138 *The Complete Illustrated Book of Divination and Prophecy*

If Monday: Plan carefully and apply yourself to higher achievements. Your capability should extend to your greatest desire if you apply it.

If Tuesday: Use your ability from now on with all the aggressiveness that you have. Follow new trends and move along without resentment.

If Wednesday: Follow your intuition, but seek advice from family or a trusted friend, then formulate a plan before plunging into something new.

If Thursday: Thinking big will help you if money is concerned, but do not waste your efforts in small things that are irrevelant. Relax.

If Friday: This is a time when dependability is most prevalent. But do not expect too much co-operation from others. Good results will be cumulative.

If Saturday: This is a period of change, so patience must be exerted because of differences of opinion with those around you. A little vacation can relieve any strain.

WHEN BIRTH NUMBER IS 9

AND DAY'S NUMBER IS 1

If Sunday: Give your full time to your immediate occupation. Avoid extravagant spending. If you must speculate, do not invest in a bad risk.

If Monday: Act now to demand more for your efforts, but do not exceed the established maximum. There are other people nearby who can offer the same or more depending upon the individual talents.

If Tuesday: You have the ability to cope with the situation before you. Try to make a better average today and wait for the good fruition of your effort and work, another day or week or month.

If Wednesday: If you feel that you must make a change, take a chance, try it, but you must maintain some sort of balance so that you will not find yourself at the brink of a precipitous downfall.

If Thursday: If on the verge of a decision, personal or in business and it involves money, better wait awhile until a more appropriate time when you become more influential. Act independently.

If Friday: Put imagination into your ideas, then play your hunches. Stay cheerful and tolerant of those near you. Take a holiday later.

If Saturday: Use your intellect for creative channels, then set your goal within your capabilities. Avoid complexities but cling to your ambition. Be positive but be ready to adjust to circumstances.

DAY'S NUMBER IS 2

If Sunday: Cultivate new friendships through your fine personality. Follow your natural traits. Good news is ahead, but release all tension lest you fail to balance the good with the bad.

If Monday: Your talents are great, but do not extend them beyond your capacity. Not too many things at one time, but talent you have and use it.

If Tuesday: Monotony is not for you, but there will be many changes whereby you can profit. Do not take the easiest way out, look for a reasonable solution.

If Wednesday: Fill your obligations to the utmost of your mental and physical strength. Your season should be filled with remunerative compliments.

If Thursday: This may be a period for speculation, adventure, or some definite change. Leave the drudgery to others. Live up to your ideals.

If Friday: Devote time to both business and your home life. Both are very important. If things are not as you wish, keep trying, because planetary changes sooner or later will swing your way for the best.

If Saturday: Use your influence to help those in need. Be fair with everyone. Make the best of every opportunity.

DAY'S NUMBER IS 3

If Sunday: Stay with your present routine. Any change could mean disappointment. Leave boasting to others. Work ahead silently.

If Monday: Consider the future as well as the present. You need plenty of security, so combine your plans for a solid front. Keep the glamour for holiday time.

If Tuesday: Use all of your versatility to further your ends. Enjoy the pleasures that come your way. Add your own buoyant traits to increase your own happiness.

If Wednesday: Study new ideas thoroughly even though you grasp their meaning quickly. Be sure all things are right before proceeding.

If Thursday: Your initiative is fine, but at this period it should be a good time to co-operate with other people even though it is not to your liking.

If Friday: This is the time to start to improve conditions. Depend upon your own forcefulness to establish good will and earn the respect of others.

If Saturday: Make the weekend interesting. Turn to study that will increase your knowledge. There is always room for improvement.

DAY'S NUMBER IS 4

If Sunday: Join with your friends in a little fun and excitement. Take time to read a little, too. Do not let your interests conflict with other people who may be with you.

If Monday: Take things a little easier lest pressure makes you irritable. You will accomplish more. Compliment those who help you. Honesty and your reliability are great assets.

If Tuesday: Try to plan for the more distant future. You may need advice to gain success at top level, so do not hesitate to seek it. Do not get bewildered at any opposition.

If Wednesday: Continue to work steadily. Treat any difficult problem with ease and patience. Stability is the secret of your success.

If Thursday: This could be an adventurous era for you; however, it is wise to avoid any extravagant spending just to impress people. You can celebrate after you have attained your rightful place in the world. Experience is necessary to you.

If Friday: Kindliness will help you to achieve your goal, though you may be faced with aggressiveness. Do not let this disturb you. If you have a chance to take a trip, do so. New vistas are good for you.

If Saturday: A good time to study one of the arts or a skill that may interest you. Take a change of pace. Do something different. Enjoy it all.

DAY'S NUMBER IS 5

If Sunday: Neither resort to nor listen to gossip. Seek honorable achievements that improve your talents. Stay busy; never give up your ambition.

If Monday: Let not your ambitions be too lofty. Stay within the bounds of your capabilities. A good, moderate, sound investment is your own intellectual ability. Apply it.

If Tuesday: Your own versatility and intuitive qualification make planning a very natural attribute for you. Be cheerful and proceed.

If Wednesday: Time to concentrate on your own affairs. Be good to yourself for a change. Check all your personal needs, then do something about them.

If Thursday: Put your ideas to work for the home or the office or for the good of others. Procrastination is no help. Travel if you must, but you can find adventure right where you are.

If Friday: A time to accomplish something worth while. Create confidence so that people will depend upon you. Make yourself indispensable.

If Saturday: Buy no more than you need, even food. Luxury items can wait for a later date. A period of solitude can promote inspiration for you.

DAY'S NUMBER IS 6

If Sunday: Look for opportunities to mix with the young people, people your own age or older or perhaps younger than you. Accept them as they are, not as you might wish them to be. Analyze your own problems with keen eyes. Do not believe everything you see or hear.

If Monday: Complications may lead to conferences. Be ready to substantiate every phase of your argument or agreement. Leave antagonism to the opposition. Rely on the judgment of a superior authority.

If Tuesday: Use all of your inventive originality to help mold the particular niche where you are. Deal only with the powers that be. Let nothing deter you.

If Wednesday: Your relationship with associates could become very tense and strained if you join a partnership financial transaction. This is not a good time according to past planetary movements. This could cost you a pretty penny and alienate your friendship.

If Thursday: If you have confidence in your undertakings, go ahead, otherwise forget the whole deal. This is a time to think carefully. If there is an angle that is foreign to you, give it a long, long time of perusal.

If Friday: Be sure all your possessions are safe and really protected. Whatever may be your plans, keep them to yourself for the present. If you have a negative reception, do not be discouraged; another time will present itself.

If Saturday: Sometimes mystic powers work for us, and this can be a help to you, so that you have time to think and plan. Keep social activities at a minimum.

DAY'S NUMBER IS 7

If Sunday: Face the issues before you. Meet them squarely and use an honest approach to solve them. Make a schedule that you can meet. Do not be afraid to accept the co-operation of others.

If Monday: Resort not to moodiness. Find solace in your very own pursuits. The artist to his niche, the musician to his, and so on down the alphabet to whatever may be the occupation.

If Tuesday: Evasion is not the solution to difficulty. If you cannot find the answer, let associates step in and try. Rivals can produce competitive blocks, but nothing is impossible to unravel.

If Wednesday: Your creative ability places many responsibilities upon you. Do not be afraid to allot some of them to others whom you well know. You also need time for home and social matters.

If Thursday: You may soon want to make an investment. Even if small, consult with someone who knows more about it than you do. Do not be impulsive. Take your time to think about any further move.

If Friday: Small, irksome disturbances can be very annoying to you, but your best bet is to finish every task no matter how troublesome. Integrity is your valuable asset. Move with discretion.

If Saturday: This can be a day or beginning of relaxation, or it can be one of work and achievement that is just the beginning. Either way you hold the key of knowledge and can direct the way to new ventures.

DAY'S NUMBER IS 8

If Sunday: This is an interesting period in which you should promote your personal ambition. Be tactful, avoid any personal opinions that could upset advancement.

If Monday: New friendships, new contacts will become valuable to you in the professional, social, or financial life. Never be discouraged.

If Tuesday: Material success and business are important with these first numbers. Adding the gaiety of the number three of Tuesday brings a charming accumulation of happiness. So may it be.

If Wednesday: Try something new, but do not take chances. Forget routine and take surprise situations with ease and grace.

If Thursday: You will probably make new friendships during this interim. Use them if need be to further your ideals, but never really impose upon them. All is reciprocative.

If Friday: This is a favorable era for you. Keep your family circle happy and contented, then proceed to enlarge and publicize your occupational interests.

If Saturday: Devote your time to your ambitions. Friends, you may have many, but if they do not help you in your field of endeavor, let them go their way. Time is of the essence.

DAY'S NUMBER IS 9

If Sunday: Be sure all is well and protected in your home, then take stock of occupational or business needs. Time to recapitulate and set your house and financial condition in order.

If Monday: This is a propitious time to spend at home while planning for new ventures. Keep your social life within the bounds of your home surroundings.

If Tuesday: Let people and press know what you are doing. Time to apply your talents and aim for the highest possible place of honor and distinction. Money will follow.

If Wednesday: You may encounter difficulties, struggles that you did not anticipate, but planetary influence is good and you should have great satisfaction in your resulting gains. Do not be careless or wasteful.

If Thursday: Business aspects are good. Just do not go too heavy on investments. For the artistic person this is a test of your ability and initiative.

If Friday: Time to plan a nice social get-together with your nearest friends. Do not spend more than you can really afford, but do make it interesting for yourself as well as all your guests.

If Saturday: A time for fun, relaxation, even romance if that is what you want. Make new friends but keep the old ones, too. Listen while you learn.

V. Tasseomancy or Tasseography

Back in the Middle Ages, there were numerous methods of telling fortunes in which diviners used their intuitive abilities to interpret various symbols formed from blobs of molten lead, wax, and other substances. Some of these were remarkably significant, and the fortune-tellers themselves became very adept at such practices.

By the fifteenth century, tea drinking was introduced in Europe and became a widespread habit. Soon, people began noting that dregs left in a teacup or bowl resembled the symbols used in old-time divinations, and they were adapted to that purpose, initiating a custom that has remained popular ever since.

Telling fortunes from tea leaves is a pleasant diversion. By careful study of the following directions and interpretation of the symbols you can become very expert at translating the hidden meanings for yourself as well as those of your friends.

If you try it often enough, you may discover that you possess psychic ability. Although we have included this chapter merely for entertainment purposes, there are many readers who actually demonstrate psychic powers while interpreting the so-called divinations or predictions.

Imagination plays a strong part in the interpretation of the forms or shapes that chance to form when the tea dregs are swished around in a teacup and *only after* the consultant has drunk the tea in the self-same cup. Exactly how the tea is brewed does not really matter, but you must have enough residue from real leaves to obtain adequate impressions. Since the stems and leaves form shapes that are called symbols, the fun of it all lies in the visualization and interpretation of them in order to make predictions.

Two teaspoonfuls of a very good grade of tea dropped into a pre-heated small teapot and boiling water over it all, placing the lid on tight, are the secret of good tea and good grounds for divination. Study the symbols and the fortune will be spelled out for you.

Time is denoted in various parts of the inside and rim of the cup.

Present Time is represented on the rim of the cup and the areas near it, meaning days, weeks; the distant future is on the bottom; everything in between gauges the variance between the immediate, the not so distant, and the very remote. The closer the symbol lies to the handle, the sooner the prognostication will be fulfilled.

The HANDLE represents the consultant and respective house, surroundings, and occupation.

INITIALS represent people in connection with a symbol or, if close to the handle, are very important to the consultant.

A LARGE STEM on the rim edge of the cup refers to a man who has an interest in the consultant. A SMALL STEM indicates a woman.

NUMBERS refer to money, an address, a date or time, which can be minutes, hours, days, weeks, months, or years. The symbols give the clue to the number. The closer to the handle the sooner the prognostication.

DROPS OF TEA that remain in the cup (or plate as in coffee) mean tears or sorrow for the consultant.

DOTS like little specks in a cluster, made up by odd sizes of leaves and stems, indicate money. The larger the dots the more money but it can mean more work to obtain it. Dots that lie in a straight line mean a journey. Three dots in a group mean a wish will be granted.

STRAIGHT LINES that look as though they are one continuous unbroken line denote tranquillity, a sort of peace of mind that results from careful planning.

WAVY LINES, uncertainty due to aggravation, sometimes loss of money.

LETTERS, capital or small, refer to friends, business acquaintances, or relatives.

SQUARES are considered a protection often covering a mistake or a danger that has been or can be averted.

STARS AND TRIANGLES always mean good luck in themselves. When close to another symbol they magnify the value of the symbol.

INTERPRETATION OF THE SYMBOLS

ACORN—Success regardless of difficulties. If the acorn is very clear, luck will play an important part. If cloudy, more effort is necessary.

AIRPLANE—On the bottom of the cup, a trip may be postponed or a disappointment is unavoidable; on the side, a wish to escape present problems by actually making a plane flight even though it seems improbable; near the handle, something new should be done for home or self.

ANCHOR—A sign of success. Near the top, love and constancy; on the side, more interest in business and travel than in the pursuit of love or sex; on the bottom, success with any project that involves travel. If the anchor is cloudy or indistinct, there are temporary disappointments that concern a loved one.

ANGEL—Unexpected happiness and good news. A time for rejoicing.

ANTS—Forecast of bad times and difficulties. Hard work ahead.

ANVIL—Laborious efforts needed to achieve desires.

APPLE—Ability can meet the demands for success in business; good health, too; cultivate your personality.

APRON—About to meet strangers who will become good friends of yours.

ARROW—An agreement may be reached by means of a letter; if the arrow is partial or cloudy, the message may be disappointing.

AX or HATCHET—Obstacles; a warning of a dangerous situation. If cloudy the danger lessens.

BABY—On the side, troubles involving finances; near the handle, unexpected honors; on the bottom, unhappiness in love.

BALL—Conditions indicate a change.

BARREL—A full barrel, near the handle, augurs a time for celebrations in your home; if empty, you need a rest; on the bottom, save your money.

BASKET—If full, a surprise and news of a birth; if empty, reduce your expenditures.

BAT—Disappointment caused by jealousy of someone who resents you. A trip you planned may be useless.

BEAR—Always a warning against misfortune; stay home.

BED—Subconscious desire for rest and quiet; dreams can be your means of escape from worries.

BELL—Good news; many bells, notification of an important event; a marriage.

BIRD—Your luck will be improving; on a branch, a journey in the near future; with short lines or dots close by, you will travel with other people; several birds, a prognostication of happiness; a bird always means news, good or bad, depending upon other symbols.

BIRD CAGE—Guard your affections; do not commit yourself without lengthy consideration.

BOAT—If it be a sailboat, proceed with your plans; if a large ship, wanderlust and desire for escape can change your present situation.

BOOK—If closed, do not make a hasty decision; if open, proceed with your scheme.

BOOT—A desire to travel, but your finances may need boosting to meet your dream. If you are thinking in terms of business, your trip would be successful.

BOTTLE—Refrain from overindulgence; at the bottom of the cup, it is a warning for someone close to you.

BOUQUET—Usually an indication of happiness in love that continues through married life.

BOX—If closed, you are troubled; if open, your instability will soon be over; sociability is yours if you simply exert your amiability.

BRACELET or RING—A union that is very important to you; congratulations are due.

BRANCH—If bare, opposition socially or in business causes temporary unrest; with leaves, new friendship ahead; announcement of a birth.

BRIDGE—Your decision regarding an obstacle will result in ultimate success.

BROOM—Look for new prospects, new interests; time for a change.

BUILDING—Your ambition may cause you to change your ideas; you may need a change of surroundings.

BULL—Danger ahead; curb your temperament.

BUSH—A symbol of unexpected money; the larger the bush, the more money.

BUTTERFLY—Social pleasures that may have implications that could end in trouble but usually finish in a jovial manner; be discreet.

CAB—Your secret may be discovered; do not act in haste.

CAGE—This usually means marriage; otherwise you have a problem that confuses you; time takes care of both issues.

CAR—A change for the better.

CASTLE—An unexpected legacy; something very pleasant is going to happen.

CAT—A bad omen; deceit may cause you a lot of trouble.

CHAIN—A symbol of love, an engagement or marriage.

CHAIR—Look for an unexpected visitor; take time out for your own relaxation.

CHESSMEN—Many complications engross you.

CHURCH—An invitation to a ceremony.

CIRCLE—Traditionally the circle means money; the larger the circle the larger the so-called moneybag; it also means success after arduous, persistent endeavor.

CLOCK—Plan for the future.

CLOUDS—An adverse sign; trouble brewing; the more the number of little grounds around the clouds, the more complicated will be financial turmoil; try a completely new project.

CLOVER—Whatever your problem is, you will emerge very happily.

COFFIN—Bad news; sometimes a death.

COMET—Do not worry about something that may never happen; relax.

COMPASS—You should travel; look for some new interest, something occupational.

CROSS—You will make a sacrifice that will be very taxing; on the bottom of the cup, very serious trouble for someone near you; near the top, the trouble will soon be resolved; within a square, you can soon divert the trouble.

CROWN—Good luck and success through honorable achievement.

CUP—A symbol of plenty; a new friendship that will bring a lot of joy to you.

DAGGER—Danger; a loss because of enmity.

DAISY—Love and happiness ahead.

DANCER—Avoid frivolity; you may have a misunderstanding.

DEER—Be calm; try not to become involved in arguments or disputes.

DIAMOND—Lucky in love.

DOG—You have a very trustworthy friend; on the bottom of the cup, a friend of yours needs your assistance; a dog's head, you are a valuable friend to someone close to you.

DONKEY—Cultivate patience; do not be stubborn; study all sides of a problem.

DOOR—If open, you will receive surprising news; if closed bide your time and you will receive your wish.

DOVE—Peace and good news.

DRAGON—Start a new year right now; try something different; take a new viewpoint.

DRUM—Beware of bombast; look for a change, something exciting.

DUCK—A cheerful attitude will help to improve your situation.

EAGLE (see Bird)—The eagle is a very large bird; so, too, your desires are stronger and bigger than you realize; try to enlarge your home or your circle of friends; need for protection.

EGGS—A new baby has arrived; double or triple the nests of eggs and you increase the blissful news.

ELEPHANT—Harbinger of health and happiness, but you need a trustworthy friend.

EYEGLASSES—A surprise is due; if in business, be cautious.

FACES—New acquaintances will enlarge your list of friends.

FAN—Be careful that you do not commit an indiscretion; your flirtatious appearance may get you involved.

FIREPLACE—Time to have a party; expand your social aspirations.

FISH—A lucky symbol; good news and the possibility of travel.

FLAG—A warning for you to be on the defensive; act slowly and wisely.

FLIES—Annoying details that you can dismiss.

FLOWERS—Happiness and honors; on the bottom of the cup, an unfortunate love entanglement; on the side, marriage or an amour.

FOUNTAIN—Your plan will be completed. Joy and prosperity.

FOX—Deceit will ruin a nice liaison or friendship.

FROG—An appropriate time to make a change in business or social matters.

FRUIT—Always a fortunate symbol; push your ambitions.

GATE—An open gate means a satisfactory solution to a vexing situation; a closed gate means further negotiations must be made before arriving at suitable conditions.

GOAT—Unhappy news from someone traveling; avoid obstinacy or too many conflicts of personal ideas.

GRAPES—Happiness through confidence in a loved one.

GUITAR—Desirous of ardent love and affection.

GUN—Look out for trouble; service in the home can be rough too.

HAMMER—Consistent trial and error will reward you with eventual success.

HAND—Someone needs you as much as you need that person; understanding and friendship keep you active.

HARP—Romance; lofty ideas.

HAT—Money; on the bottom of the cup, balanced marital bliss; on the side, an exceptional talent of diplomacy.

HATCHET (see Ax)—Difficulties; do not be impetuous; avoid arguments.

HEART—A lover or a very close friend; if the ring symbol is close, a marriage is near; little dots, money; if the heart is not clear, you are not serious.

HEAVENLY BODIES—These require some imagination, but they are the sun, the moon, the Milky Way, the stars, and other planets. They all indicate a state of happiness and prosperity.

HEN—Take care of your money; good foresight and financial provision bring peace and happiness.

HORSESHOE—A promise of good luck; look around the cup for the key to the lucky streak.

HOURGLASS—Danger is imminent; especially a bad warning if the hourglass is on the bottom of the cup. Do not make hasty decisions.

INITIALS—These can be any of the letters of the alphabet. They refer to people you know or will soon know.

JUG—Conviviality and fun should soon be yours; guard against excesses, overindulgence, and procrastination: you will have many happy social gatherings with your friends.

KETTLE—Domestic harmony should be your aim; a steaming kettle indicates struggles and a lack of tranquillity.

KEY—You are a lucky person; all avenues and doors to business and friendship are open for you; whatever your problems, they will be solved reasonably; continue the search for new interests.

KITE—Gambling and chances are not for you; maintain a constant balanced outlook on everything.

KNIFE—An unfortunate symbol; take very good care of your health; do not make contracts without expert advice; misunderstandings can involve you financially; if the knife is on the bottom of the cup, lawsuits may threaten you; if pointed toward the handle, it means temporary separation from family and business. If the knife is partially covered with a square, you will have some good luck and avoid some of the difficulties; however, bonds of friendship and love will be sorely tried.

LADDER—Your idealistic ambitions will increase your advancement, but the demands upon you will grow in proportion.

LAMP—Unexpected co-operation during a time of loss if the lamp is on the side of the cup; if it is on the bottom, a disappointment or postponement of a social event; at the rim, a happy reunion and celebration; near the handle, a special legacy. Two lamps indicate a business merger or two marriages.

LEAVES—Simple open formation of the tea grounds so they look like little leaves, hope never dies, so you can start again; if they are on the bottom of the cup, you will attain your ambitions even though late.

LETTERS—If well defined, good news; if poorly formed, bad news; if dots are near it, money; if close to a heart, emotional disturbances.

LILY—A symbol of friendship and constancy; at the rim of the cup, a fine marriage; at the bottom, angry words, opposition.

LINES—Straight and unbroken, peace, tranquillity; parallel, a journey; wavy or broken, uncertainty, indecision, losses.

MAN—An unknown man will contact you; an initial nearby will give the clue to the name.

MASK—A warning to guard your innermost thoughts and secrets; if a bell or a flower is in close proximity, a gala time will soon be your pleasure.

MOON—A symbol of honors; if near the handle, romance; at the bottom of the cup, a good time for travel; if it is the first quarter of the moon, start something new; if the last quarter, take your time to make decisions; if cloudy or indistinct, your worries will soon pass.

MOUNTAINS—Rough work ahead, but a staunch friend will assist you.

MUSHROOM—A sweethearts' quarrel of short duration; business or domestic complications; may need mental or physical adjustment.

NUMBERS—Indication of days or weeks; several numbers refer to money or an address; any or all will be related to other symbols. Old interpretation—lucky in a lottery.

OWL—Bad omen of illness, perhaps a death.

PALM TREE—A sign of good luck, happiness, and marital contentment.

PIPE—A time for thinking and listening; do not be opinionated, try to be fair-minded.

RING—The symbol of marriage; an engagement; check for an adjoining number and initial; if the ring is on the bottom of the cup, an unforeseen difficulty or misunderstanding will mean a postponement of an engagement or marriage, sometimes a cancellation.

SAW—Interference by someone who will cause trouble.

SCISSORS—An unfortunate omen; if near the handle, unhappy domestic relations; near the rim, separation of husband and wife; on the bottom, occupational disputes.

SHIP—Travel; if the ship is near the handle, travel may combine business and family; near the rim, you will pack and leave in a hurry.

SNAKE—Bad luck; an enemy wishes you misfortune.

SPADE—Your hard work will be rewarded with honor and ample remuneration.

SPIDER—In spite of your secretiveness and artifices you will receive money and unexpected gifts.

SQUARE—Always a good sign; a protection that modifies mistakes, lessens danger and accidents.

STAR—Always a lucky sign; health, wealth, and happiness are associated with this symbol. Your destiny should be the completion of your ambitions and hopes.

SWORD—Be alert for domestic and occupational quarrels.

TENT—Travel is your answer for your unrest and discontent.

TREE—Life will reward you with health and many possessions. Many trees indicate a practical wish for a change that should materialize.

TRIANGLE—Luck increases with a triangle unless it be upside down, in which case it indicates the need to study every possible step before undertaking a new enterprise or interest.

UMBRELLA—If closed, you will be thwarted in your present situation; if open, proceed with caution and don't be afraid to consult with your friends.

VASE—Gratification and peace of mind are yours through service to others.

WHEEL—A symbol of achievement by your own hard work; if the wheel is near the rim, you will be remunerated with an increase of salary plus possible dividends.

WOMAN—The symbol of wishful thinking, of every aspiration, every desire.

SAMPLE INTERPRETATION OF TEA LEAF READING

Hold the cup with the tea grounds away from you to get a good general picture. Try varying distances. Look for groupings, dots alone, dots in a line. Crosses, squares, circles, triangles, letters, or numbers may be in a partial formation so that you must decide upon their degree of importance and relativity to the nearest plainly visible symbol. Look for clouds, trees, flowers, animals, birds, a house, a ship, anything that seems to form a picture or an outline. If the symbol is large, it is important; if small, it has less bearing on the message for the consultant. Look for signs such as a square or rectangle near a letter of the alphabet. This indicates news by mail for the consultant. If there are also a lot of dots nearby, money is involved. The closer to the handle and the nearer to the rim, the sooner the letter will be received.

Turn the handle to the left to serve as a base or starting point, termed "South". Lines, formed by the grounds between South and West, mean an immediate journey; between West and North, later on. Between North and East, they mean an unexpected visitor; between East and South, the visitor will arrive soon, perhaps imminently. If the grounds form a path that circles the inside of the cup, the consultant will take a lengthy trip and return home again. So when the symbols are on the west half of the cup, the consultant is the motivating force; on the east side, the action is brought to the consultant, which again means the house, surroundings or occupation. Lucky and unlucky signs must be balanced by comparative sizes. The smaller, the less important and the less bearing upon other symbols.

Should the cup show nothing but a mess, consider it a state of confusion or indifference. Unless the consultant is very insistent, do not try again, because it is not considered lucky to read the grounds for others or self more than once a week.

The consultant, represented by the handle, appears about to receive a communication by letter. The dots and lines toward the north mean a journey because of the letter (envelope). Since the handle is considered south, the journey may be westward. At about the same time, a message will be sent to the consultant by someone else; this is because the symbol, the bird, is situated toward the south of the cup, showing that the motivation comes from an outsider. The large stem on the rim

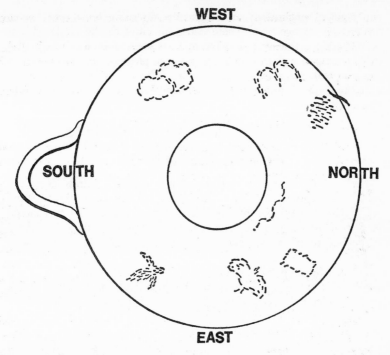

5) Tea leaf divination. Interpretation of the leaves remaining in the teacup, noted in clockwise rotation from the handle.

Clouds—trouble
"M"—initial for place or persons
Dots and lines—journey
Large stem on rim—a man
Wavy lines—uncertainty
Letter (envelope)—news
Butterfly—pleasure
Bird—news, message (from far away)

In the reading that follows, these symbols are taken in irregular order according to their comparative importance or their relation to one another.

of the cup indicates that a man will have some interest or negotiation with the consultant in the course of a few days, perhaps in connection with the journey. The clouds show uncertainty as to the outcome of the meeting because of a little trouble or misunderstanding. Since there is no unlucky sign near, such as a cross, the culmination should be favorable for the consultant.

Again the wavy line and cloudy appearance in the bottom of the cup warn of uncertainty and vagueness regarding some very remote business or engagement. There being no clues to the cloud, this is purely worry or conjecture in the mind of the consultant. The butterfly at the right of the word "East" promises pleasure and a most happy event to take place in the near future. The initial "M" close to the butterfly concerns a person who will contribute greatly to that pleasurable meeting.

DIVINATION FROM COFFEE GROUNDS
Directions for the Preparation of the
Coffee Grounds and the Cup

For best results use a mixture of two different grinds of coffee, preferably "regular" and "fine." Allow two tablespoons of regular grind coffee and one teaspoon of fine to each cup of coffee. The cup should be a standard wide-rimmed cup without decoration so there is nothing to detract from the symbol formation of the grounds. Also use a saucer.

Prepare the cup by warming it with very hot water, then dry it quickly. Place the two tablespoons of regular and one teaspoon of fine ground coffee in the cup. Keep a saucer under it to avoid soiling a table or cloth on which it rests. Pour boiling water in the cup, cover and let steep a minute or more. Remove cover, stir, then hand to the consultant, who in turn must drink a little of the coffee or all. When finished, the consultant must pour off the remaining coffee liquid, leaving about a tablespoonful in the cup.

This done, take hold of the handle of the cup with the left hand, make a wish, and swish the cup around three times counterclockwise so the grounds will scatter around the sides of the cup. Next, turn the cup upside down on the saucer to drain, then place the cup, rim upward, on the saucer. The grounds will be scattered around the inside of the cup, forming groups of designs, dots, and lines which the reader must study and interpret.

At about the time when tea leaf reading came into vogue, coffee grounds were used for the same purpose, particularly in countries where coffee was a more popular drink than tea. Many people prefer it and the two types of readings are interchangeable.

In the eighteenth century Italians claimed that the process of coffee reading was really invented by them and its results were supposed to be the work of demons. Coffee had to be ground and placed in a coffeepot, water added, boiled, and then certain words were to be spoken by the consultant: "*Aqua boraxit venias carajos*"; while stirring with a spoon (it might boil over) repeat the words "*Fixitur et patricam explinabit tornare"*; then, pouring the coffee water off and subsequently pouring the very wet grounds (dregs) on a white unglazed plate, recite: *"Hax verticaline, pax Fantas marobum, max destinatus, veida porol."* Witches who forgot to repeat the foregoing quotations, or never knew them, were likely never to make correct predictions.

As the interpretations of the coffee symbols are identical to those of tea leaf reading, refer to page 144, starting with *Time,* then check the list of symbols that follow.

VI. The Hand of Fate

Here we have a unique form of divination, based on letters in names, as applied to palmistry. Only one name should be used, such as a person's given name, though an adopted name, a pen name, a professional name as used in the theater, or even a nickname may be utilized. In any or all of these, you may find something of importance to yourself.

Each letter is interpreted individually, according to its position upon the palm. Of the various choices, one or more may apply to you or have some significance that you will recognize. To begin, take the letters of the selected name and write them in a column at the left margin of a sheet of paper. Then fill in appropriate definitions at the right, so you will finish with a running account from top to bottom.

A person desiring to take a new name can change it to conform to this simple delineation by first choosing the interpretations, then forming the nearest meaningful name and waiting to see if it changes your way of life.

The Hand of Fate provides an excellent way to liven up a party. You can let other people take your name and choose the statements that they feel are most appropriate to the "you" that they see or know.

A

Your strong vitality will always stimulate others.

You may have periods of poor health, but care and common sense will overcome weakness.

Irritability and nervousness must be avoided or you will face domestic and financial problems.

You will overcome your timidity and sensitivity if you engross yourself in some new activity.

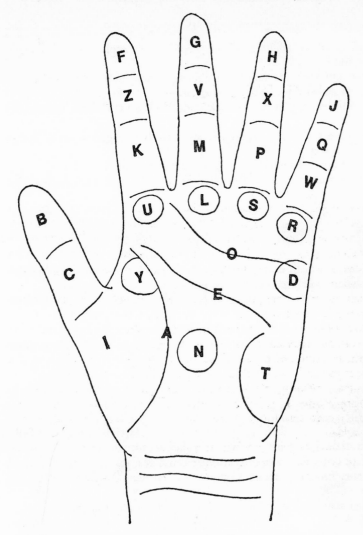

6) Letter designations for the Hand of Fate.

Unforeseen events may cause you to move to another place.

You will travel far and may not return due to your own desires.

Your fickle temperament must be controlled or you will hurt yourself.

Your ambition will be attained if you apply your energy and skill.

B

You have the ability to direct people if you apply yourself thoughtfully and honestly.

You are very adaptable and able to handle any problem that you have, provided you do not go to extremes.

Think before you act, because your careless nature may defeat your plans.

You are not happy unless you are actively engaged in every project that faces you.

Generosity will interfere with your artistic talent.

Stubbornness must be controlled or you will meet with discouraging situations.

C

Your practical understanding of people is excellent, but lengthy discussions will often defeat your purposes.

Common sense will overcome your unwillingness to reason out little problems or situations.

Your brilliant intelligence will force you to places of importance.

Your impulsive tendencies must be modified by analyzing situations before jumping into them.

D

You have excellent judgment when you weigh things carefully, so let nothing discourage you, success lies ahead.

Your brusqueness and forcefulness can defeat you.

Your inferiority complex must be overcome. Patience will reward your efforts.

You may be afraid of nothing, but stay out of physical fights.

E

You will overcome your timidity as you grow older.

Your secretiveness and selfishness will give you power, but you may lose good friends and family unless you modify your ambition for money and fame.

Your ambition will be achieved if you use your intelligence and diplomacy.

Your versatility will bring you honors, but do not get careless.

You have great imagination, use it, develop, and apply it, but do not be irrational or you will not succeed.

You will be surprised if you know what people really think of you.

F

You have great pride; watch out for a fall.

Don't go by your superstitions.

Your desire for justice will bring you great friendships.

You work well under direction, so join an organization.

Don't let your artistry make you conceited.

Your intelligence will take you far if you pursue your talents with diligence.

G

Don't be so morbid; this disturbs those around you.

You like to be alone, and sometimes it is good for you.

You need outdoor occupation and activities.

Your indifference will hurt you yourself most of all.

Realism is for you, so proceed accordingly.

You will attain your desire if you become more careful in money matters.

Avoid excesses; they are harmful to you.

Science will carry you through your roughest times.

H

Pursue your ideal; it will bring you happiness.

Music or art will add to your achievement.

Avoid criticism; it may hurt you.

Don't concern yourself about the arts or literature.

Your talents are numerous, but concentrate on one for your fame.

Bragging will not further your status.

I

Your efforts will reward you with a beautiful family life.

The opposite sex is a nuisance to you; your talent will be your great love and inspiration.

Inconstancy will cause you untold anguish.

Sympathy and humane understanding will bring you big dividends.

Your cleverness may rob you of your physical desires.

Do not confuse sensuality with your great family love.

Idealism must be your goal.

J

Your intuition will be very useful to you.

Eloquence will add to your gifted mind.

Business schemes are dangerous for you, so be alert.

If you manage your inventiveness, you will acquire wealth and high position.

Put your energy to some useful occupation that will help others.

K

If you love your home, you will increase your security.

Your desire for independence is fine, but it will be dangerous if you go to extremes.

Control your zest for power lest it overwhelm you.

You have the instinct of a good director, but too much meddling will weaken your position.

Discretion and moderation will be an important factor in your accomplishments.

L

Sobriety and deep thought will promote your talent.

The secrets of magic and mystery are yours if you so desire.

Your sexual urge must be kept under control, otherwise it will place you in unpleasant situations, even relationships.

Do not get involved with the supernatural; it has nothing for you.

Hatred and jealousy must be wiped out of your mind before you can achieve success and happiness.

Theological studies will aid you greatly.
Outdoor occupations will make money for you.

M

Physical comforts and wealth will mean everything to you.
Excesses in eating, drinking, or bad habits will do you no good.
Your respect for religion will aid you and give you peace of mind.
Do not take risks; they will destroy your stability.
Keep your expenses under control lest they destroy you mentally.
Morbidness must be avoided to succeed in any field of endeavor.

N

Indecision is your worst enemy, so your stumbling can be conquered by you alone.

Overcome your fear of everything by developing your personality and following your latent talent.

Control your impulsive nature before it gets you into serious trouble.

Your irritable, unpredictable character must be subordinated, and then you will find many friends and prosperity.

Imaginary problems will hound you until you make up your mind to stay with your immediate interests.

O

You are constant and true as friend or lover, which in turn will always reward you with happiness.

You are ruled by your head, not your heart, so you must search far and wide for your innermost aim in life.

Your selfishness will defeat your plans, so modify your demands.

Sedentary habits are no good for you; keep active.

Misfortune will follow you unless you stop your recklessness.

Imaginings will mar your love life; control yourself.

Your devotion will see you through.

Your flirtatious habits will bring you bad luck, disappointment.

You are an idealist in love, hence take time to consider your choice for a mate.

P

Follow your artistic ability and you will have a brilliant career.

Do not follow your artistic trait; one of your practical abilities will bring financial rewards.

You need lots of common sense with your attractiveness.

Literature, music, some form of art will bring you what you want.

A great future is yours if you concentrate on your most obvious talent.

Q

Look to something scientific for your best plan of action.

Your cleverness will go far in business or industry.

You need management for your ideas.

Love for humanity will place you in the right profession.

Your schemes border on risk, which may get you into serious trouble.

Look for the best in everything, but do not get too optimistic.

R

Your persuasive power can place you in a prominent position.

Your evasive nature will sooner or later mark you as a schemer.

Your money will be made in business.

Select a profession for your career.

Your scheming mind and eloquence would do well in politics.

If you must invent something, stay with a practical idea.

You expend too much energy on too many projects to succeed.

Your adventurous spirit will bring you many changes.

S

You have great talent, but do not overrate it.

Pursue your best talent and you will have luck as a bonanza.

You are very gifted and will add gaiety to everyone in contact.

You have an enchanting personality that will help others along the road to prosperity, as well as yourself.

Your versatility and fearlessness will make you a spectacular career; however, you must provide for your old age.

You are aesthetic and by dreaming about unrealistic attainments you must be practical and carve an everyday career.

You have great vision, but do not lose what you have already attained.

You have great originality, but do not scatter your energy and talent.

You are articulate, unorganized, and a pinchpenny, so it is up to you to seek advice in all transactions.

T

Great imagination is your talent, and if you can place it you will enjoy riches and honors.

You are restless, nervous, petulant and so need companionship.

Change of surroundings often help.

Fantasy and love of the weird will assist you in new endeavors.

You are factual and need the study of history of some sort whereby you learn facts.

You are impulsive and do not need the satisfaction of intensive study in any of the arts or professions. Your boredom requires extra-sensory interests to divert you. You are a good imitator and should be with a group of progressives.

U

You take great pride in your achievements and rightfully, for they are noteworthy and will succeed.

Family and home are your pride and joy and will be so long as you maintain them.

Bragging about your success may end in disappointment.

Common vulgarity has no place in your life; forget it.

Your lack of respect may become retroactive to you. Give the other fellow a boost and see how your life will change.

Your unselfish and charitable characteristics will bring you unexpected happiness and prosperity.

Stay with your ideals; they will bring you great acclaim.

Beware of egotism, it may be your undoing.

Your honesty will bring you honors and distinction.

Your devoutness is your present and your future.

Intolerance and fanaticism can ruin you.

Your creativity and adaptability will place you in enterprises of the highest order.

Exaggeration is not for you; stick to the truth.

You should be practical in every way and help to keep stability in your family circle as well as with business and social contacts.

You may be a perfectionist, but you must not go to extremes or you will become a martinet.

V

You have your own ideas about values, usually correct, too, but keep them to yourself.

Your interest in land should make you money with real estate.

Music or poetry or both make an excellent outlet for your introspective, melancholy nature.

Apply your mathematical ability to another science and forget your sensitivity.

Overcome your abhorrence of socializing and you will have a happy life.

You have no interest in serious studies, but your practicality will keep you in a good position.

The occult and world of superstition hold nothing for you, so forget them and follow the ways of your family.

W

You like a lot of money, so give up your indolent ways and put your talent to work.

Your keen mind should make a fortune in business.

Comedy is your forte, so develop it more and use it in your profession.

You have excellent business talent, but it will be useless to you if you let your schemes get out of line.

Use your originality and try not to be impulsive.

Throw your sympathetic nature into a profession or service that will help others.

Your inherent love of science should be activated to your full capacity of research.

X

Fortunate you are that with your wonderful talent you have common sense to direct it.

Your artistic interest should be combined with merchandising in a manner that you like.

Your interest should be directed toward some division of engineering until you find a niche for an artistic skill.

Try writing only as a hobby until you have proved its worth to you.

A fabulous career can be yours if you apply yourself and not just dream.

Your love of excitement and publicity makes you vulnerable, but this can be a boon in public appearances.

Y

Put your aggressiveness in a selling capacity and you will find success.

You are a fighter both physically and mentally; apply these qualities in sports until you have achieved your desire.

You have courage to stand by your decisions, so do not let opposition discourage you.

Do not look for trouble; you will find it and quarrels will not solve it.

Seek advice before you place yourself in a troublesome spot.

The military world is for you, so it may be difficult to choose between home and country.

Z

The calculating idealist; how far will you go? This depends upon you.

Your pride will not let you concede to others, yet your ability to appraise a situation accurately will make you successful.

Your respect for others may be minimized, yet your ability may exceed them.

Apply your vanity to your home and surroundings; nothing can harm it.

Whatever business or enterprise you undertake, avoid bragging, do not be commonplace; maintain your ideal and you will attain your goal.

VII. The Modern I Ching

A MODERN INTERPRETATION OF
AN ANCIENT FORM OF DIVINATION

The I Ching, or Yi King, known also as The Book of Changes, dates back approximately 5,300 years, though it was not until nearly 2,000 of those years had passed that it was put into written form. Originally, it was a simple form of oracle, involving two lines, one solid, the other broken, which gave the consultant an affirmative or negative answer to a question, just as an issue can be decided by tossing a coin and noting whether it falls heads or tails.

From this developed a series of diagrams, combining two such lines in vertical formation, and those were later followed by trigrams, in which eight combinations of three lines each were loosely defined as follows:

SKY   **EARTH**   **SUN**   **MOON**

AIR   **WATER**   **MOUNTAIN**   **THUNDER**

7) Yin and yang trigrams of the modern I Ching.

The basic lines are known individually as *yang*, for solid, and *yin*, for broken. Yang, originally used for "yes," and yin, originally "no," therefore represent "positive" and "negative," but not in an opposing sense. Rather, yang is projective; yin, receptive. Where yang initiates, yin sustains. Other connotations of yang and yin would include: light and shadow; hard and soft; expressive and contemplative; strong and weak; firm and pliable; day and night.

Many other contrasts could be suggested, but never are they classed as outright "good" or "bad." There are times when yang is specially needed and times when yin is specially needed. Always, one complements or modifies the other, and a blending of the two functions constitutes what may be termed the life principle itself.

This becomes increasingly apparent in a study of the trigrams with an extension of their meanings. The trigram representing "sky" is all strength, with its triple yang, hence it also signifies "heaven," which is all-powerful and showers its blessings upon "earth," which is appropriately responsive and receptive, being represented by a triple yin.

Similarly, the trigram for "sun" can be extended to signify "fire" or even "lightning." The trigram for "moon," by still broader interpretation, can be anything that supplants sunlight; thus it may symbolize clouds, rain, or even the dangerous torrent in a deep gorge. Among other trigrams, "water" may specifically refer to "lake" or "marsh"; "mountain" to "height" or "summit"; "thunder" to "strife" or "tumult."

It is easy to see how "lake," as an extension of "water," can be further expanded to signify "sea" or "ocean," but there are other long-accepted equivalents that are puzzling indeed. The trigram for "sun" may signify "wind," which, like sunlight, has a penetrating effect; and that simile can be further extended to signify "wood," because tree roots penetrate the soil.

But the meanings went beyond that, including not only elements as detailed and expanded, but associated factors, such as "danger" for "moon" or "water," "immobility" for "mountain" and so on. In addition, family relationships were drawn into the over-all picture, with "sky" representing "father," "earth" symbolizing "mother," and other trigrams standing for "sons" and "daughters."

Next, the trigrams were doubled, forming hexagrams of six lines each, producing a total of sixty-four combinations as shown in the diagram, with a traditional numbering in the order given there. Thus "sky above sky," "earth above earth," "moon above thunder," and all the rest lent themselves to more elaborate interpretations. This led to skillfully shaded meanings, wherein one particular line might be stressed according to its position or its importance to the person consulting the oracle, who thereby could gauge his actions to suit his individual circumstance.

8) Table of Modern I Ching

Thus the I Ching developed into a Book of Wisdom and as such won the acclaim of the famous Chinese sage Confucius, who added his interpretations to those of the philosophers who had preceded him. Fortunately, however, it retained some of its oracular status, for at a period in Chinese history when philosophical works were banned and burned, the I Ching was spared on the claim that it was a Book of Divination, and, as such, its popularity has continued to the present.

Many scholars have probed deeply into the interpretations of the I Ching, and it is claimed that even Confucius, at the age of seventy, wished that he could live fifty years more to explore the subject properly. But times have changed since then. Today's questioners prefer a brief but pointed interpretation of each hexagram that expresses its ancient essence in terms of modern purpose. That rule has been applied to the listings that follow.

But first, the procedure of the divination must be discussed. In the traditional method, forty-nine stalks of the yarrow plant were used to determine which hexagram applied to some given situation or personal problem. These were divided into two random heaps that were subdivided by an almost ritualistic process, resulting in a group of stalks that represented yang, if odd, and yin, if even. By repeating the procedure, a hexagram was built, line by line, and its meaning was consulted according to its number.

A simpler and more practical method involves three ordinary coins or tokens and is therefore the best to use. Simply take the three coins, shake them, and let them fall upon a table or flat surface. If the majority fall heads, they represent yang; if tails, yin. This is registered as the *bottom line* of the hexagram. The coins are gathered, shaken, and dropped again to form the next line above, and the procedure is continued thus until the hexagram is complete, whereupon the consultant checks its meaning and applies it to his case.

Another and perhaps more popular method is to take six coins, preferably of the same size, and shake them between the cupped hands, finally forming them into a stack that is set on the table to represent the actual hexagram. Five of the coins are lifted and moved forward—or above—the first coin, then four are lifted and advanced in the same manner. Three, two, and finally one are then advanced, so that all six form a column of heads or tails that can be translated directly into the corresponding hexagram.

Even simpler is a method requiring only a single coin, which is tossed six times in succession, and each result, heads or tails, is recorded as yang or yin, starting with the bottom line and ending at the top.

Whichever method is used, the question in mind should be a

serious one, well weighed before the divinatory process is employed. In any case, the answer is left to chance, but that is a good reason to use the three-coin method, for since it takes longer than the others, it gives chance "more of a chance," so to speak. The answer, upon being read, should be interpreted by the questioner as it fits his own individual need.

For example: A man borrowed money with a piece of property as security, and after several years his finances improved to the point where he could easily reclaim it. But the value of the property had not increased, so he wondered whether he should let it go and invest the money in something else, even though he had been carrying the property all that time. So he used the I Ching system and came up with Hexagram 40, which indicated that since the storm that had forced him to shelter had lost its threat, he should free himself from past encumbrances and make up for lost time. So he let the property go.

The list of hexagrams follows:

1

A mighty dragon uncoils deep in a hidden cavern, ready to emerge. Watchful at first, he will rise high in the sky, winging his way to a well-planned objective or a deserved triumph. Once that is gained, he will return to earth without delay. So pattern your own course to that of the great dragon. Do not try to outrace, outdo, or outlast him, as it may cause you great regret.

2

The happiness that you seek should come your way, but only if you bide your time. Let others take the initiative, while you establish your own merit through willing co-operation. Those whom you serve or assist will recognize your virtues yet overlook your faults, as long as you are content with modest gain. In due time this will bring great fortune if a firm policy is maintained throughout.

3

As a plant struggles upward through the earth, so should you be content with slow attainment of your present quest. Learn to crawl before you walk; and once you walk, do not attempt to run, for the faster you try to go, the more often you may fall. Guidance is needed or you may be lost in a maze of your own making, for the very symbols that betoken small success may prove the undoing of anyone who undertakes anything too large.

4

Lessons must be learned, just as distinctions must be earned. So be simple and sincere in whatever you may do; and not only ask the advice of those who are qualified to give it; having asked it, above all, follow it. Ignorance is the only form of insincerity that can really hurt you, for the more advice you shun, the less you will be given.

5

Danger threatens as you approach the brink of a raging stream. Strong though you may be, it is better not to cross until your strength is greater or the risk is less, as added danger may await upon the other side. By waiting, you may ensure your chances for withdrawal, should that need arise, with friends ready to support you if you do. Good fortune is in order.

6

Strife and conflict are justified on your part now, but the longer you persist in such contention, the more futile it may become, with lack of gain or glory. Better to sway as a tree in the wind, while stormy clouds blow over, or to accept criticism and even temporary obscurity until you can gain the goal that you seek without senseless struggle.

7

A time for battle may be close at hand. Whether to fight, advance, or retreat is for you to decide, but you must be ready to strike when the vital moment arrives, as to hesitate then can mean sure loss. Those upon whom you depend must be of the same mind, so ensure yourself on that score. Firmness and decision are in order here.

8

Now is the time for peace and harmony; and with it, the urge for mutual effort. So make sincerity your watchword, but withal choose your partner or associates well, in order that your intentions be truly reciprocated. The chain that proves strong enough for those who pull together may snap when strained in opposite ways.

9

When dense clouds gather in abundance, rain must surely follow. Should it be delayed, there is no reason to prepare hurriedly for drought instead. Rather, wise men will plan to utilize the expected downpour, even guarding against floods that it may cause; and they will thank the clouds for granting a respite. So with our own actions, brief restraint at the right moment will signify sincerity and regard for others.

10

Walk firmly and gaze constantly along your chosen path and you may tread upon a tiger's tail, yet still stride steadily onward before the beast has roused to action. But those whose feet stumble or whose eyes wander may hesitate too long and fall prey to vengeful claws. This symbol, too, is likened to steppingstones across a stream, where one loose stone may yield beneath a careless foot and plunge the wayfarer into the torrent. So be firm!

11

As the gentle breath of spring presages a fruitful planting and the glory of autumn betokens a fine harvest, so should the gifts of heaven be showered upon earth. Thus those who are great and powerful in this world should show understanding and compassion for those who are small and weak that all may share happiness and good fortune.

12

From small beginnings or humble surroundings, it is possible to improve your status or ability without attracting undue notice or arousing envy. Thus, though seemingly at a standstill, you may later emerge as though sprung from earth, yet possessing gifts of heaven. Wait for doors to be opened, but plan to be ready when they are.

13

Amid absolute darkness, the tiniest flicker of light can be seen from afar. Thus, from obscurity, you can spark yourself to action and encourage others to kindle kindred lights. United in fellowship, such flames can grow to a mighty conflagration illuminating the entire sky. Success, once yours, should therefore be shared with those who helped you gain it.

14

Progress and prosperity may be mingled in great measure, with emphasis on scholarly pursuits. If you approach a task with proper understanding, you can carry a great burden and win much acclaim, but do not become conceited over early success. Your one weakness is a tendency to overshoot your mark, and you can cover that by impressing people with your built-in sincerity.

15

Humility and condescension can be more than virtues; they can mean power when properly and intelligently applied. Like a majestic mountain, modesty is impressive because of its very stability. Through it, you can inspire others to aid you in your aims. Their help will be needed, so encourage it; but again, like a mountain, be firm when needed. They will then look up to you and admire you for your deeds.

16

To gain the success that you deserve, you must arouse enthusiasm in others, so that you can shape their actions to conform with yours when the time comes to use them to advantage. Hence any arrogance must be avoided in the early stages, as it may curtail such fervor. Similarly, indulgence or self-satisfaction on your part may cause others to lose their zest for your ideas, and you may fall victim to your own illusions.

17

Let someone choose the course and show the way. By drifting comfortably along the stream, you can avoid the rocks by watching the craft ahead. The fact that you have reached a harbor safely and unscarred will encourage others to accept your guidance when you embark anew and on your own.

18

Your obligation is to rectify some wrong, redeem what has been lost, or correct some misunderstanding. Much energy is better than too little, for it may enable you to accomplish even more than you set out to do. Think right, act right, and you can proceed with impunity, even risking a rift with friends who disagree.

19

From strong beginnings, you must adapt yourself to later conditions. First, gain authority through self-assertion, then advance with caution, ease, wisdom, even outright generosity, as each new facet of your career offers its own beckoning brilliance.

20

As the wind, you can sweep across the earth and penetrate to every cranny. This covers all stages from the gawking of the callow youth, the prying eye of the inquisitive neighbor, consideration of one's own status, analysis of affairs of state, and finally the art of heavenly contemplation, which is mastery of life itself. Where to begin is the question, but progress is essential, otherwise the wind will do more harm than good; or, worse, blow itself out.

21

A little man thinks little of his accomplishments, because they are disregarded. Conversely, he disregards his small failings; but later, he is surprised when other people magnify them. So, by being careless or indifferent, he lets a case be built against him, to his undoing. To avoid this, you should stress your virtues, seek acclaim, gain it, and proclaim it. Later, it may swing the balance in your favor, if petty quibblers try to discomfort you with trifles.

22

Outward show may bring immediate success, if kept within its proper orbit. Appearances are good as long as they bring results; after that, be willing to give up luxury and self-indulgence, in order to live a simple life. Fire and light reflect a tinsel glitter, which should be abandoned to seek the solitude of the mountain heights. There, you can revel in the greatest and most illuminating of all spotlights—the sun itself.

23

Odds may be against you now. The better off you are, the more severe your fall. But weakness or decay may be rendering such changes inevitable; if so, the sooner they occur, the sooner your opportunity to build on new foundations. Meanwhile, guard against borers from within and strengthen your position until the time when you can safely and openly oppose such forces.

24

As the seasons return in endless procession, so will your prospects be reactivated at constant intervals. Renewal of energy is the keynote for the awakening to come, so if you seemingly reverse yourself, you cannot be blamed. Only poor timing is a fault: do not force a change when you are unready, nor excuse yourself from action when the time is right. Attune yourself to nature and your lot will improve.

25

Be not among the fools who rush in where angels fear to tread. Heaven itself will help you if you faithfully follow its dictates. Be simple, honest, unselfish in all you do and wait for progress and success to follow. No reason then for temporary setbacks to perturb you; they can be taken as tests of your innocence and integrity.

26

You have the power to rise skyward to great heights, but, greater still, you can use that power toward restraint. By curbing impatience while you wait, you can consolidate your efforts and gain greater strength for the take-off. Advance is your great aim, but until the time is right, it may bring misfortune. So wait for that right time.

27

Like the wide-open mouth that it depicts, this symbol stands for watchful waiting. Strong at the start, it is followed by a succession of weak steps, all discouraging decisive action, until the final line is strong again. The mouth also betokens acquisition of nourishment, whereby vigor is gained during the intervening stages, promising full strength when the time for action arrives.

28

As a beam of sturdy appearance may be overweighted until it sags and breaks, so can a man of courage and ambition take on too many burdens and collapse beneath them. To know your own strength, you must also recognize your own weakness.

29

Fear of the pitfall before you may encourage you to steps that may prove worse. Forward, backward, sideward may plunge you into abysmal depths. So do not move; do not act. Wait for some kindly light to reveal the path that you may safely follow.

30

Fire and light intermingled, though fitful and flickery at first, promise a double brightness of intellect and action, but this double power should be restrained as it nears its zenith, or, like a meteor, it may consume and extinguish its brilliance through its own ardor.

31

Envy not the mountain peak that juts sharply to the sky. Far better to be a rounded, hollow summit, containing a lake whose placid depths reflect the heavens above and provide water for the foliage of the mountainside below. In turn, the mountain gathers clouds whose rain replenishes the lake. Thus can a lofty and receptive mind give what it gains and thereby gain all that it gives—and more.

32

To occupy a place and make the most of it is often very wise. When perseverance brings results, it becomes preferable to hasty action. Do not worry over suppressed desires; being casual of manner may prove clever policy, until the time for self-assertion has arrived. Be yourself and heaven may fulfill your hopes.

33

When small snares increase to large, no one can blame the tiger who turns tail and flees. To delay reaching the habitat where he is king would be far worse. But you can attain the same result by watching for the trapper from the start and turning a quick-tailed retreat into a slow withdrawal, much to your delight and the discomfiture of those who expect you to fall victim to their wiles.

34

Thunder that rumbles mightily high in the sky is meaningless unless rain follows. Therefore, your strong words should produce the action that they promise. Otherwise, they will be branded as loud talk and empty boasts that will haunt your memory like the fading reverberations from futile storm clouds.

35

As the sun rises high in the clear sky, so may your fortunes be on the rise, brightening your outlook like the glow of the sun itself. So continue with confidence, regardless of opposition, remembering only that, as you advance in the full glare of the sunlight, so must your deeds be open, that all persons may view them. Think right; be right; do right.

36

When darkness and gloom are settling over all, you must be cautious in dealing with whatever they produce. Daylight will dawn later, so to waste time now would be foolish. You may do well to feign obedience, even ignorance, to hide your misery from those who deal in ways of darkness.

37

Now is a time to consider duties close at hand. If you are happy in your present surroundings, make them happier, rather than stray afield in response to fleeting whim. If you are unhappy, find the cause and rectify it. The accent is on family life, where understanding is attained by tempering severity with indulgence.

38

Since disputes over trifles may lead to opposition in greater matters, it follows that to give and take in small things can pave the way to larger understanding. Even when you are right, stubborn insistence upon that point can make you wrong, if it irks others to such a degree that they resolve to thwart your aim.

39

When faced by an obstacle, rather than bemoan your luck, find a way to remove it or go around it; or in an emergency act boldly, for even a path that narrows may lead somewhere. Seek aid from others when you can and give them help if called upon, for the obstacle that confronts them now may be one that could obstruct you later.

40

The very thunderstorm that forces you to shelter may clear the air, allowing you to advance with vigor and confidence, now that the threat of the storm has passed. But to turn such opportunity to rapid action, you must free yourself from past encumbrances or fellow travelers who may retard you from making up for lost time on your appointed course.

41

When you acquire wealth or possessions through the efforts of others, it is unwise to nurse the surplus in jealous or miserly fashion. It is better to distribute it freely, but sincerely and intelligently among those who deserve it, thereby encouraging them to perform further services in your behalf.

42

When heaven smiles on earth below, it is wise to make the most of every opportunity, for in times of progress, even incompetent people find their services needed. But to expect such prosperity to endure continually, or to regard mere luck as personal accomplishment, can prove to be the height of folly.

43

When the heavens release cloudbursts, or floodgates break wide open, the deluge may sweep away the mightiest of men and their possessions. To be watchful for such danger is wise indeed; to apply the rule to human affairs is even wiser. The flood can represent small minds, uncontrolled, carrying away established principles. Stay firm, lest torrents of evil swallow what is good.

44

When darkness encroaches upon light, it is easy for the strong mind to be influenced by the weak. That should be checked, not by violent action, but by calm persuasion. As the wind sets things in motion, so can you influence people from afar and dispel darkness as the wind scatters obscuring clouds.

45

To fight your way against opposing forces is difficult indeed; hence those who are reckless and insincere are the first to take that course, sometimes with quick returns. But for real results, it is better to join with the crowd and ride the incoming wave. If the crowd is unwilling to accept you, attach yourself to someone identified with it and be carried along on the crest of the tide.

46

As a seed buried deep in the soil thrusts upward, so must your will to do be strong and constant. Grow without haste, but likewise without rest. Let the sun within you seek the sunlight above, for to push up blindly will merely exhaust your efforts. The longer the climb, the greater your strength will become. So do not falter or desist.

47

When things go bad, your urge may be to flee afar and seek new fields. Instead, you should look into yourself. Adversity itself can be right for the right person; one who can conquer troubles inwardly and profit by the test. Don't beat your head against a wall and blame the wall. Rather, have confidence in yourself, knowing that as your strength returns you can break the bonds that now restrain you.

48

Up-down, up-down, up-down—a tedious, monotonous action, but one that is worth while, when you are drawing water from a well. But first make sure the well is neither muddy nor leaky; and when you find one that is fresh and spring-fed, do not demand it for yourself, for water is heaven's gift to all. Yet be watchful while you toil, lest someone break the jug that you hope to fill!

49

As the spots of the growing leopard sharpen and the stripes of the growing tiger broaden, so can you undergo a change within that will brighten your outer self. Await development and, while you do, be neither hasty nor ruthless, but once the time is ripe, do not hesitate.

50

While building fire beneath a bronze caldron, do not worry if it overturns, for only an unwanted residue will pour out. But once fresh food is placed therein, and the fire is kindled, take care that the handles are away from the flame, or you cannot lift the caldron from its tripod. Watch also that the tripod does not weaken, or your meal may spill and spoil.

51

When great thunderclouds meet and clash like two mighty dragons fighting in the sky, men tremble with fear at each succeeding shock. Thus presence of mind is lost when it is most needed. It is better to be stout of heart, letting heaven and fate decide the issue while you plan the course to take when the storm abates.

52

If mountain summits loom invitingly across your path, remember that an attempt to scale them will retard your present progress. Any extra effort you apply may demand a pause in which you must remain as immobile as the mountainside itself. Eagerness can exhaust the energy that you may gain by resting until you are ready for another upward thrust.

53

A tall tree grows faster than a sprouting shrub, yet being so much larger, its change is imperceptible. Similarly, a wild goose, approaching shore, circles gradually inward until its goal is at hand. So let your ability follow its natural trend. Through it you will develop the stature needed to attain the objectives you desire.

54

If you cannot get what you want, it may be wise to want what you can get. Those who demand too much are often saddled with responsibilities that they did not expect, while those content with less may be appreciated for their worth. Yet do not be too quick to throw away good prospects. Those who can be content with less should also be content to wait for more.

55

When inwardly happy, you should brighten the lives of others, like the sun beaming down upon earth at high noon. Should the outlook blacken, do not be perturbed, not even if trifling stars should appear in the sky. It will only mean that your sunlight has been briefly eclipsed by the passage of the fickle moon, which will go as rapidly as it came, making your brightness all the more vivid.

56

Be like the traveler who moves swiftly onward, as fire sweeps across the dried grass. If he should tarry, he would no longer be a traveler. Always, he must be prosperous in appearance, or he will not be welcomed; always, too, he will meet others who want to go along with him, but he should choose them carefully, to make sure they are worthy.

57

Gentle winds, moving softly and unimpeded, can accomplish much that could not be gained in any other way. As the grass bends when the wind breathes upon it, so will you find that many people will accept your ideas. Follow that rule and blow stronger and steadier as conditions demand, but never blow too hard, or you may blow yourself out —and out, and out—

58

Look to the moon high in the sky, then to the lagoon in the earth below. There, you will see the reflection of one within the other. Reflect upon your own affairs in that same placid way. Heavenly happiness may be found on earth. Earthly pleasures may bring heavenly bliss.

59

When wind sweeps water, waves result, only to dissipate in foam. When winds become colder, water freezes into ice, to await the warmer winds of springtime, which restore it to its original state. This carries a double admonition: Do not let your opinions and ideas dissolve like so much froth, nor should you allow them to harden and turn cold.

60

Recognition and acceptance of established limitations can bring good fortune, much as money saved in times of plenty may prove indispensable in times of need. When doors or gates are barred against you, an attempt to crash them may be a waste of strength, but once they are opened, you should be prompt to use them, if only to prove your right to do so. By following rules, you can make rules work for you.

61

When sportive dolphins and playful porpoises leap up from the placid sea, mariners regard it as a sign of an approaching storm. Thus does water relate to wind. Conversely, the mother crane, snug in a hidden nest, sends a call that is carried by the breeze to her fledglings wading in the shallows of the lake, to bring them to safety. Thus does wind relate to water. So you should watch and listen for such warnings, that you may duly heed them.

62

A young bird finds safety fluttering to perches in the brush, rather than by flying vainly toward an imaginary refuge in the thunderclouds that gather on the mountainside. The hunter who blindly follows that evasive trail may lose his way and become mired when the storm bursts and the rains descend. Whichever you are, the hunted or the hunter, do not press onward too eagerly or too far.

63

Fire blazing below a kettle heats the water therein, but beyond that, the water, boiling over, may extinguish the flame and rapidly cool itself, turning gain to loss. Thus the man who has crossed a raging torrent may turn back to view his triumph and plunge headlong into the current that he just eluded. Accordingly, once you have built a difficult past into a solid present, your aim should be to consolidate your gains and ensure a happy future.

64

The crafty old fox moves cunningly across the ice-clad stream, listening for any crackles that may betray a weakness. The young fox, eager to reach the bank beyond, is suddenly immersed and is lucky to emerge, dripping to the end of his drooping tail. Remember this when tempted to advance too rapidly, but otherwise, do not try to move too soon. Do what the moment calls for, but do it wisely—and do it well!

VIII. The Tarot Pack

The tarot pack consists of seventy-eight cards, which fall into two distinctive groups called the Major Arcana and the Minor Arcana. Of these, the Major Arcana, consisting of twenty-two strikingly individualistic cards, is seemingly the more important; while the Minor Arcana, composed of fifty-six cards, divided into four groups of fourteen each, are of lesser significance. However:

The art of divination, as interpreted through the tarots, originally emphasized the Major Arcana, because of the obvious importance of the cards involved, giving lesser importance to the Minor Arcana. All that was understandable, until the Minor Arcana became so notable that it was turned into a royal diversion that eventually became a popular pastime, from which developed our modern playing cards.

From those, in turn, came modern cartomancy, a form of divination in its own right. But there are persons, steeped in lore and transition, who still prefer to read directly from the tarots particularly because of the additional interpretations obtainable from the cards composing the Major Arcana, though some of these have found their way into various forms of modern cartomancy, as applied to the standard playing cards of today.

Comparing the ancient with the modern, the Major Arcana has been linked to the mystic Cabala, as represented by the twenty-two letters of the Hebrew alphabet; while the Minor Arcana, consisting of Cups, Scepters, Swords, and Pentacles, can be classed as the direct forerunner of the modern cards with their corresponding suits of hearts, clubs, spades, and diamonds, respectively. Each is numbered from one to ten, with four court cards, running in ascending order: knave, knight, queen, king. Modern packs have reduced those to three by eliminating the knight, or combining it with the knave, under the now more common name of jack.

The traditional tarot cards, and most of their later adaptations, have "one way" designs, making it easy to distinguish the top of each card from the bottom. This is particularly true with the tarots forming the Major Arcana, with one exception, Number 12, the Hanged Man, who is hanging upside down, thereby giving the impression that the card itself is inverted, though a close scrutiny will prove otherwise.

Thus, in reading the tarots, their meaning should be modified and in some cases given a contrary interpretation whenever a card is inverted, or, in tarot terminology, "reversed." Usually, although not always, a reversed card signifies something for the worse rather than the better.

The first step, therefore, is to consider:

THE TAROTS AND THEIR SIGNIFICATION
The Major Arcana

1. *The Conjuror* (or *Juggler*) represents the Questioner, if a man. Also: Confidence, dexterity, capability.

If reversed: Deceit, chicanery, weakness.

2. *The High Priestess* represents the Questioner, if a woman. Also: Love, mystery, romance.

If reversed: Passion, remorse, ruin.

3. *The Empress* symbolizes initiative, progress, and fertility, sometimes in overabundance.

If reversed: Passion, infatuation, superficiality.

4. *The Emperor* betokens ambition, authority, achievement, and determination, often intermingled.

If reversed: Sincerity, sympathy, recognition, but marked by indecision and instability.

5. *The Hierophant* is a sign of faith, inspiration, and co-operative effort. Someone who may aid the Questioner.

If reversed: Harmony and understanding, but ineffectual.

6. *The Lovers:* This is a token of happiness, mutual attraction and affection, with promise of a lasting marriage.

If reversed: Quarrels, disappointment, separation.

7. *The Chariot* is a highly mystical sign, promising excitement with triumph, but with strife and vengeance apt to figure strongly.

If reversed: Obstacles, disputes, failure.

8. *Justice* symbolizes truth, honesty, and integrity as guiding forces in all personal affairs or aims.

If reversed: Litigation, unpleasant duties, law, and order.

9. *The Hermit* is an enigma in itself. Its depiction of a man with a lantern suggests a watchman making his rounds, thereby symbolizing caution and foresight, yet at the same time hidden danger, or evils that the Hermit should shun. So it may apply either way.

If reversed: The meaning is identical, but with emphasis on fear rather than hope.

10. *Fortune* is perhaps the oldest of all known symbols, the sign of chance, luck, and therefore destiny. The wheel alternates good and bad, gain or loss, as "around, around, around it goes—and where it stops, nobody knows."

If reversed: It means about the same. A wheel, of all things, can never be upside down, though the card, when reversed, may mean a born loser.

11. *Strength* means exactly that: Vim, vigor, and vitality, bringing the success and rewards they deserve, if exerted fairly.

If reversed: Oppression, tyranny, dictatorship.

12. *The Hanged Man,* curiously, is not the bad token that it would seem to be. It symbolizes endurance, suffering, and therefore an intelligence far higher than those that gawk up from below.

If reversed: A show-off. Pretended sacrifice for personal gain.

13. *Death,* though grimly significant, is not as unlucky as the Number 13 indicates. It may simply mark an end to present hopes or purposes, which in turn may lead to newer, brighter prospects.

If reversed: Loss of the old may be regretted; future aims may not materialize.

14. *Temperance* is a warning to economize, to make the most of what you have rather than count on more. Conservative and practical.

If reversed: Self-interest, self-indulgence may work against you.

15. *The Devil* betokens a great but uncontrollable force; hence fate, violence, retribution, superstition, illness all figure here.

If reversed: Much the same, but on a lesser scale, involving rage, animosity, hate, suspicion, and financial problems.

16. *The Tower,* being struck by lightning, symbolizes disaster, downfall, and destruction, either physically or in personal affairs.

If reversed: The same, but in lesser or limited degree.

17. *The Stars:* Variable, basically denoting hope and destiny, but therefore indicating some preliminary loss or struggle, with future prospects depending on new friends or associations.

If reversed: Hope frustrated through lack of foresight.

18. *The Moon* is a warning against gambling, speculation, self-indulgence, and hidden dangers in personal relations. A bad sign that can be counteracted by a calm, complacent outlook.

If reversed: Fear, incompetence, trifling worries.

19. *The Sun,* the brightest symbol in the Major Arcana, represents health, wealth, and happiness. A sign of material success.

If reversed: The same, but despite obstacles or losses.

20. *Judgment* denotes completion and should bring satisfaction and recognition where personal policy or projects are concerned.

If reversed: Disappointment and loss of status.

21. *The World* symbolizes success and therefore involves such factors as travel, opportunity, knowledge, and happiness.

If reversed: Immobility, inaction, fixed ideas.

22 (or 0). *The Fool* denotes a happy-go-lucky, individualistic nature; adventurous, artistic, but with wasteful, reckless trends.

If reversed: Carelessness, indifference, indecision.

The Minor Arcana

CUPS: Pertaining to Love, Friendship, Emotion.

King: A man of importance or authority. Generally a friendly adviser, but this may be a pose covering deceit, especially *if reversed.*

Queen: A romantic and practical woman, but *if reversed,* self-centered.

Knight: A friend or lover. Also, attractive offers or social contacts. *If reversed,* chicanery or deception.

Knave: A helpful, faithful youth who may bring good news, but wayward and irresponsible *if reversed,* betokening bad news.

One (or *Ace*): Joy from love and family, but marred by spite and discord *if reversed.*

Two: Affection and friendship despite petty squabbles; *if reversed,* more serious misunderstandings and possible breakup.

Three: An objective fully realized; *if reversed,* delays and excess.

Four: Outside obstacles to love and friendship, producing anguish or resentment. *If reversed,* new contacts may change the outlook.

Five: Deep love or friendship tinged with sadness. *If reversed,* a parting.

Six: Happiness dependent on old memories. *If reversed,* a renewal of past associations.

Seven: Fulfillment of love and desire. *If reversed,* somewhat visionary.

Eight: Disillusionment in love or friendship may force solace through solitude or resignation. *If reversed,* a cause for celebration.

Nine: Security through love or friendship. *If reversed,* the same, but endangered by false sentiment and exacting demands.

Ten: Complete composure. *If reversed,* problems through mismanagement.

SCEPTERS:

Pertaining to Enterprise, Purpose, and Glory.

King: A friendly, worthy man. Usually married, with a family. Ready to aid a good purpose. *If reversed,* critical and exacting.

Queen: A kindly, helpful, matronly woman; a good adviser. *If reversed,* overcautious with money and often mistrustful.

Knight: A well-disposed young man, but too much on the go to be relied upon regularly. *If reversed,* may interfere with plans.

Knave: Symbolizes either a helpful youth or a message from a friend or relative. *If reversed,* expect false rumors and indecision.

One (or *Ace*): New or current projects offer great future promise; but *if reversed,* overeagerness for gain may bring unhappiness or ruin.

Two: Well-laid plans faced by choice between happiness or success, with no compromise. *If reversed,* the choice is apt to be wrong.

Three: A very fine token. Whatever is planned will succeed to the degree that it is pushed. *If reversed,* a quick end to any troubles.

Four: Obstacles to be overcome. Prepare for every problem or emergency and meet it. *If reversed,* exactly the same.

Five: Rebellious youth, beating itself down. Friction, trouble in any project. *If reversed,* litigation, perhaps the best solution.

Six: Failure amid success; *if reversed,* disappointment will be less.

Seven: Success is assured, but only through sustained effort. So do not relax. *If reversed,* don't hesitate; that would mean sure loss.

Eight: Action, travel, changes, mergers—a card with a modern touch, generally favorable. *If reversed,* disputes may force such changes.

Nine: Issues and problems will be counteracted if met squarely. Success assured against all antagonists. *If reversed,* the same, but delayed.

Ten: Too many burdens or worries. Shed some. *If reversed,* false friends.

SWORDS:

Pertaining to Enmity, Conflict, Rivalry, Change.

King: A powerful personage, dangerous as an enemy; therefore to be avoided or mistrusted. *If reversed,* the same, with a cruel, evil streak.

Queen: A sad, morose woman; one who may be harsh, yet wise and sometimes helpful; but *if reversed,* given to gossip, spite, or revenge.

Knight: A younger man of military type. Bold, capable, but conceited. Very dangerous as an enemy. *If reversed,* impulsive; often in trouble.

Knave: A youthful type; not dangerous, but apt to be as obnoxious as precocious; a natural spy. *If reversed,* trouble from that source.

One (or *Ace*): Strife and enmity loom as immediate threats. Curb them now and success will follow. *If reversed,* avoid all anger and violence.

Two: Antagonists or problems nullified by pitting one against another. *If reversed,* conniving enemies defeated by gaining new, strong friends.

Three: Issues that must be met with added courage and firmness after each setback. *If reversed,* defeat likely if odds prove overwhelming.

Four: Hatred rampant. Knowing that, ignore it; remain calm, while it burns itself out; then move. *If reversed,* all to the better.

Five: Very deceptive. Great triumph marred by trifling enmity. Pride before a fall. *If reversed,* worse; severe loss, even death.

Six: New opportunity; a trip abroad. *If reversed,* an alluring proposal.

Seven: Hopes realized despite opposition and disputes. Losses may be offset. *If reversed,* pettiness, quibbling over past mistakes.

Eight: A period of restraint, but with eventual freedom. Illness or criticism. *If reversed,* accidents, toil, worries.

Nine: Severe, disheartening loss; unexpected sorrow and disappointment in someone. *If reversed,* desperation, dishonor, deep dread.

Ten: Prolonged suffering and uncertainty. *If reversed,* temporary relief.

PENTACLES:

Pertaining to Wealth, Welfare, Interests.

King: An important personage, symbolizing wisdom, financial gain, but apt to show indifference. *If reversed,* grasping, miserly, corrupt.

Queen: A high-minded, generous woman; a patron of arts and worthy causes; very intuitive. *If reversed,* distrustful and unscrupulous.

Knight: Someone both responsive and responsible; helpful in fields of science and culture. *If reversed,* limited outlook and indolence.

Knave: A serious, scholarly, youthful person or a group; highly appreciative. *If reversed,* defiant, unconventional, irrational. Bad news.

One (or *Ace*): The foundation of fortune. Every desire is attainable if properly nurtured. *If reversed,* the same, but with added urge.

Two: Division of interest between wealth and welfare. Count on letters or messages from friends for guidance. *If reversed,* difficulties through uncertainty may lead to extreme measures.

Three: Small artistic efforts promise great reward and should be followed through. *If reversed*, demand for money may ruin creative talent.

Four: Sit tight and wealth will come your way. *If reversed*, some delay.

Five: Material problems will produce other problems. Unity, togetherness can solve them. *If reversed*, trifles can spoil such prospects.

Six: Prosperity is present. Make the most of it. Be nice to people and they will be nice to you. *If reversed*, smallness will spoil it.

Seven: By faithfully following your own inclinations, you can ensure success. *If reversed*, worry over money can spoil such chances.

Eight: Success in certain efforts will offset disappointment in other fields. *If reversed*, frustrated ambition may lead to dishonesty.

Nine: Great wealth and attainment. *If reversed*, disastrous losses.

Ten: Accumulation and culmination combined. A happy outcome from all endeavors. *If reversed*, some loss or doubt may injure such bliss.

DIVINATION THROUGH THE TAROTS

Among various methods of divination with the tarot pack, the following procedure is specially intriguing, due to its comprehensive coverage:

Separate the cards composing the Minor Arcana from those of the Major Arcana and shuffle each group thoroughly, face down. Deal the top twelve cards of the *Minor Arcana* face up in a large circle, like the dial of a clock; but begin at nine-o'clock position, regarding that as Number 1, and deal the cards counterclockwise; that is, downward to the right. Do not point the cards outward; keep them all perpendicular, so that each card can be classed as *upright* or *reversed*.

The cards forming the circle represent four stages of the Questioner's career, each merging into the next, thus:

The Past, represented by positions 1, 2, 3, 4.

The Present, indicated by positions 4, 5, 6, 7.

The developing future, signified by 7, 8, 9, 10.

The ultimate or distant future, shown by 10, 11, 12.

These are read in sequence, like a running narrative from 1 to 12, according to the cards that appear at the various positions, thus forming a continuous chain from past through present and future to ultimate.

From the *Major Arcana* packet deal four cards within the circle, as the points of a compass, starting with west, and rotating north, east, south. These points represent governing factors in the Questioner's career or situation, namely:

A: *Origin*, or chief preliminary factor. (West)

B: *Ascendant*, bearing upon an anticipated climax. (North)

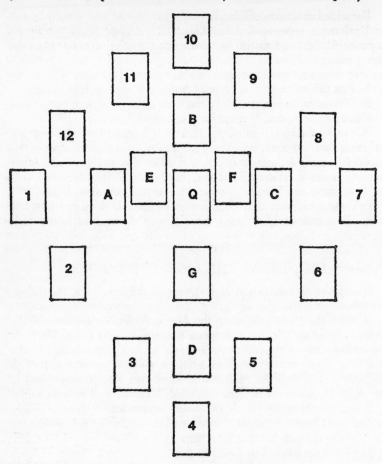

9) Card pattern to follow in dealing out the tarot pack.

C: *Descendant,* or reaction to such a climax. (East)

D: *Decline,* a resultant factor. (South)

These are interpreted in terms of the outer sequence, although their periods do not necessarily correspond. Theoretically, the zenith, or climax of a Questioner's fortune, should be reached midway between B and C, but it may occur much sooner or much later. It may even be divided, like twin peaks, or there may be no actual climax to the Questioner's plans or career. Those possibilities should be considered and treated accordingly.

For added consultation: *The Triangle.*

Deal three more cards from the *Major Arcana* pack, within the square (ABCD) to form an inverted triangle (EFG) that shows underlying influences that have a direct bearing on the Questioner's actions or reactions to the projected sequence of events. These are:

E. *Past Influence,* point at upper left.

F: *Present Influence,* point at upper right.

G: *Future Influence,* lower point of triangle.

All these tarots of the Major Arcana are interpreted according to whether they are *upright* or *reversed,* but as a final touch, one card is always set upright in the very center of the circle, at position Q, which represents the Questioner. For a male Questioner, *The Conjuror* (Tarot 1) is used for that purpose; for a female Questioner, *The High Priestess* (Tarot 2) is placed there. If the Questioner's own card should happen to appear in either the Diamond (ABCD) or the Triangle (EFG), it should be moved to Q and replaced by another card from the Major Arcana packet. The Questioner's card does not actually figure in the reading but serves as a focal point throughout the interpretation.

SAMPLE TAROT READING

The High Priestess, in the center of the circle, represents a matured woman with artistic ability and business acumen, with preference for an independent career.

Minor Arcana: (1) The *Nine of Cups* showed an early life secure in love and friendship, therefore free from worry, but (2) the *Five of Scepters* is the mark of a rebellious urge with choice of similar companions, which helped her gain (3) the *Ten of Cups,* a complete composure through her own self-sufficiency and assertiveness, until:

(4) The *Ten of Swords, reversed,* marked her advent into the present, with a growing uncertainty that was temporarily relieved by (5) the *Eight of Pentacles,* reversed, blaming frustrated ambitions or actions that she once might have classed as shady but that now seem justified, particularly because of (6) the *Seven of Scepters,* her sustained effort to further her more selfish and perhaps ruthless aims. Now, on the verge of the future:

(7) The *Seven of Pentacles, reversed,* shows a continuation of her confidence that her own inclinations will succeed, but money problems, emphasized by the card's reversal, threaten an actual reversal of her aims, indicating (8) *Two of Swords, reversed,* a real need for new friends or purposes to counteract persons whom she antagonized by her highhanded tactics. Indications on that score are strongly favorable, because (9) the *Seven of Swords* promises a realization of hopes, despite opposition and disputes, the very factors she must conquer.

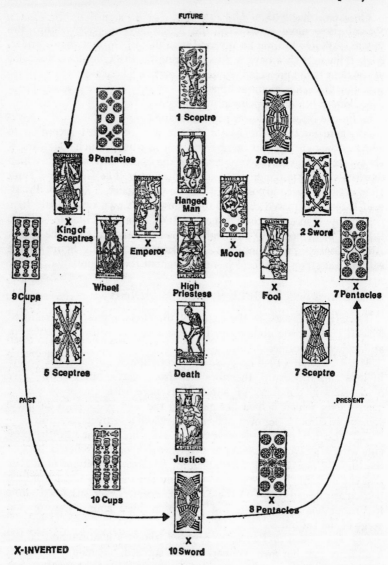

10) Tarot pack: sample interpretation.

Once past that crisis, she should find that through (10) the *One of Scepters,* her new projects will not only prove promising, but (11) *Nine of Pentacles* should lead to great wealth, high attainment, or both. This will be due in some measure to (12) the *King of Scepters, reversed,* a friendly, well-established man, who will be critical and exacting but whose advice or aid will be all the more acceptable because of that. So the ultimate future should be happy.

Major Arcana: The governing factors in the four periods represented by the Minor Arcana are as follows:

A: *Fortune* (Tarot 10), very definitely confirms that chance was responsible for the Questioner's present situation. While the "wheel" of all the tarots is much the same either way, its position in this case is significant, as it correctly intimates that the Questioner, who always had things her own way, never realized how lucky she was.

B: *The Hanged Man* (Tarot 12) shows that in the immediate present, intelligence and endurance are involved, but with greater suffering than other people know. Unless it is all in the Questioner's mind, which it could be in this case.

C: *The Fool* (Tarot 22 or 0), *reversed,* marks the same individualistic trend carried into the future, but with a careless, indifferent attitude that is responsible for indecisive action, which must be curbed. This is the critical period.

D: *Justice* (Tarot 8), as the ultimate sign, shows a rebound to truth and integrity that fits the situation to perfection. The only regret is that it might have expedited matters if it had appeared earlier, but perhaps that would have been too soon.

The Triangle: These three points, representing past, present, future, carry an added emphasis where the Questioner is concerned. Being closest to the Questioner's own tarot (in the center of the circle), they can be construed as an inner motivation, which the Questioner may not even recognize, but should; namely:

E: *Past: The Emperor* (Tarot 4), *reversed:* Early ambitions gained sympathy and even recognition that they did not deserve; hence they deteriorated to indecision and instability.

F: *Present: The Moon* (Tarot 18), *reversed:* Self-indulgence, no matter how natural or justified, produces fear, incompetence—real or imaginary—and worry. These are self-defeating as of now.

G. *Future: Death* (Tarot 13): The end of present purposes, which can open the way to a newer and happier future. In this particular reading, where a change is already signified, this stands as an excellent token, despite its ominous aspect.

Note: The example just given is a "general reading" covering an extensive period of the Questioner's career. Such readings may be repeated after a reasonable interval, as any marked variance can usually be attributed to a change of circumstances or to the fact that certain factors have come more to the fore.

Specific readings relating to love, money, or some immediate problem or event can be made in the same manner, but all interpretations should be considered in direct terms of the matter concerned.

IX. Divination with Playing Cards

USING THE THIRTY-TWO-CARD PACK

After playing cards became popular, it was only logical that they should supplant the tarots as a device for divination. Being based on the Minor Arcana, it was possible to employ them in short readings at the very start. But before the practice became general, card players had taken up games involving a thirty-two-card pack, with each of the four suits running in descending order, A, K, Q, J, 10, 9, 8, 7, and stopping there.

This was particularly true among the nobility and gamesters, the very classes who worried most about what fortune had in store. So "short readings" became still shorter, until the significations were expanded, with added stress on special groups or layouts. Many such methods are still current and form the basis for this chapter. However:

Since early playing cards had "one way" designs that could be studied in upright position, like the tarots, special meanings are given to those that are "inverted" or "reversed" when using a thirty-two-card system. As modern packs are "double-ended," most of their cards look the same whether right side up or upside down, so it is customary to put a pencil mark on one end of each card to distinguish the top.

A better and more modern plan is to use thirty-two cards from a bridge pack that has an ornamental or pictorial design on the back, making it easy to tell top from bottom when they are dealt face down. In turning them face up, inverted cards can be set at an angle to show that they are reversed.

Significations of the thirty-two-card pack follow, as preliminary to the methods that are detailed later.

LIST OF COMBINATIONS AND THEIR MEANINGS WITH THE 32-CARD PACK

When the entire thirty-two-card pack, or most of it, is dealt face up, the most obvious thing to note is whether certain types of cards appear in clusters. When smaller groups are dealt, the same thing can occur, but in this case actual clusters are not necessary. The mere frequency or prevalence of certain types may be noticeable in itself. Either way, interpretations are in order, along the following lines:

Picture Cards: These include Aces, along with Kings, Queens, and Jacks. When clustered, but in no particular order, these denote a gay social life, with parties, pleasure trips, and special occasions setting the tempo. Even with conservative persons, cordiality will be highly apparent. This applies both to a full deal and to smaller groups, but in both cases clusters are what count. In a group of ten or twenty cards, the fact that picture cards are in the majority is not enough; they must be bunched, at least four—and preferably five—together. The same applies to lesser groups, though there, a cluster of four is strongly significant. Upright and inverted cards count the same in any cluster.

Spot Cards: Here, frequency is the important factor. When most of the pack is dealt at once, in a single group, "pictures" and "spots" naturally equalize, as there are four varieties of each—A, K, Q, J for pictures; 10, 9, 8, 7 for spots—so there is no majority. With lesser groups, a predominance of spots is an indication of general good fortune, dependent on the size of the majority, but it should be stronger than 60 per cent to be really significant. Beyond that, the greater the percentage of spots, the better. If there are more Clubs among such spots than any other suit, prosperity is just about assured.

Suits themselves follow significant patterns, each unto each, and these become increasingly apparent when cards of one suit appear in sequences or dominate any particular group. Their meanings run as follows:

Hearts stand for love, romance, and affection, or the opposites. There is an intensity here that may work for good or bad, but Hearts are essential to sympathy, hence are usually helpful when clustered or in the majority, provided they can be controlled. Harmonious relations with family and friends are involved here.

Clubs symbolize prestige, strength, and promise of riches, as well as what goes with them—comfort, pleasure, self-satisfaction, and the like. Home life, influential friends are indicated by this suit, so its frequency is much to be desired.

Diamonds are a business sign, denoting the ups and downs of life, with results dependent on attendant circumstances. Anything involving finance should be favorable when Diamonds are clustered or strongly prevalent. Otherwise, it is a tossup between profit and loss. That leaves it up to other suits to settle the uncertainty.

Spades bring misfortune, hence they depend upon other suits to break the chain. When in sequence, they are bad indeed; the longer the run, the worse the luck. But, as a dominating suit in a group, Spades are not too serious when scattered. Strong intervening cards can pull them up from despondency, but they still spell trouble.

Next in line are the denominations: Aces down to sevens, according to their frequency, with this proviso:

In a complete deal of thirty-two cards, they must appear in sequence, or nearly so, to be significant. Any wide separation destroys the setup. In shorter deals—twenty cards, ten cards, or less—the need for sequence is eliminated. Frequency itself is a sufficiency, as follows:

Four Aces: Sudden change, often for the worse. Following cards may soften the situation, and any that intervene are still better. Curiously, if all the Aces are upright, they are at their worst. The more that are inverted, the more easily it may be handled.

Four Kings: Good indeed. Good business, good friends, good luck. Everything should come your way and plentifully, if upright. The more Kings inverted, the sooner things will come your way, but not with such plenty.

Four Queens: Here is society at its highest. You may move in circles beyond all reasonable hope. But beware! If all are upright, fine; but each inverted Queen means disappointment afterward.

Four Jacks: Fun, conviviality, excitement—but too much of it. This can mean trouble if joy goes unrestrained. However, each inverted Jack helps to control the situation. One, fair; two, good; three, fine; four, a total washout. Why get together to begin with?

Three Aces: Changes, but not too consequential. Personal problems, but not serious, as they can be forgotten, unless the Aces are inverted. In that case, you will take the problems all the more seriously and probably too much so.

Three Kings: Direct, concerted action in some important project, but any inverted King means opposition that must be overcome. With all three inverted, chance of success is about nil.

Three Queens: Social affairs involving women, with friendly small-talk degenerating into gossip and disputes, in proportion to how many happen to be inverted.

Three Jacks: Petty annoyances of a social nature, often caused by treacherous friends. Here, any inverted cards are helpful, as they cross up the troublemakers.

Two Aces: A meeting of minds. Fine results if both are upright.

Doubtful if opposite. Disagreement if both are inverted. Diamonds and Spades denote conspiracy, so they are better off if they disagree.

Two Kings: Both upright, you can count on the co-operation of a friend. One inverted may mean the ending of a partnership. Both inverted, mutual interests concern trifling matters only.

Two Queens: A chance meeting or an exchange of ideas or sharing of a secret. Pointed opposite, there will be a clash or conflict of interests. Both inverted, any plans will go awry.

Two Jacks: Schemers at work, so beware. If both are upright, your loss will probably be slight or avoidable. With both inverted, it is due to hit right away. Pointed opposite, it may strike after all danger seems to be over.

With *spot cards*, combinations pertain more to things than to personalities. Typical indications include:

Four Tens: Attainment of desired aims, particularly anything now pending. Ability will figure strongly if the majority are upright, but with two, three, or four inverted, luck becomes increasingly necessary, as those are hurdles in your path.

Four Nines: These symbolize the unexpected, usually to your great advantage. If all are upright, the surprise will be immediate; for each inverted card, there will be delay, demanding patience. All inverted is best of all, as it signifies some special honor as the climax of the long wait.

Four Eights: This is the unsettled sign. Mix-ups, changes of plans or jobs, with travel also indicated. The more that are inverted, the greater the confusion.

Four Sevens: Spiteful persons will seek to harm you or belittle you. Inverted cards are helpful here; the greater their number, the more likelihood that such acts will backfire on the instigators.

Three Tens: Monetary problems, possibly involving legal matters or other complications. The more that are inverted, the less you will suffer from such causes, but watch out for other problems.

Three Nines: Prosperity and gladness, if upright, but each inverted card may mean a dispute or some monetary setback that will mar expected happiness and possibly ruin it if all three are inverted.

Three Eights: These indicate love, romance, and family relations, all serious if upright, with prospect of marriage. Inverted cards reduce this to frivolity and indifference.

Three Sevens: Sorrow, weariness, or other difficulties that must be met with fortitude. Inverted cards indicate that such tribulations will be of short duration or fewer in number.

Two Tens: A change of luck or circumstances, usually for the better. One inverted card will delay it briefly; two for a long time.

Two Nines: A substantial gain or improvement of position. One inverted may delay this; two may presage an offsetting loss.

Two Eights: Fleeting love, or brief happiness, which may bring greater expectations, unless one or both cards are inverted.

Two Sevens: Intensive love, but with ups and downs if one card is inverted. Misunderstandings and remorse with both inverted.

TABLE OF CARD SIGNIFICATIONS WITH THE THIRTY-TWO-CARD PACK

HEARTS

Ace
Upright: Favorable home life. Satisfaction with present surroundings. Expect glad tidings, perhaps a romantic sort.
Inverted: Unsettled conditions. Unexpected visitors. A possible change of residence or present connections.

King
Upright: A liberal, fair-minded friend or adviser. Often a professional man. Helpful and influential. Light complexioned.
Inverted: A changeable, hesitant person, unlikely to keep promises. Friendly but unreliable. Often bombastic.

Queen
Upright: A kindly, considerate woman. May be romantically inclined. Lively and sparkling. Dark hair, medium complexion.
Inverted: A person given to spiteful moods and deeds, especially when slighted romantically. Otherwise can be mollified.

Jack
Upright: A happy, carefree person. A convivial friend. In line for romantic involvement, particularly if young and unattached.
Inverted: Shows frustration or annoyance. May involve someone with a military connection. Antagonism should be softened.

Ten
Upright: Achievement of ambition. Joy and gaiety. Triumph over all obstacles. Strengthens good indications and neutralizes bad.
Inverted: Temporary disappointment or uncertainty. May demand a change of plans, possibly involving relatives. Success limited.

Nine
Upright: A fulfilled wish. Coming honors may bring affluence. Harmony gained through sincerity and effort. A big good luck card.

Inverted: Brief unhappiness. Weariness through overwork or burdens. Luck and confidence can overcome such problems.

Eight   *Upright:* Romance or affection, with realization of long-cherished hope. Friendship, invitations, end of problems.

Inverted: Indifference toward affection. Need for responsive friends. Great personal joy, with exciting fun unless marred by petty quarrels.

Seven   *Upright:* A sign of wisdom. Complacency and meditation coupled with imagination. Self-sufficiency with love of solitude.

Inverted: Strong urge for recognition. Without it, may become bored and dejected. Affectionate but flirtatious and jealous.

CLUBS

Ace   *Upright:* Wealth, health, and happiness. Checks, letters, legal documents link with fortune and success. A harmonious marriage.

Inverted: Success delayed or only temporary. A letter may bring disappointment. Unexpected love or happiness may make amends.

King   *Upright:* A reliable, generous friend. Ideal companion or business associate. A faithful husband. Dark in appearance.

Inverted: Worry and disappointment through failure or lack of good intentions. A friendly front may mask a mean disposition.

Queen   *Upright:* A highly romantic woman, apt to be talkative and excitable. Cordial, sympathetic and likes display. Dark appearance.

Inverted: Person depending on intuition more than intellect. Crafty, vengeful, and dangerous if crossed or slighted, especially in love.

Jack   *Upright:* A skillful, youthful, enterprising person. A good friend and a sincere lover. Very dependable. Slightly dark.

Inverted: A specialist in flattery. Insincere and deceitful, but usually harmless unless roused to anger or desperation.

Ten   *Upright:* A money card. From steady gain to a great financial future. Luck and adventure may figure. But be ready for some grief.

Inverted: Quarrels may hinder quest for wealth. A long trip, probably by air. Minor losses should be offset by luck.

Nine   Upright: The symbol of immediate results. A gift, a legacy, an offer—any may come unexpectedly. Watch for sudden opportunity.

Inverted: A trifling present, smaller than expected. An urge here to gamble on future prospects. Danger of losing all.

Eight   Upright: Affluence and affection. Double or nothing, as one will encourage the other. Choice of proper partner or mate is vital.

Inverted: Misplaced affection will bring unhappiness and financial embarrassment. Here, a mistaken choice should be avoided.

Seven   Upright: Small but important. A debt repaid or collected produces good will and friendship. Children may be involved.

Inverted: The same but literally reversed. Small financial problems can disrupt harmonious relations. A warning to be heeded.

DIAMONDS

Ace   Upright: Of highest importance. It signifies a message: a letter, gift or promise that is generally good but must be treated personally, as to whether you should give or receive.

Inverted: Almost the same, but with this slight difference: the message is more apt to be bad, placing the burden more on you.

King   Upright: Man of long experience with military or official background. Powerful and can be helpful, but apt to prove self-centered and dangerous.

Inverted: The same, but here the person may betray himself in trifling treachery, which will warn against greater threats.

Queen   Upright: A woman who spreads rumors and scandal, often to mask her ignorance and appear important. Light-complexioned.

Inverted: Similar, but more frustrated, ready to involve innocent persons in serious affairs. Also a flirtatious type.

Jack   Upright: Someone in official position. Reliable if important; in lower brackets, deceitful, seeking favors or bribes.

Inverted: A true troublemaker, exaggerating his own importance or falsely claiming authority. Denotes a swindler.

Ten   Upright: High attainment if linked with favorable signs. A big job, a big town, big success will beckon anyone who thinks big.

Inverted: Similar opportunities but more care needed in early steps. Changes may bring problems, so weigh them carefully.

Nine   *Upright:* Denotes enterprise. Putting own interests first may mean loss of friends and other sacrifices while ensuring gain.

Inverted: Failure through family and business wrangling. Lack of initiative will raise obstacles. Try to curb obstinacy.

Eight   *Upright:* Pleasant journeys or vacations in happy surroundings. Love and romance with great promise. Sometimes a late marriage.

Inverted: Overeagerness for new places and new faces. Hasty romance may bring sorrow or vexation. Look before you leap.

Seven   *Upright:* A social card, denoting idle talk, a coming party, surprising news. Things that are pleasant but unimportant.

Inverted: Trifling problems or criticism that can rise to undue proportions. Welfare of children or pets may be involved.

SPADES

Ace   *Upright:* Pleasure and high purposes, but with caution needed in legal matters. Adjacent picture cards may signify ardent love.

Inverted: Bad news, which may pertain to injury or death. Also a warning against bad luck, unwise ventures, or false friends.

King   *Upright:* Man of position and prestige, but doubtful as a friend and deadly if an enemy. Romantically trustworthy, however, sometimes denoting a reliable widower.

Inverted: Beware of a greedy, unscrupulous person whose urge to do harm is curtailed only by lack of ability.

Queen   *Upright:* A generous, friendly woman, often easily flattered, but, once misled, may become mistrustful. Maybe a dark widow.

Inverted: A highly romantic and purposeful person, ready to spite anyone to gain her way. Too crafty for her own good.

Jack   *Upright:* A rough, ill-mannered person, though often intelligent and studious. Can be a helpful friend if not too critical.

Inverted: An eager beaver, friendly on the surface, secretly a petty spy. Not to be trusted with anything of importance.

Ten   *Upright:* Unhappiness, waste of time, and perhaps outright misery. Usually the result of jealousy or emotional distress.

Inverted: Severe shock or illness. Loss of a friend or personal property. Accompanying cards may be keys to trouble.

Nine   *Upright:* Conflict, defeat, sickness, mourning—all are betokened by this unfortunate card. Look for others to soften it.

         Inverted: One misfortune followed by another. Main hope is that both will be minor, therefore less serious than one hard blow.

Eight   *Upright:* Threat of approaching illness or anxiety. Possibly prevented by due precautions. Avoid anything involving risk.

         Inverted: Disappointment in love. Waste and extravagance may follow. Artistic or spiritual ambitions may offset troubles.

Seven   *Upright:* A worry card. One sorrow may cause dread of another. Imaginary problems can be solved by building future hopes.

         Inverted: A token of indecision, in both love and business. Advice from friends and avoidance of rash or foolish actions will bring stability.

Note: In most fortunes, one of the cards listed serves as the "significator," representing the subject whose fortune is being read. Such cards will be specified in the description of the system and can be treated accordingly.

With the "Square of Thirty-six" (see page 235) four extra cards are used; namely, the deuces, 2 H, 2 D, 2 C, 2 S. While any of these may represent the subject, the 2 H usually serves that function, while the others run as follows:

2 D   A person very close to the subject, often a lover.

2 C   A friend or associate of the subject.

2 S   A stranger or someone concerned in the subject's affairs.

PAST–PRESENT–FUTURE

This is a direct, effective card-reading system, one of the best for a beginner. The pack of thirty-two cards is thoroughly shuffled, care being taken to turn the two sections inward, so as to ensure reversals. The shuffle completed, the top and bottom cards are taken from the face-down pack and placed aside—still face down—to serve as a "surprise."

The thirty remaining cards are then cut and gathered with the left hand. They are then dealt in three heaps of ten cards each. Just how does not really matter. Some cartomancers deal ten above, ten between, ten below. Others deal cards singly: below, middle, above. Whichever way is adopted, the general rule is to adhere to it, but the right to switch is still an individual privilege.

These cards are dealt face down. Then the top row of ten is turned face up, singly, in an overlapping row from left to right. Inverted

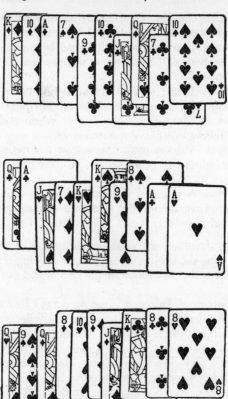

11) Divination with playing cards—thirty-two-card pack.
   Past (top row).
   Present (middle row).
   Future (bottom row).
   Surprise (bottom two cards).

cards, if noted by the backs, are drawn downward (as shown in the diagram) to distinguish them from uprights. If already marked for "tops" and "bottoms," there is no need for that.

The top row represents the *past*, so far as the subject is concerned, and is interpreted in such terms. The middle row stands for the *present* and is interpreted next. The bottom row prognosticates the *future* and is read in due turn. The two cards originally peeled from the top and bottom of the pack are placed further below—still face down—so they can be turned up finally as the *surprise*.

Each row is studied for combinations, then for individual interpretations. How they may turn out is perfectly illustrated through a card-by-card delineation of the following deal:

The Past: Assuming that the subject or person consulting the cards is represented by the Q S, we see immediately that past events are important as the significator—as this personal card is termed—is found in the Past Row.

A man of importance (K D) with some military or official status had much to do with the subject's career and early success (10 D), and some gift or promise (A D) was involved. The combination of three diamonds shows that business and finance were favorable until worry entered (7 S) and the subject received less money than anticipated (9 C inverted), but by boldly risking it, results were gained financially (10 C) with promise of still more.

Here, the flattery of an insincere individual (J C inverted) directly affected the dark-haired lady who is the subject of this reading (Q S), and a breakup came because of monetary losses (7 C inverted). This, although not necessarily great, disrupted the subject's financial progress—as represented by four successive Clubs with the significator card in with them—and the result was unhappiness (10 S) caused by great emotional distress, which may still affect the subject. This is confirmed by the combination of three tens, which signify monetary problems and indicate that legal complications were involved.

The Present: The subject is closely associated with a friendly, sympathetic woman who is either wealthy or influential (Q C) but also talkative and fond of show. This friendship points both to good times (A S) and high ideals, but care should be taken to avoid any resultant entanglements. Annoyance may come from a somewhat adventurous but persistent young man (J H inverted) of military bearing, who is turning trivial matters into big issues (7 D inverted) involving the welfare of somebody or something very close to the subject. A boastful friend (K H inverted) is doing nothing to help, but someone of high position (K S) is ready to handle the situation, and is probably hoping to break it up completely, as indicated by a pair of Kings, pointed opposite.

Since the K S matches the significator (Q S) in suit, romance is budding here, with prospects of marriage, particularly if the man is a widower, or on the rebound from a previous love affair. At present, however, the subject is unresponsive, due to overwork (9 H inverted), which is bringing on illness (8 S) or anxiety. Disappointments and bad tidings (A C inverted) are keeping the subject in an unsettled condition (A H, inverted), which only romance or a sudden change can cure. Note that the three Aces confirm the existence of personal problems, which are exaggerated, because two are inverted. Those same two Aces (A C, A H, both inverted) also verify that persons conspiring against the subject are gaining nothing thereby.

The Future: A spiteful, inconsiderate woman (Q H inverted) will hinder the subject's quest for happiness, causing new but hopefully small misfortunes (9 S inverted), which will also involve a frustrated, flirtatious woman (Q D inverted). The troubles may be mostly their own, so they will cancel each other out, for the subject can look forward to pleasant surroundings replete with love and romance (8 D) even though marriage may be a late one. Gaiety, happiness, and achieved ambition (10 H) will make all previous troubles seem as small as they really were, providing new and greater vistas, all for the subject's own best interests (9 D) even if old friendships are forgotten.

The only problem here will be a run-in with a false friend or outright swindler (J D inverted) who might even bring up the subject's past to threaten her good fortune. Such machinations will be spiked by a keen, capable friend or business adviser (K C) whom the subject should have met long before. Prosperity and companionship will be assured (8 C) particularly in the case of a well-matched marriage, causing past problems to vanish as fondest hopes are realized (8 H) perhaps beyond all expectations.

Here, again, there is fine confirmation, covering past and present, as well as future. It appears in the form of three eights, which predominate this portion of the deal. They show harmony in love and friendship, as well as married life; since all are upright, the indications are both serious and sure. The two eights (8 C and 8 H) that are both together show only brief happiness, but with greater expectations, which the third eight (8 D) certifies. Thus, the two eights link with the past and present, where newer and greater love was in the early stages of future development.

The Surprise: The two cards originally laid aside form a pointed sequel to the general reading, which may sometimes be a disturbing factor but are nicely controlled in the present instance. There will be petty annoyance from a shrewd, prying person (J S inverted) who may be linked with troublemakers mentioned earlier. Simply keeping alert for such a double-crosser should be sufficient, as the subject personally will acquire enough wisdom to meet problems calmly (7 H) yet with imagination and self-sufficiency, to whatever extent is needed.

TWENTY-ONE-CARD ORACLE

The thirty-two-card pack is used in this effective form of divination, but only twenty-one of them are required for the original deal. The pack is shuffled to start, cut by the subject, and given a preliminary reading if requested. In that case, the pack is gathered and given a further shuffle, followed by the usual cut. With the pack face down, the reader counts off the top eleven cards and lays them aside as unneeded.

From the remaining packet of twenty-one, the top card is dealt face down, to serve later on as the "surprise." The next twenty are dealt face up in a long row, being turned sideways during the deal, so that each will remain "upright" or "inverted," exactly as it was in the pack. Here, if the reader is using a pack with a "one-way" design on the back, the simplest procedure is to draw each "inverted" card about an inch downward, to distinguish it from the "uprights."

To save space, the cards can be dealt in overlapping fashion, as shown in the accompanying diagram; this also helps to keep the cards in position. During the deal, the reader can interpret the cards individually, and then in relationship to each new card that turns up. This is a very intriguing procedure, adding a touch of suspense throughout the reading.

Once the cards have been interpreted according to the accepted Table of Card Significations on page 201, the reader may modify the findings according to the List of Combinations, which is fully detailed on page 198. Many cartomancers do this in reverse, laying out the whole line of twenty to start and interpreting the "combinations" as an over-all reading, before treating the cards consecutively.

This is purely a matter of personal choice, which adds to the zest of the reading. Some readers mix the two procedures, providing that much more fun, as a series of cards coming up in unexpected succession is sure to demand an unusual interpretation. Whichever course is followed, after the twenty cards have been duly interpreted, the twenty-first is turned face up. Whether "upright" or "inverted," it is given a specially strong significance pertaining to the entire deal, thus fulfilling its "surprise" quality.

That completed, the reader gathers the twenty-one cards, shuffles them, cuts the packet, and deals three face-down heaps of seven,

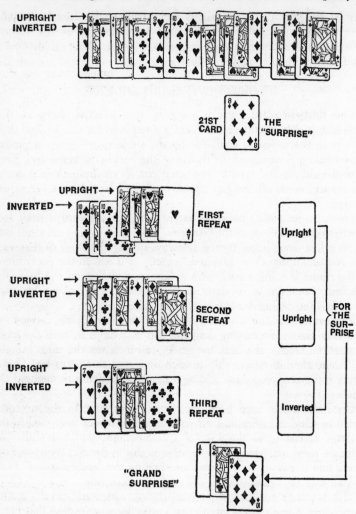

12) Divination with playing cards—thirty-two-card pack. A sample hand for the twenty-one-card oracle.

seven, and six (7+7+6=20) with one card laid aside toward a new surprise. The subject picks any heap of the three, and the reader deals its cards face up, interpreting them one by one, as a modified or supplementary reading to that already given.

Now, the reader gathers the twenty cards, shuffles them, has them cut, and deals three face-down heaps of seven, six, and six (7+6+6= 19) with the extra card added toward the new surprise. Again, the subject chooses a heap and the reader interprets it card by card in supplementary fashion. Then:

The reader gathers and shuffles the nineteen cards, deals them face down in heaps of six each (6+6+6=18) with the extra card being placed as the third in the new surprise. The subject chooses a "six heap," which the reader interprets as a further modification. Then, the "surprise heap" of three cards is turned up, with due care to keep all cards "upright" or "inverted," and from it, the reader draws the final conclusions.

Here is a sample reading taken from the cards shown in the diagram, starting with the individual interpretations:

You may be troubled by brief but pressing problems (10 H inverted) that may involve relatives, but that can be straightened through the aid of a straightforward friend or business associate (K C)—probably a dark-complexioned man—who may visit you shortly (A H inverted), or you may meet persons who come to see you unexpectedly. During this unsettled period, you should guard against a shrewd troublemaker (J D) whose underhand methods can be nullified only through a generous, understanding person (K H) who can provide any required aid.

This may lead to a long plane trip (10 C inverted) with hope for better luck, which definitely should be gained (9 H) through your own sincerity and effort, and deservedly so. However, you are apt to be tired of the whole situation (7 H inverted) after you have gone through it without proper recognition particularly as it will take too much time (10 S) and cause too many emotional complications.

You will find people generally unresponsive toward your problems (8 H inverted), which will turn any enjoyment into petty quibbles, particularly if you mistakenly rely on an equally petty individual (K D inverted) whose word is worthless. You, as the subject (J C), are really in the middle of the muddle, which may be muddled further by the spiteful attitude of an unhappy young woman (Q H inverted) whose demanding ways may fortunately be counteracted by a talkative, excitable woman (Q C) who at least will be sympathetic and helpful to a marked degree. However:

Between them they will hinder your enterprises (9 D) unless you put your own interests first, which in this case may be very necessary, even though it may mean losing a few friends while getting rid of troublemakers. An important message or a personal promise (A D) involving a member of the armed services (J H inverted) will greatly change the situation. This might possibly be an offer of marriage to someone concerned, and it should bring success to your plans (10 D) if you think in big enough terms to eliminate further difficulties. These may include a spiteful, flirtatious woman who may meddle in everyone else's affairs (Q D inverted), but a keen, hard-boiled friend (J S) will help to curb such nonsense.

Matters still may be touch and go depending on the turn-up of the surprise, or twenty-first card, which proves to be the 8 D. This points to pleasant journeys with happy landings, studded with romance and the prospect of a belated marriage. This card is doubly lucky: being upright, it steadies a situation that would be very shaky if the card happened to be inverted, and it indirectly speaks of money in the offing, as a good financial condition would be necessary to fulfill the surprise promise.

Checking the combinations, *Hearts* prove to be the prevalent suit (eight out of twenty cards), proving that romance is the dominating factor, confirming the general indications of the individual cards. *Spades* are in the minority (only two cards), which is a protection against loss or poverty, thus strengthening the intimation of the surprise.

Two runs of picture cards—K C, A H, J D, K H and K D, J C, Q H, Q C—point to parties, gala occasions, and other social activities, in close accord with the romantic trend of the Hearts. Going on to the various denominations, the fact that less than two thirds of the cards are in the layout (twenty out of thirty-two) means that "fours," "triplets," and possibly "pairs" have special significance, even when not closely grouped. Among these are:

Four Jacks, which mean that gaiety and excitement will take a wild, perhaps rebellious trend. The inverted J H may act as a restraint, but two Diamonds between a *pair of Jacks* (J H and J S) point to reckless extravagance or monetary loss through fines or legal expenses.

Four Tens show chance of attaining all desired aims, but luck will be needed to overcome the hazards of two inverted cards (10 H and 10 C). Two Hearts enclosed between *pair of tens* (10 C and 10 S) can mean a sudden change in love and affection, perhaps for the better.

Three Kings mean that important affairs should work out well, but a setback may come from the inverted card of the trio (K D).

Three Queens: Chummy get-togethers may turn to bickering and even hostility because of two inverted cards (Q H and Q D). Clash of personalities due from *pair of Queens together* but pointed opposite.

Two Aces, but widely separated, show occasional divergence between love (A H) and money (A D), as they are pointed opposite.

Two Nines, though well separated, are both the same color and both upright, indicating good cheer and well-being.

With the *first repeat deal* of the twenty-one cards, we assume that the *first heap* at the left is chosen and that its seven cards are dealt face up in the order shown in the diagram. The reader interprets this sequence as follows:

A severe shock or loss (10 S inverted) may seriously hinder the subject's plans, causing him a real upset (J C inverted), forcing a drastic change or a long trip (10 C inverted) to avoid further quarrels and to recuperate. A romantic, sympathetic woman, possibly the subject's sweetheart (Q C), will help solve his problems by enlisting the aid of someone in authority (J D) whose co-operation—which may be hard to get—will be clinched through the efforts of a powerful, friendly adviser (K H) who will ensure a favorable home life (A H) or happy surroundings, as a truly romantic climax.

Note: The fact that the J C is the significator in this reading links it with the subject. Otherwise, it might concern someone else's affairs. The friendly adviser (K H) is apt to be an older man—a lawyer, banker, financier—with some personal interest in the subject's affairs.

With the *second repeat deal,* we assume that the *middle heap* is chosen. Its six cards are dealt face up and read in sequence:

A happy-go-lucky friend (J H) will open channels to a highly profitable future (10 C), dependent on hunches and calculated risks, which depend upon the whims of a gossipy woman (Q D) who may help matters without realizing it, since happy times in pleasant surroundings (8 D) are promised through the aid of an experienced man with a military background (K D) unless a swindling troublemaker (J D inverted) moves in and spoils it all.

With the *third repeat deal*—which by now is really needed!—the wise, self-sufficient course (7 H) that may have been adopted will be seriously impeded (10 S inverted) unless the constant adviser (K H) comes to the fore again, which he may, despite the interference of a crafty woman (Q S inverted) who may have been awaiting this very opportunity to injure the subject (J C inverted), who is still in a topsy-turvy mood and is ready to take off to anywhere (10 C inverted) if it will only change his luck.

That leaves everything more or less dependent upon the *"Grand Surprise,"* consisting of the three cards laid aside during the repeat deals. Turned up, they are the A D, Q C, and 10 D inverted. They show that:

Fortune and success should prove in the subject's favor (A D) if only he will rely upon the romantic, sympathetic woman (Q C) who appeared earlier and who has been striving steadily in his behalf. Opportunities are still within his reach (10 D inverted) but only if care is being taken toward attaining them. By weighing the factors covered in the reading—particularly those which the subject recognizes as pertaining directly to himself—it should be possible to chart an effective course to a specific goal.

MODERN ROMANY METHOD

Though based upon a time-honored system utilizing the thirty-two-card pack, with its standard Table of Card Significations, this modernized version involves the present-day pack of fifty-two cards, which is gradually winnowed down to the lesser size. The reason for this will become apparent as you proceed; for the moment, there is just one important reminder. Be sure to use a pack with a "one-way" design on its back, or pencil-mark one end of every card from Aces down to sevens, as they will be given "upright" and "inverted" interpretations.

The full pack is thoroughly shuffled, the ends of each half being reversed each time the cards are riffled, so that some will point opposite to the others. The pack is then cut, turned face up, and cards are dealt in threes, which are treated as follows:

Should all three cards be of the same suit, they are put in a special group, which is to be used in the reading. However, all such cards must be above a seven in value; any that are lower are laid aside as a discard, which plays no part in the divination.

If two cards are of the same suit, the higher of the two is put in the special group, provided its value is seven or above. Example: J C, 8 C, K D. The J C is put in the special group; the 8 C and K D are laid aside. With 6 H, 3 H, J S, all are laid aside.

If the three cards are of different suits, they are all laid aside in the discard.

While weeding thus, the dealer keeps watching for a suitable significator card to represent the subject; for example, the K H, signifying a light-haired or light-complexioned man whose fortune is under consideration. He also keeps count of the cards that go into the special group, which are supposed to total fifteen, including the significator. Generally the pack runs out before that number is reached, so in that case, the dealer gathers the discard, which represents the bulk of the pack, shuffles it, and continues to deal by threes, adding more cards to the special group.

If the significator is not among the first fourteen cards that form the special group, the deal stops there, and the significator is taken from the pack and added to the group. If the significator is already present, the deal ends on the fifteenth card. Only the special group is used in the series of readings that follow:

The First Reading: Deal the cards in a circle, beginning with a single card at the top and running them in clockwise fashion, so that there are two at the bottom. The cards are dealt face up and in the example shown (see Diagram 13) the significator (K H) was added to the group to make the fifteenth card, hence it is at the top.

13) Divination with playing cards—thirty-two-card pack. Modern Romany method: sample first reading.

The circle is studied for combinations, which are interpreted in the usual fashion. In the example, a cluster of seven *picture cards* show gaiety and sociability, but with the hazards that accompany such life. It should be noted that picture cards normally predominate in this type of reading, because high cards are given first choice, but seven in a row is a strong score.

Hearts, as the predominant suit—six out of fifteen—confirms the sociable trend by stressing romance and friendship, but here, too, there can be complications. Any trend toward sympathy and understanding will be helpful. So the reader looks for such indications in the following:

The subject can expect good results in business and friendship (four Kings) with the one inverted card (K C) being helpful rather than hurtful, as it may quicken those results. Good planning (two Aces) will be a strong factor as this pair (A H and A C) harmonizes sentiment with prosperity. Any arguments because they point opposite (A H inverted, A C upright) should prove constructive and helpful.

Bickering and backbiting may be expected (two Queens, both inverted), but affinity between the subject (K H) and his true love (Q H) means that he should stay strictly on one side, his own. He has a bigger problem, in that people are plotting against him (two Jacks), but since both are upright, he may ward off trouble with very little loss. Luck and changes for the better (two tens) are coming soon, as they are opposites, and, being red (10 H and 10 D), they promise happiness and romance.

As already strongly indicated, love and romance are the most important factors in the subject's life, and they may be hanging in the balance (9 S inverted) because there will be ups and downs (7 S upright, 7 H inverted) of a minor though very disconcerting nature. The care and handling of these can be determined by further readings.

The Second Reading: Start counting with the significator (K H) as "one" and continue to five in clockwise fashion, in this case ending on the A H. Lay the first card (K H) aside and count five more from the new card (A H), ending on the 7 S. Place the A H so it overlaps the K H and start another count of five from the 7 S, ending on the Q H. Place the 7 S on the K H and A H. Start another count of five from the Q H and continue thus until the whole circle has been formed into a single line (Diagram 13).

Note the inverted cards, which can be drawn downward from the uprights, as shown in the diagram, so that the cards can be read in sequence. This example would run:

The subject (K H) is unsettled (A H inverted) and wants a change because of worries (7 S) and heartaches over one he loves deeply (Q H inverted) but who is inclined to spiteful moods. A good job and new opportunity (10 D) will straighten all that, as wealth and success

(A C) are promised by a highly important person (K D) who may be in an official position. The subject should make the most of this, however, for a run of bad luck (9 S inverted) will follow and a carefree friend (J H) may be more hindrance than help, leaving the subject in a dejected state (7 H inverted). Another important man (K S) can help the situation but may betray the subject's trust. Fortunately, a vigilant young friend (J C) will keep an eye on this and may also alert the subject regarding a frustrated woman (Q D inverted) who is plotting trouble for him, bringing disappointment (K C inverted) under the mask of friendship. Such setbacks will not be long-lasting (10 H inverted), but they may limit the subject's success. More can be determined through:

14) Modern Romany Method: sample second and third readings.

The Third Reading: This is done by pairs, a favorite process with many veteran card readers, who often place special significations on such combinations. However, a long list of such couplets would be superfluous, for careful analysis of many cases shows that they go back to the accepted meanings, but with the doubled interpretation regarded as a single unit. Here, the reader may balance the factors and project imaginatively to come up with full interpretations.

In the present method, the pairing is done thus: Take the cards at the extreme ends of the row (K H and 10 H inverted) and pair them. Then, the next cards from each end (A H inverted and K C inverted) and so on until a lone card is left, in this instance the 9 S inverted, which is a "consolation card." The pairs are duly interpreted and linked, with the "consolation" as an added unit bearing on the whole. Our example—shown in Diagram 14—runs as follows:

The first pair (K H as significator with 10 H inverted) accentuates the subject's uncertainty and verifies his need for change. The second pair (A H inverted and K C inverted) further stresses his uneasiness and worry, which can be attributed to the third pair (7 S with Q D inverted), where a scheming, flirtatious woman is shunting her own troubles onto the subject and trying to blame him for them.

This threatens an estrangement in the subject's home life, but the fourth pair (Q H inverted with J C) indicates that the subject's true love will heed the advice of a trusted friend, so that a reconciliation should be close at hand. The fifth pair (10 D with K S) denotes the wealth and power of some person or organization that can work strongly to the subject's welfare; while the sixth pair (A C with 7 H inverted) shows financial success and eventual happiness in marriage, even though the subject may not gain the recognition he once anticipated.

The seventh pair (K D with J H) is highly important, as it combines the influence of a powerful man, possibly an official, with a youthful, carefree friend. Whether these two clash or harmonize, the subject's interest and future may be dependent on the outcome, so he should be tactful indeed. The consolation card (9 S inverted) confirms this, for it betokens a series of lesser troubles and setbacks, the very sort that could come from continually playing policy with a sticky situation. Its very title, "consolation," softens any adverse trend represented by such a card, which is nice to know in this case.

The Fourth Reading: Though the same fifteen cards are used, they are first gathered, shuffled, and then cut before the final deal. In the old versions, the cards were assembled without changing the direction of the ends, but this had two glaring faults: the interpretations of the cards were limited to the original "ups" and "downs," while any carelessness in handling the cards might inadvertently turn a few, thus changing the context of the reading anyway.

Since the chief purpose is to gain a fresh viewpoint within the existing framework, it is better to turn the cards deliberately and repeatedly, thus letting chance take control, as is customary in all forms of fortunes. This can be done by sweeping the outspread pairs toward the center of the table with a swirling motion, so that the ends meet haphazardly. When the gathered packet is shuffled, the halves should be turned end to end, then reshuffled, adding that much more to chance.

The packet is then turned face down and dealt into five heaps of three cards each. One card from the fifth heap is then pushed aside as an extra. These are defined as follows:

1) *For the person,* namely, the subject, or significator.
2) *For the house,* people or conditions surrounding the subject.
3) *The unexpected,* pertaining to associates of the subject.

15) Modern Romany Method: sample fourth reading.

4) *The expected,* how or whether it will be realized.

5) *The surprise,* directly concerning the subject.

Extra card, the Consolation, with final bearing on the reading.

The heaps are turned face up in order, care being taken to turn them sideways so that upright and inverted cards will maintain their status. If one-way backs are used, each can be drawn downward when inverted as in Diagram 15, to keep track of inverted cards during the reading, which proceeds thus with the sample groups:

1) *For the Person:* Since the significator is the K H, the subject's romantic outlook is high indeed, as his ladylove (Q H inverted) is between the 10 H, with its sparkling gaiety, and A C, symbolizing wealth, comfort, and above all harmonious marriage. But gaiety can be fleeting and prosperity slow in attainment. Hence, due to the inverted Q H, the lady may be petulant, easily slighted, and more swayed by present whims than future prospects. The subject must be patient, confident, and willing to do more than just promise if he wants the romance to be intact when the glad times finally arrive.

2) *For the House:* Repeated troubles will disturb a favorable home life, involving a young, reliable friend or relative (9 S inverted with A H and J C). This combination corroborates indications of earlier readings, making it all the more vital. The danger here is that petty grievances may swell to undue proportions, so that the friend, although normally helpful, may be in the middle of a breakup if one occurs and may change his policy entirely. Chances are that happy circumstances will weather the strife, but any laxity may prove serious.

3) *The Unexpected:* Here, a real shocker will directly affect the subject, as the significator is in the very middle of an adverse trio (7 S, K H, Q D, all inverted). The subject's plans will be totally upset through his own utter indecision, which will spell golden opportunity for a frustrated, ignorant woman who likes to belittle anyone she envies. Fortunately, she regards all that glitters as "golden" so the opportunity may be reduced to cheap "brass." However, the subject's trifling acts may be magnified into something scandalous, so beware!

4) *The Expected:* The subject has a good friend whose hopes are similar to his own. How will he fare? The cards tell thus: A reliable, generous man, with ultrafine intentions, seeks recognition that he may not gain (K C, 10 D inverted, 7 H inverted). Should he be told? Yes, most certainly. But from the subject's standpoint, it means that he cannot expect much from the friend until the friend has gained what he expected.

5) *The Surprise:* A real dandy. It may explain something that has really worried you but that can now be cleared. The combination

(K S with J H inverted) marks antagonism resulting in annoyance and frustration. Whether personal or impersonal, it has come from a powerful source and may have been working secretly against you. Find the cause, relieve it, and the grudge, if personal, will rebound on anyone who instigated it.

Extra Card, the Consolation: Always to the significator's advantage, this points to a man of wealth (K D) and possibly high official position whose influence can be enlisted in the subject's behalf, although until now, it may have seemed adverse. Actually, this may represent something that has been to the subject's advantage all along.

X. The Square of Thirty-six

This intriguing system of card reading has been attributed to the famous Madame Lenormand. If so, it could very well account for some of her remarkable prophecies, as the cards cover a wide variety of interests, some thirty-six in all. The interpretations of these are brief but pointed, being based on suits alone, but this is followed by a more detailed reading, in which each individual card has its own significance according to established rules.

Hence the Square of Thirty-six may be regarded as unique throughout, even to the number of cards in the pack, which also happens to be thirty-six, consisting of the "short" pack of thirty-two cards (Aces down to sevens) plus the four twos; which with this method represent the subject and various other persons, during the later stages of interpretation.

The first requirement is the Chart, which consists of thirty-six blocks, preferably placed in six by six formation, as shown in the diagram opposite. These run from one to thirty-six, row by row, and each represents a different interest, as listed. By having a copy of the chart handy, you can check the position of any card after all are dealt; or, if preferred, the listings can be written or typed on separate slips of paper, which can then be taped to their proper positions on a card table.

In either case, it is a good plan to use half-size packs of "play" cards, which require much less space than the standard size and are generally printed with a "one way" design on their back, so they can be recognized as "inverted" when turned with the design pointing downward. With a "two way" design, one end of each card can be marked with a pencil to indicate the top.

The pack is shuffled, cut by the subject, and given a preliminary reading if desired. It is gathered in exact order by the reader, who

1 Present Purpose	2 Accom- plishment	3 Recog- nition	4 Expec- tation	5 Specula- tion	6 Wishful Thinking
7 Wrongs	8 Ungrate- fulness	9 Contacts	10 Reverses	11 Problems	12 Posses- sions
13 Gladness	14 Love and Affection	15 Welfare	16 Matrimony	17 Worries	18 Harmony
19 Windfalls	20 Dishonesty	21 Opposition	22 Presents	23 Friendship and Affection	24 Advance- ment
25 Co-oper- ation	26 Under- takings	27 Circum- stances	28 Sorrow	29 Appre- ciation	30 Scandal
31 Future Prospects	32 Affluence	33 Neglect	34 Awards	35 Influence and Power	36 Health

16) Square of Thirty-six. Chart of thirty-six squares.

deals the cards directly from the face-up pack, without inverting them, to fill the spaces from one to thirty-six. The reader then proceeds with a general interpretation of those spaces, according to the following list, which applies only to the suit of each card.

1: PRESENT PURPOSE

This refers to an immediate project or whatever else the subject has uppermost in mind, provided it is something of a practical or definite sort. The suit interpretations are:

Heart: A symbol of success. Proceed with present plans.

Club: Prospects are good but will need the help of friends.

Diamond: Expect obstacles, especially if business or financial matters are involved.

Spade: Failure probable, due to delay or misplaced confidence.

2: ACCOMPLISHMENT

This covers a broader range, namely the gain that may ensue, not only from an immediate purpose, but through various factors that attend it, making it something of a follow-up to present aim.

Heart: Your satisfaction will be great, exceeding expectations.

Club: Strengthening of friendships will be a major accomplishment, outweighing any doubtful factors.

Diamond: Any satisfaction may be lessened by petty spite.

Spade: Fraud and unfair tactics will nullify your accomplishments, leaving you little satisfaction.

3: RECOGNITION

This represents results rather than prospects, hence can be regarded as a gauge of success, which depends on recognition.

Heart: Your success will be complete, with recognition sure.

Club: Only through friends can you gain the recognition that you truly deserve.

Diamond: Recognition will be much less than you expect. But partial success may pave the way to something better.

Spade: Recognition is hopeless. Antagonism and mean methods will balk success. Either begin all over or try something else.

4: EXPECTATION

This deals with any hope that is actually in the balance or dependent on a halfway promise, the more tangible the better.

Heart: Your expectation will be realized, perhaps in greater measure than anticipated.

Club: Your hopes depend on friends. If old ones cannot help, find new ones. Your own efforts must be persistent throughout.

Diamond: The more trifling your hope, the less chance that it will be realized. Look to bigger things.

Spade: No chance of gaining expectations. Persistence will make it worse, perhaps with maddening results. Better abandon it.

5: SPECULATION

This refers to outright risks or sheer chance, as betting on races, buying a lottery ticket, playing the stock market, gambling at Las Vegas, or anything else that is beyond the questioner's own control.

Heart: Look forward to an unexpected gain. Any contemplated risk is likely to succeed. A good time to follow a hunch.

Club: Luck will be in your favor if you deal with reliable people and follow sound advice.

Diamond: Losses are likely but may be offset by some unexpected gain. If money is due you, go after it now, or you may lose it.

Spade: Avoid all risks and speculations, no matter how sound they may seem. Keep your insurance paid up, as you may need it. This may symbolize anything from robbery to bankruptcy.

6: WISHFUL THINKING

This approaches the fanciful, covering things you would like to have but cannot gain through your own efforts. The more bizarre, the better.

Heart: Your utmost desire may be realized sooner than you ever hoped.

Club: If you don't get what you want, turn things about and want what you can get. The results may really amaze you.

Diamond: Somebody is due for something wonderful, but it may not be you. Friends will help you if you urge them, but despite their support, you should be satisfied if your wild wishes are only partly realized.

Spade: Remember the old saying, "If wishes were horses, beggars would ride." That about sums your chances; namely, zero.

7: WRONGS

This has to do with any grievance suffered by the subject and what can be done to rectify it, particularly if laboring under it now.

Heart: Any wrong will soon be remedied and turned to your advantage.

Club: The more friends you have, the sooner you can wipe out an existing wrong. As go-betweens, they will correct misunderstandings.

Diamond: Be cordial toward persons who have treated you unjustly and they will make amends, at least in part.

Spade: Any injustice will become worse, the more you try to better it. Expect the worst and do your best to ignore it.

8: UNGRATEFULNESS

Here, the subject's worries are largely imaginary but may threaten to become more serious. The suits tell what to do:

Heart: Be confident. Full appreciation will soon be expressed.

Club: Persons who have failed to express proper gratitude will do so if you approach them through mutual friends.

Diamond: Other factors are behind the ungrateful attitude. Look for spite and malice as the real reasons, then take proper steps.

Spade: You have been too generous toward persons who are naturally ungrateful. Ignore them and avoid similar mistakes with others.

9: CONTACTS

These have to do with fellow-workers, business partners, and anyone with whom the subject expects to make important deals.

Heart: All signs are for the best, with profits assured.

Club: Keep all transactions on a friendly basis, otherwise misunderstandings may develop, with resultant loss.

Diamond: Avoid taking sides if associates quarrel. If you do, you may be blamed for everything. Use tact and make the best of it.

Spade: Trust no one but yourself. Take immediate profit in preference to future promises. Others may already be squeezing you out. Get clear before they can.

10: REVERSES

These are to be expected. Rather than regarding this as a bad sign, take it as a warning with the cards disclosing the following:

Heart: Loss of some person or connection that has given you great benefits, on which you have depended—perhaps too greatly.

Club: You may lose a good friend. Regardless of the reason, it may bring a severe setback to your present prospects.

Diamond: Loss of money or property is an imminent threat.

Spade: Your most important interests are at stake. Watch out for wheeler-dealers. Lack of foresight may bring misery and remorse.

11: PROBLEMS

This has to do with personal matters, from petty annoyances to deep sentiments, though it may carry into business affairs as well.

Heart: Disputes with family and relatives may reach serious proportions unless curbed. Handle them tactfully by showing due affection.

Club: Misunderstandings with friends may bring a serious break.

Diamond: Quarrels involving money or other obligations.

Spade: Envy and rancor may cause you great anguish.

12: POSSESSIONS

This covers all assets from job security and personal effects to stocks, bonds, and real estate. Indications regarding them are:

Heart: Expect a steady and even surprising increase. The latter may be due a sudden upturn in business or an inheritance.

Club: You should definitely prosper through steady effort and the aid of good friends who appreciate your ability and will recommend you.

Diamond: Expect opposition and difficulties involving land or other property. These can be overcome, but if too much time is wasted, your great opportunity will be lost.

Spade: You are losing ground and may have to sacrifice many possessions unless you work twice as hard and gain new aims.

13: GLADNESS

This is gained by everyone to some degree, though how much, how often, and how soon are difficult to predict, due to conflicting factors. The cards, however, may indicate the source, as follows:

Heart: Gladness will come through inspiration and appreciation of the finer things of life.

Club: By cultivating friendships and taking pride in your work, you will experience continued gladness in everyday affairs.

Diamond: Worry and personal conflicts are your obstacles to gladness. Eliminate them and you will learn what joy really is.

Spade: Through helping others, you will help yourself. Your loyalty will be rewarded through persons in high positions, unless the Spade is the Ace. It presages utter disappointment.

14: LOVE AND AFFECTION

This is a very ardent sign, which may influence the entire reading. Since it shows the relationship of the subject to close companions, it naturally should guide the actions indicated elsewhere.

Heart: Complete contentment and mutual understanding.

Club: Those you love will be constant and dependable.

Diamond: The clash of interests may produce resentment and mistrust. A rival may try to win the one you love most.

Spade: Love is fickle, affection swayed by whim. Patience and perseverance may overcome this, but the outcome is doubtful. New objects of affection may be the only answer.

15: WELFARE

Progress and prosperity come under this head, hence the interpretations generally cover a range well beyond the immediate present.

Heart: A highly prosperous outlook, limited only by the extent to which you deserve it. Aim for a big goal. It may be yours for the asking.

Club: If you seem to be working too hard to make necessary progress, don't slacken, or you may lose out. Accept advice and help from friends, keep plugging, and accept whatever prosperity you gain.

Diamond: Your welfare will be hampered by persons who envy your progress and will scheme to outdo you. You must keep alert to succeed.

Spade: Outright antagonism and interference with your plans are hindering your immediate progress. Unless counteracted, such malice will endanger your future prosperity as well.

16: MATRIMONY

Interpretation here depends upon the age and present status of the subject. With teen-agers, it is strictly a future, and perhaps distant. Young married persons will find a present signification. Older folks may look back in retrospect when they read the following:

Heart: A good and happy marriage. Mutual interests, if furthered, will lead to greater understanding. Often romantic, particularly if the Ace of hearts appears.

Club: This indicates a well-planned marriage, often brought about by friends. Both are helpful but unneeded, provided both husband and wife are practical-minded, which is more important than romance.

Diamond: Jealousy and conflicts can mar this marriage. No need to delve into details. The participants can provide those themselves. If clashing individuals will declare a truce, they will succeed. Otherwise, they must take what comes for better or for worse.

Spade: Outsiders may prevent this marriage, or they may try to break it up once it has been consummated. Spot cards, 7, 8, or 9, point to separation or divorce.

17: WORRIES
Though seemingly trivial, these can go quite deep, leaving a more devastating effect than something encountered bravely. Indications:

Heart: Worries will be close at hand. Love, relatives, friends, in that order. They will soon pass, so forget them.

Club: Real worry here. A conflict with a close friend—or friends—can threaten serious consequences. Smooth it over and restore mutual understanding, regardless of all else. Usually it will work out that way by itself. Just make sure that it does.

Diamond: Anger, haste, uncertainty will cause arguments and misunderstandings. Dismiss such strife and happines will follow.

Spade: The subject is the helpless target of mean and vicious critics or outright enemies. Any action will be futile. Let the storm blow over and disintegrate into the nothingness it represents.

18: HARMONY
All cards in this category can prove helpful if properly interpreted. But watch for warnings. Experience has proven their worth!

Heart: Close friendships will bring mutual benefits and understanding. Don't neglect them, or you will regret it.

Club: Push friendships slowly, steadily and they will grow to your great advantage. Remember your friends and they will remember you.

Diamond: Avoid all jealousy or arguments where friends are concerned. Otherwise, you will lose them. Side with them, even when you don't agree, and you will keep them.

Spade: Your friendships are apt to prove passing and trivial. Enjoy them now, but cultivate new ones. Keep ahead of the game, but don't burn your bridges behind you. You can renew old acquaintances later.

19: WINDFALLS
Back in the staid old days, this referred almost exclusively to legacies, as they were about the only way whereby anyone could experience unexpected good fortune. Today, with inheritance taxes running high, there are better ways. Here are some indications:

Heart: You should soon receive a gift or opportunity that will go beyond all normal expectations. The longer you wait, the better, as it may then exceed your wildest dreams. And it will be all yours.

Club: Some friend will remember you in a substantial way. One such gift may foreshadow another, often from a different source.

Diamond: Claims or interests that are properly yours will be disputed. The stronger your rights, the more costly it may prove to gain them. Better be satisfied with whatever you can get.

Spades: Someone may defraud you of property you have overlooked or know nothing about. You may have time to prevent it by checking your affairs and looking well ahead. Otherwise you may never learn the truth.

20: DISHONESTY

Here we are dealing with outright cases of fraud and deceit, the sort that everyone encounters. The suit of the card will tell you what to expect; a picture card—Jack, Queen, or King—makes the situation more precarious, the higher the worse, and may help to identify some person involved.

Heart: Any scheme directed against you will backfire on the persons who started it. Be confident and let them take the consequences.

Club: If you suspect double-dealing, seek the advice and help of friends. They will turn the tables on the malefactors.

Diamond: Any fraud or conspiracy will collapse or be nullified. Be firm and remain calm, as your loss, if any, should be small. Worry will hurt you most, so avoid it.

Spade: A bad token. Deception and double-dealing will hurt your reputation and ruin opportunities. Your only course is to grin and bear it.

21: OPPOSITION

Here, the situation is more forthright. Anything from competition to conflict may be expected in all phases of life. Many such phases are covered under other heads. Here, the cards indicate the outcome:

Heart: Complete triumph over all opponents, great or small, fair or foul. Love, business, fame, all are covered by this token.

Club: Rivalry will be keen and perhaps unfair. Count on friends to prevent opponents from ganging up on you. With such aid you are sure to win out.

Diamond: Odds favor the opposition, but disputes among rivals will work to your advantage. You may either score a surprising triumph or come out better than you expected.

Spade: Better face it. You are being outwitted and outclassed. The meaner the tactics of your opponents, the worse it may be for you.

22: PRESENTS

Like a few other categories such as "Wishful Thinking," the receiving of presents or tokens of esteem usually depends on the consideration of other persons. However, gifts are often to be expected, which puts them in a practical realm. Here is what the cards indicate:

Heart: You will receive fine gifts or high honors that are either totally unexpected or far beyond your expectations.

Club: You are apt to receive practical gifts from generous friends or relatives.

Diamond: Useless or unwanted gifts may put you under obligations that you should avoid. It may be better to return them.

Spade: Someone may offer you presents to inspire false confidence. Watch out for "free gifts" with a catch to them. You are apt to be victimized by some shady scheme.

23: FRIENDSHIP AND AFFECTION

This goes deeply into the subject's personal life and therefore should be checked against other categories in which personalities are involved. Here, the cards disclose the dependability of those you trust:

Heart: Close friendship or deep affection will be ever constant.

Club: You have sincere friends upon whom you can fully depend.

Diamond: Disagreements among your friends will work to your disadvantage. Deal with then individually and humor their moods.

Spade: Friends may prove false and your affections may be misplaced. Rely only on those whom you have proven through a test.

24: ADVANCEMENT

This runs the range from improving your present status to high attainment, through which you may gain celebrity. The cards show:

Heart: A sudden promotion or a rapid rise that can scale to lofty heights, with fame and honor as the ultimate goal. If success is limited by present surroundings, a change will be wise.

Club: Your advancement depends upon your friends, so don't neglect them. How high you go will hinge on how hard you work.

Diamond: Determination is needed here to meet competition and counteract criticism. The sooner you overcome such factors, the greater your chance for fame. Delay can ruin your chances.

Spade: Malicious rivals will block you with unfair tactics. Fulfill lesser duties capably and constantly, and you may be in line for something bigger. But the obstacles are too great to warrant hope for fame.

25: CO-OPERATION

A most important adjunct, as it shows how much you can depend on outside aid when under pressure. Check this with other categories.

Heart: Aid in any project will be gained for the mere asking, often beyond the actual need and even from unexpected sources.

Club: If your friends are really sincere, they will help you when you need them, but don't overtax them, or they may hesitate if you call on them again.

Diamond: Don't count on co-operation from anyone if you are involved in complications. Clean the slate, then things will come your way.

Spade: Help that you need and deserve will be usurped by unscrupulous competitors or rivals. You must seek co-operation elsewhere, or get by on your own—if you can.

26: UNDERTAKINGS

This covers long-range enterprises in contrast to any immediate purpose, though obviously, present projects may influence the future. Hence this strengthens or weakens various points covered elsewhere, and should be judged accordingly.

Heart: Success will crown any well-planned enterprise; the more ambitious the project, the better.

Club: If your friends will back you in any undertaking, you can count on financial gain. To chance it alone would be unwise.

Diamond: Avoid competition and seek success in some new field. Make sure that all parties are in full accord. Disputes will bring ruin.

Spade: Any enterprise you start may meet with unforeseen difficulties. Let others take the risk and be sure you are not involved.

27: CIRCUMSTANCES

Everyone wonders about the advantages or disadvantages of a change, either in occupations or surroundings. Read what the cards suggest:

Heart: Unless present circumstances are ideal, any opportune change is for the better. Following your own inclinations may prove lucky.

Club: If a friend offers you a better situation, take it. If it comes from an outsider, accept it only on advice of reliable friends.

Diamond: Avoid any change to new conditions, as you may be caught between, or become the object of contention. It won't work out.

Spade: Unscrupulous persons may be trying to crowd you from your present situation so that they can take over. Hold fast if you can.

28: SORROW

Anything from doom to disaster is to be expected here. Whatever the card, it symbolizes an end of life, but the consequences vary:

Heart: As the result of a death, the subject will receive or learn of something that is totally unexpected.

Club: This presages death of a friend or acquaintance. A study of other categories may show how it will affect the subject.

Diamond: Whatever the subject's present plans, they are due for a change because of a sudden or unexpected death.

Spade: A death will solve a pressing problem for the subject.

29: APPRECIATION

The older the subject, the more important this card, as it covers rewards for services rendered, which often come near the close of a career. Sometimes it refers to appreciation already expressed.

Heart: You will receive a reward far beyond your expectations.

Club: Loyal friends will show appreciation that you well deserve.

Diamond: You will be surprised by sudden recognition, but do not be surprised if someone tries to belittle the honor due you.

Spade: Any appreciation you anticipate will not be forthcoming.

30: SCANDAL

A bad card at best, so cushion yourself for the following shocks:

Heart: Through some mistake, you will be roundly criticized or even confronted with disgrace. Fortunately, it will soon blow over, so keep calm.

Club: This is a double-edged blade. An "honor card" (A-K-Q-J-10) may mean dishonor to a friend, which will cause you equal suffering; a lower card (9-8-7-2) indicates an embarrassing situation of your own, in which even your best friends desert you. Wait and see which happens.

Diamond: Spite, jealousy, and malice will create a furor in which you will be involved. Keep to the fringe and it won't matter.

Spade: Whether right or wrong, you will have a rough time.

31: FUTURE PROSPECTS

Good things coming up—let's hope! Luck enters as a factor with all future prospects, for after all, life itself is luck, like the turn of a card. For instance:

Heart: You are due for a wonderful streak of luck. Stay with it!

Club: Friends, old or new, will toss you a real opportunity.

Diamond: Jealousy aimed against you will turn out to your favor.

Spade: You will be in real danger, whether mentally, physically, or morally. But if things really get bad, friends will rally to your cause and pull you to safety. Nothing will be shattered but your nerves.

32: AFFLUENCE

Money, wealth, solvency—here is how the cards foretell them:

Heart: Whether through business, profession, or outright speculation, you should acquire a big bank roll. Bigger than you dreamed.

Club: Hard work, good deals through friends, with a dash of brains, will put you in a higher income bracket.

Diamond: You will make money, but it will go to other people if you aren't careful. Very probably you won't be, despite warnings.

Spade: Don't count on anything. Any profits due you will be intercepted on the way. Just work hard, make whatever you can, and keep it.

33: NEGLECT

This represents a negative quality, which makes it all the more important. It shows how the subject, by ignoring people and opportunities, may lose out in the long run. The suits indicate:

Heart: By indifference toward other people, you let your own interests lag, so that life becomes drab. Snap out of it. Have fun!

Club: Your neglect of friends is causing you to wonder why they are neglecting you. End worry by renewing old acquaintances.

Diamond: People are taking advantage of your careless attitude to strengthen their position and weaken yours. Prompt action on your part will reverse the trend and solve other problems as well.

Spade: Take care of your possessions, or people will take them from you. Whatever you have lost, you can still lose more. Halt this neglect, or you will wind up with nothing, not even friends.

34: AWARDS

Broad coverage here, from slight favors to substantial emoluments. In any case, whatever you may get will depend upon the cards:

Heart: Everything will come your way from everybody you know. The wealthier and more important your connections, the bigger the awards.

Club: Friends will remember you, both in kindly and practical ways, provided you quietly and sincerely further such friendships.

Diamond: Any bounty due you will be sought by others, so don't be disappointed if you don't get all you should. People may lend you money or offer you an opportunity instead of a bonus, so make the most of it.

Spade: Don't expect anything, not even a trifling handout.

35: INFLUENCE AND POWER

How far your ambition can carry you depends upon factors covered elsewhere. Here, the cards tell how strong you will be in your own field.

Heart: You will gain influence and power to your heart's content.

Club: Whatever authority you acquire will come through friends.

Diamond: Your aims will be blocked by envious persons. By secretly furthering your real ambition, you can surprise the opposition when you suddenly attain it. But don't expect it to meet your full hopes.

Spade: Your ambitions belong under the head of wishful thinking. A good card there may help you gain influence and power, but only to a moderate degree.

36: HEALTH

How far accident or illness may figure in a reading is a question asked by every subject. Too many factors are involved to give a positive answer, but in general the cards supply these indications:

Heart: Any indisposition will usually be brief and trifling.

Club: A warning of impending illness.

Diamond: Indicates an attack of some known ailment.

Spade: Ill-health may interfere with business and social life.

SAMPLE READING OF
THIRTY-SIX SQUARES

This interpretation is keyed to the random deal of thirty-six cards shown on the opposite page. This basic reading, involving suits alone, will be followed by a more detailed interpretation of the cards immediately surrounding the significator (2 H), which represents the subject. However, in the basic reading, the 2 H is interpreted simply according to suit, like any other card.

The *Spade* at *Number 1* bodes failure for your *present plans*, but it may not prove hopeless, as elements of delay and misplaced confidence are offset by the *Heart* at *Number 2*, which promises great satisfaction through *accomplishment*. However, there is uncertainty as to gaining *recognition* for your efforts, due to the *Diamond* at *Number 3*, and this can dwindle to a hopeless state where *expectation* is concerned, because of the deadly *Spade* at *Number 4*.

Against all such misfortune, any *speculation* should be to your advantage if you deal with reliable people, as indicated by the *Club* at *Number 5*. Even your *wishful thinking* may bring surprise results if you keep it within realistic bounds, as suggested by the *Club* at *Number 6*. Those favorable signs build to a peak with the *Heart* at *Number 7*, which should almost certainly remedy any *wrongs* you may have suffered earlier, but you will have to ignore the *ungratefulness* of certain persons, indicated by the *Spade* at *Number 8*.

Here, you should check back to any helpful dealings (as specified by Number 5) to find which friends will be the most dependable *contacts* shown by the *Club* at *Number 9*. You will need all such support that you can obtain, because you are due to lose one of your best connections, a severe *reverse* marked by the *Heart* at *Number 10*. This in itself could produce quarrels over money among the *problems* shown by the *Diamond* at *Number 11*; so if bad goes to worse, you may even wind up losing most of your possessions, as betokened by the *Spade* at *Number 12*. Sacrifices, debts, even bankruptcy may result, according to how deeply you have become involved in difficult situations with the wrong people.

So far, it has been a losing struggle at best, so don't be surprised if worry and conflict spoil all chance of *gladness,* for the *Diamond* at *Number 13* says exactly that. Persons toward whom you feel *love and affection* should remain constant and dependable according to the *Club* at *Number 14*, but your *welfare* will be threatened by the *Spade* at *Number 15*. The fact that it is a baleful spot card (8 S), followed by another *Spade* of the same ilk (7 S) at *Number 16*, indicates that

17) Square of Thirty-six: sample reading.

romance or *matrimony* is due for rough going, perhaps an actual parting.

Truly, the saying, "When poverty comes in at the door, love flies out at the window," can apply here, as the *Club* at *Number* 17 denotes further *worries* through conflict with friends, who are the people you need most at this crucial period. If you can smooth over the storm and avoid arguments, you can restore *harmony* through the *Diamond* at *Number* 18. Don't expect any lucky breaks in the way of *windfalls*, for another *Diamond* at *Number* 19 may mark a further struggle for any rights that you think you still have. All this uncertainty could complete your royal road to ruin, but your friends—if you have kept a few! —will forestall any *dishonesty* that threatens you, as indicated by the timely *Club* at *Number* 20, which turns the tables on double-dealers.

You will need that friendly aid, for you are due for more serious *opposition*, shown by the *Spade* at *Number* 21, but if you accept it as a warning and play things safely, you will receive a still stronger warning against accepting *presents* from false friends, covered by the *Spade* at *Number* 22. Here, the appearance of two bad cards in a row really fits with the old rule that "Two negatives make a positive," as they are so closely linked that you can treat them as a single issue, thus avoiding both the plots and blandishments of your adversaries. The A S in particular is a warning card, making it all the better.

From there on, you can trust in *friendship and affection*, symbolized by the *Club* at *Number* 23, a highly dependable token. A second *Club* at *Number* 24 promises that friends will also contribute to your *advancement*. A third *Club* at *Number* 25 guarantees *co-operation* in every way by those sincere friends upon whom you know you can depend in full. Ordinarily there might be a proviso on one of those counts, such as taking care not to overtax a friendship, but three Clubs in a row add strength to one another. They are strong enough to back you to success in your next *undertaking*, providing you avoid disputes and seek some new field, as advised by the *Diamond* at *Number* 26, as your past pitfalls show that you may do better by avoiding too much competition.

Success is practically sure at this stage, for the *Heart* at *Number* 27 favors any change of *circumstances*, so opportunity is yours at last, with your own representative card (2 H) to certify it. Even the *sorrow* of *Number* 28 will be softened by the *Heart* that appears there, indicating some further upturn in your fortune. As for *appreciation*, you will receive it from the *Heart* at *Number* 29, which makes three in a row, truly a triple triumph. As if that were not enough, the *Heart* at *Number* 30 hits just as *scandal* rears its ugly head. Don't let it disturb you, for with four Hearts in a row, you are immune to anything, so any criticism will be trifling.

Your *future prospects* gain a real boost from the *Diamond* at *Number 31*, where even jealousy will turn to your advantage. Those prospects include *affluence*, according to the *Diamond* at *Number 32*, but much of your profits may go to other people; particularly so if you show *neglect* of your own interests because of the *Diamond* at *Number 33*. With three Diamonds in succession, the pendulum is swinging dangerously wide and a bad card following could mean disaster, but happily, you have a *Heart* at *Number 34*, which promises *awards* in fullest measure. Whatever you may have lost will be trifling compared to the bounty indicated here.

Curiously and also happily, even *influence and power* may come your way despite the *Spade* at *Number 35*, for it refers back to the *Club* at *Number 6*, where "wishful thinking" was the theme. There, you were advised to be satisfied with what you could get, which meant rather meager pickings back in the early stages of the reading. But now, with big "awards" just promised by the *Heart* at *Number 34*, you can ride along with your imagination. Hope of realizing your wishes should be clinched by the *Heart* at *Number 36*, which adds *health* to the wealth and happiness that you may already have gained.

Over-all, this reading indicates an upward climb, limited only by how well you overcome adversity during the fitful starts and stops during the early stages. Any weakening there will throw uncertainty into the more favorable phases that are promised later, even to the point where their benefits may be lost.

INDIVIDUAL INTERPRETATIONS WITH THE SQUARE OF THIRTY-SIX

After completing the basic reading according to the general meanings of the suits, the reader can proceed with individual interpretations based on the position of the significator, or card representing the person who is the subject of the reading. Usually the 2 H serves in that capacity, so it will be considered in the present case.

Using the significator as the center of a nine-card square, the cards in the left column represent obstacles or complications that must be overcome; those in the right column are helpful or favorable to the subject; while the middle column stands for realization, whatever its degree. The middle cross-row denotes the present, while the row below is past and the row above pertains to the future. Since the significator is in the very center, it properly covers the status of the subject as of now.

This pattern holds with various types of readings, but with the Square of Thirty-six, it has special applications. The subject's present status is interpreted in terms of the square on which it appears, and the surrounding cards are read according to their respective squares. This serves the subject as a guide to the course that he should follow in relation to the general reading already given.

Continuing with the sample reading, the chart on the opposite page shows the significator and its surrounding cards, with the number and key definition of each space. The individual interpretation follows:

The 2 H as significator, is at *Number* 27, representing *circumstances* or condition. A Heart there is good in itself, and the significator particularly so, as it shows the subject to be adaptable to almost any circumstances and therefore able to take advantage of whatever offers. However, the subject is already handicapped, as can be seen by analyzing each row, starting with the lowest of the three:

The 8 D inverted at *Number* 33 indicates the existence of ill-will and annoyance through *neglect* of important interests. That feeling may be mutual, both on the part of the subject and that of any associates. For although the ingredients of wealth and success are close at hand—due to the 10 D at *Number* 32—it lies to the left, which means that hurdles will be encountered in attaining *affluence*. Fortunately, the 10 D is upright, but the subject can still lose a proper share of whatever it represents, unless care is exercised. The subject must also be prepared for spiteful actions on the part of envious persons (7 H inverted), but those should easily be counteracted, as *Number* 34, wherein this card appears, lies to the right, greatly favoring the subject's chance of winning *awards* that are rightfully due, despite any show of spite, which will probably be confined to social matters or affairs of the heart.

Taking the significator's own central row, the subject is strongly influenced by two other persons. One is an official of some sort, the J D at *Number* 26. Being on the left, this person may block the subject's *undertakings,* but through duty rather than hostility, as the card is upright. Typical examples would be a banker hesitant about granting a loan, or an athletic coach who demands that the subject work harder to make the team. On the right, the subject must strive against unhappiness and disappointment from the inverted J H at *Number* 28, which points to *sorrow* or uncertainty involving a close friend or relative upon whom the subject depends. Some unexpected situation and possibly an inheritance may result from this token.

Taking the top row, the 2 C at *Number* 20 is decidedly a warning, as it indicates a supposed friend or adviser who may prove false, due to *dishonesty* being the symbol of that square and the card being to the left. The 9 S threatens defeat or severe loss through *opposition,* at *Number* 21, unless the subject finds some way to circumvent it. This,

18) Square of Thirty-six: with the 2 H as significator, a personal interpretation can be read from this square of nine cards.

by an odd quirk, may be possible through the A S at *Number* 22, which is both upright and to the right, so that the *presents* signified by that square may include the natural endowments of purpose, responsibility, and esteem. This does not conflict with the earlier warning from the A S, as each is a special indication.

Summarized: Ill-will and annoyance engendered by neglect of interests (8 D inverted) can jeopardize the subject's best laid plans and present position (2 H) unless a natural adaptability is applied toward outwitting or avoiding conflict with opposing parties (9 S).

Hindering this is the fact that available funds are not forthcoming (10 D) and that some officious person (J D) refuses to grant needed or promised aid. This may work to the subject's advantage by offsetting the chicanery of a false friend or unscrupulous adviser who is trying to take over on his own (2 C).

However, from the very start, the subject can count on moral support and substantial aid that will smother the spite and envy (7 H inverted) of a few small critics. The unhappiness and sadness attending the possible loss of some friend or relative (J H inverted) will be assuaged by some good fortune that will further the subject's high purposes (A S) that promise ultimate achievement.

Whenever the significator appears in an outside row or column of the Square of Thirty-six, it causes a slight complication in the individual reading that follows. That reading depends on the formation of a nine-card square, with the significator in the exact center, which is impossible under the circumstances unless special allowance is made, as follows:

Consider the Square of Thirty-six to be the center of a block of nine such squares, all numbered in the same manner. However, it is only necessary to number those that border on the central Square of Thirty-six, as shown in the accompanying diagram. If the significator happens to be in an outside row, the nine-card square can be formed by simply projecting it across the border into an adjacent square.

Two examples are shown: In one, the significator is at Position 4; hence the nine-card square is composed of 33, 34, 35, 3, 4, 5, 9, 10, 11. Cards originally at 33, 34, 35, should be moved up to their new positions. In the other, the significator is at 31, so the nine-card square includes 30, 5, 6, 36, 31, 32, 6, 1, 2. Cards originally at 30, 36, 6, 1, 2 are moved to the new positions as shown.

GATE OF FATE

In this intriguing and distinctive method, all thirty-two cards of the pack are dealt in the form of a gate, as shown in the diagram (Fig. 20).

29 30							5 6
35 36	31	32	33	34	35	36	31 32
6	1	2	3	*	5	6	1
12	7	8	9	10	11	12	7
18	13	14	15	16	17	18	13
24	19	20	21	22	23	24	19
30	25	26	27	28	29	30	25
36	*	32	33	34	35	36	31
5 6	1	2	3	4	5	6	1 2
11 12							7 8

19) Square of Thirty-six: how to adjust the significator when it appears on the outside column.

The post at the left is read from the right side of the table, so that its cards can be identified as upright or inverted and interpreted accordingly. It symbolizes the subject's *past*, with the upper line (Cards 1, 2, 3, 4, 5, 6) representing the person's life in relation to others; the lower line (7, 8, 9, 10) the subject's inner emotions.

The top of the gate, which is read from the near end of the table, represents the *present* but broadly enough so that when the cards are read in order they can be taken as a transition from past to future. Again, the upper line (in this case Cards 11, 12, 13, 14, 15, 16, 17) is related to the affairs of daily life, whereas the lower line (Cards 18, 19, 20, 21, 22) indicates the subject's inward moods.

The post at the right, which is read from the left side of the table, relates strictly to the *future* and is read in the same fashion. The top line (composed of Cards 23, 24, 25, 26, 27, 28) reveals the subject's future as the world will see it, while the lower line (Cards 29, 30, 31, 32) is the key to the underlying emotions that will govern that coming period.

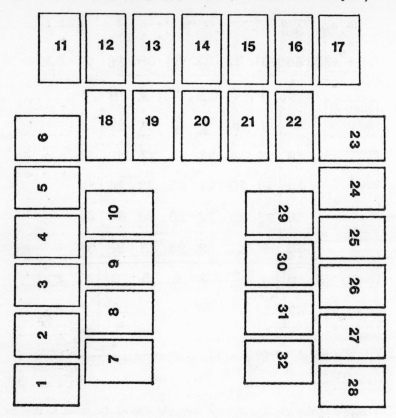

20) Divination with playing cards—fifty-two-card pack. The Gate of Fate: card pattern.

Each group of cards is interpreted in the order given, using the accepted Table of Card Significations (page 201) in the form of a running commentary.

Sample Reading for

the Gate of Fate

Subject: A young lady.

The Past

Outward Signification: A careless youth of her acquaintance (J H) caused her to lose friends and prestige (10 S reversed) through rumors

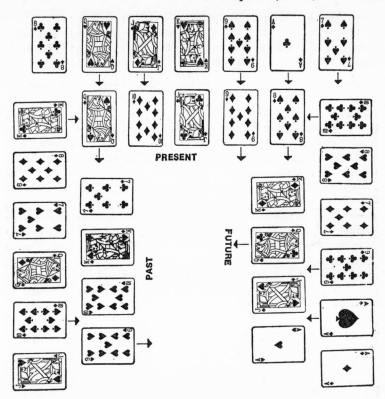

21) The Gate of Fate: sample reading.

spread by a stupid woman (Q D). However, the subject, acting wisely (7 H), found new friends (8 D) and reduced the whole episode to a minor disappointment (K C reversed).

Inward Signification: Brief unhappiness (9 H reversed) was offset by gaiety and new interests (10 H) involving a romantically inclined older man (K S) who did much to restore good will (7 C).

The Present

Outward Signification: Increasing affluence and affection (8 C) is threatened by a jealous woman (Q H reversed) and an unscrupulous man (J D reversed). A capable legal adviser (K H) is handling these recurrent problems (9 S reversed) so that future happiness is being delayed (A C reversed) only until indecision is ended (7 S reversed).

Inward Signification: The subject fears that a crafty rival (Q S reversed) may threaten her present hopes (10 D), but is depending upon a good friend (J C) to offset obstinate action (9 D reversed) that threatens disappointment in love (8 S reversed).

The Future

Outward Signification: A long trip may prove lucky for the subject (10 C reversed) with romance, realized hopes (8 H) and convivial companionship (7 D) threatened only by an urge to gamble (9 C reversed), which will bring sure disaster (A S reversed) unless a warning message is heeded (A D).

Inward Signification: A powerful and highly influential man (K D) can be of great help—if he only will!—but the subject may find it unwise to trust him too far. Her qualms on this score also include possible opposition from a crafty woman (Q C reversed) whose pose of friendliness is probably a pretense. Her only hope in such a fix would be dependence on a rough, aggressive, but dependable man (J S) who could do much to straighten matters and bring them to a highly satisfactory conclusion (A H). But it would be wise not to tempt fate too far.

XI. Divination with Playing Cards

USING THE FIFTY-TWO-CARD PACK

In the modern forms of divination with cards, a fifty-two-card pack is used, but whether these are preferable to the older thirty-two-card methods is a matter of personal opinion. In fact, many competent readers are apt to switch from one pack to the other to add variety to their work and in some cases to corroborate their findings.

Most fifty-two-card methods are better adapted to modern packs because no attention is given to "reversed" cards, which accordingly speeds and smooths the process. This reduces the total interpretations from sixty-four (two for each card in the thirty-two-card pack) to only fifty-two, but that is still enough for a good reading. Moreover, the fifty-two-card pack has its own special significations, which are broader in scope than those of the thirty-two-card pack, and its methods have their own layouts and procedures, expressly designed for added results.

The suits of the fifty-two-card pack conform to the traditional pattern but are somewhat more flexible, since no "reversed" cards are involved. Thus, *Hearts*, while denoting romance, kindness, and affection, can indicate emotional stress when adverse cards are close by. *Clubs*, indicative of prestige and influence, can offset bad signs, but only to a certain point, beyond which they may weaken.

Diamonds waver between practicality and difficulty. They are apt to represent unfinished business, a symbol that something more is needed to ensure success, so don't depend on them too heavily. However, *Spades*, so often regarded as bad cards or as heralds of misfortune, may supply helpful and timely warnings, an important factor to remember.

TABLE OF CARD SIGNIFICATIONS
With Pack of 52 Cards

ACES

H This signifies home and domestic happiness. May be news from friends or family, perhaps a change of surroundings. Can also be domestic problems.

C This represents success, wealth, renown, and many friends who help to bring the desired goal to the consultant.

D This may mean money or a gift. If there is an adjacent card, it indicates a message by letter. For a woman, an engagement ring.

S Known as the "death" card or bad luck not necessarily for the consultant, but certainly bad news. May mean quarrels with a loved one or a friend.

KINGS

H An influential man who wishes to help the consultant, but it only results in disagreement, heated arguments.

C A loyal friend and adviser, a relative of a woman consultant. To a man consultant it means a rival with great generosity, thereby causing trouble.

D Considered a ruthless man in business, a dangerous rival in love. For women this card signifies an unfaithful lover or husband.

S A man so ambitious that he can upset a business or a marriage. According to adjacent cards, it warns a woman about an incompatible, worthless man.

QUEENS

H For a man, this card represents his true love or amour. For a woman consultant, it means a rival even though unaware of it.

C A fine woman who is a wife or close confidante to a man. A close friend to the woman consultant.

D This represents the woman who interferes with a man's business affairs. Otherwise a jealous and dangerous woman even to her own sex.

S Sign of a cruel, ruthless woman who takes advantage of both men and women. Likely to appear very friendly but really insincere.

JACKS

H   A person who is very close to the consultant. Can be a friend or a relative but one who has been known to the consultant for many years.

C   A friend, male or female, who is kind and thoughtful. A helpful person who sees the consultant's best qualities and says so.

D   This card usually means bad news for women, brought by a male friend or relative. Adjacent good cards modify this. It is not especially bad for a male consultant.

S   A partner or friend who is indifferent and too lazy to help the consultant in business or social organizations.

TENS

H   An excellent card meaning success, luck, and an element of surprise. It counterbalances bad cards and strengthens good ones.

C   A very lucky card bringing happiness and good fortune. Wards off bad influences. Can also mean a long journey.

D   Money is usually involved when this card appears. It may indicate an unexpected journey or marriage.

S   This card negates adjacent good cards and doubles the troubles of bad cards. A truly unlucky card.

NINES

H   This is the "wish" card that promises fulfillment of wishes and success in projects as shown by adjacent cards. If these cards are bad, they indicate obstacles that can be overcome.

C   Not a helpful card. It indicates disagreements with friends and obstinacy by the consultant, which can harm self and success.

D   This represents money that the consultant wants for advancement, travel, or just plain adventure. If the nearby cards are bad, there may be bad news about money.

S   Loss of money, illness, frustration, everything bad are the meanings of this card, the worst in the pack. Even good cards near it cannot help.

EIGHTS

H   This card is the prediction of a pleasurable event, something that has been dated and known to the consultant. Nearby cards may be in accord or present slight disappointment.

C   A desire for money even to the point of borrowing to gamble for more. It may refer to a project undertaken with friends of the consultant.

D   Several meanings here combining courtship, marriage, and travel. It can take place early or late in life. Check adjoining cards.

S   This is a warning that the consultant may have false friends, but the warning should be in time to offset problems and possessions.

SEVENS

H   Disappointment is the keynote to warn the consultant that present plans will not materialize. Do not rely upon friends or associates who may be part of the plans.

C   If surrounding cards are good, the seven augurs good luck and success, but there must be no interference or opposition from the opposite sex.

D   A sign of bad luck. It refers to the gambler, the loser. Bad time to venture into new enterprises or change of purpose. Also warns of unwarranted criticism.

S   A card of sorrow. Avoid quarrels with anyone no matter how trying. Hold all discussions until bad luck turns to good.

SIXES

H   A warning that the consultant's generosity may be imposed upon. A weakness that conniving people will use to their advantage.

C   A success card pertaining to business, usually with friends. A time to seek advice from them or perhaps raise funds.

D   Usually signifies an early marriage ending in frustration. Threatens unhappiness if a second marriage, depending upon surrounding cards.

S   A discouraging card for work and plans that bring little or no results. However, perseverance can turn failure into good luck.

FIVES

H   Indecision haunts the consultant in personal and/or business matters. The surrounding cards sometimes indicate new surroundings just to get away from immediate problems.

C   This card indicates a marriage or liaison with a wealthy mate. Also foretells prosperity for both. Balance the related cards.

D   Good luck and prosperity in business. Great happiness in marriage. A life filled with enduring friendships.

S   The consultant may be too easily discouraged; however, with good surrounding cards success and a happy married life result in spite of reverses.

FOURS

H This is the card of the unmarried person, usually due to a personal reason or fault, but nearby cards may indicate a long-delayed marriage or a very late one.

C Misfortune, danger, or losses may injure this person's affairs because of insincere, unreliable friends. Check other cards for escape or avoidance.

D Quarrels with family or certain friends are indicated. Time to renew an old friendship. Avoid interference from relatives or overanxious friends.

S Jealousy, illness, or financial upsets will disturb the consultant's personal or business affairs. Close cards can show a way out.

THREES

H An unfavorable card threatening impulsive, bad decisions and actions on the part of the consultant. Time to slow down.

C A marriage card promising two or three marriages. It can mean a long courtship or engagement that breaks up but followed by marriage to someone else.

D This predicts marital problems ending in divorce or dissolution of some sort. Can also refer to disputes in business that end in legal action.

S Unhappiness and great disappointment in a love affair or marriage. The consultant must turn to other interests and forget the past.

TWOS

H Good fortune, greater than anticipated. If the adjacent cards are bad, it only means that the success will take a little longer in arriving because of minor obstacles.

C This card warns the consultant that all efforts must be executed alone. No use to depend upon others for help because of their opposition.

D An amour that could result in marriage if the other cards agree. If not, the love affair might hinder the consultant in future projects that could lead to a successful life.

S Known as a death card, separation, or change. It can refer to a separation from a loved one, a loss of some sort, or a journey. Adjacent cards could make the change definitive.

Note: In addition to the individual interpretations listed, there are certain cards that carry special significance when they appear in com-

♥	♣	♦	♠	
2		10		Romance and finance, happily combined.
		J	Q	A dangerous or dubious alliance, be wary!
4			A	A new influence will mean big changes.
	K		A	Someone important will shape your future.
			A-10	Impending problems should be settled now.
		9	7	Unexpected happiness may be short-lived.
5		8		Some money may be coming your way soon.
5-8				Don't be surprised if you receive a gift.
		7	6	Avoid a scheme that may cost you money.
9			5	Don't count on some promised honor.
	2	3		Whatever you don't expect, expect it.
	8		A	A big argument is due, maybe over nothing.
	ANY		10	Business problems, which may be doubled.
A-ANY				Happy friendships, doubled, big romance.
A		ANY		Plenty of money. Get all that you can.

22) Divination with playing cards—fifty-two-card pack. Sample reading of certain cards of special significance in interpretation.

bination, one adjacent to the other. These are shown in the chart opposite, so be on watch for them. In the chart, the word "Any" means any card of that specified suit. For example: Any C with the 10 S would mean "business problems; possibly doubled." Should two cards of that suit flank the single card—say, in this case, 5 C 10 S 9 C—the message becomes extremely urgent.

SIMPLEX SYSTEM

One of the quickest and most practical ways of interpreting the cards with a full pack of fifty-two is to read certain cards as you deal them, pausing to give each designated card a careful study. Beginners can refer to the list of individual meanings while doing this, making it all the easier. Yet even after proficiency has been gained and those meanings spring to mind almost automatically, this is still a good, efficient method of telling fortunes.

First, shuffle the pack thoroughly and hand it to the person whose fortune you intend to tell, asking him or her to do the same. The person then cuts the pack with the left hand and you complete the cut, holding the pack face down in readiness for the deal, which proceeds as follows:

Turn the cards face up, one by one, repeating softly, "Diamond, Club, Heart, Spade, Picture—" and continuing that rotation. Whenever a card turns up as stated, you lay it in a separate pile and interpret it according to the chart. Go through the entire pack in that fashion and at the finish you will be surprised how well the cards have formed a connected story.

For example: Suppose you deal 4 H, 4 S, 8 H. As you call off, "Diamond, Club, Heart," you would pause on the 8 H, lay it aside, and state, "You can look forward to a happy event, one that you may have been planning for a long time," and then continue the deal, which might run 10 C, 4 D, 2 S, J D, 6 S, K S. Since you are calling off, "Spade, Picture, Diamond, Club, Heart, Spade," you would pause again and deal the K S on the 8 H, stating: "There you will meet a very aggressive man who may make trouble unless you recognize his importance."

Keep on, laying aside all cards that hit according to your formula. Suppose that the following are called and laid in this order: 8 H, K S, 2 H, 7 S, 6 D, 5 C, J H, K C, Q H, 9 D, 8 C, 9 H. Your interpretation would run like this:

23) Simplex system: significant cards chosen by the "Diamond, Club, Heart, Spade, Picture" formula.

"You are looking forward to a long-planned occasion [8 H] which involves a man who is assertive and apt to make trouble [K S] unless you win his friendship, in which case he may be helpful [7 S], particularly if an early marriage is involved as it can end unhappily [6 D] unless those concerned have enough money to enjoy it and live harmoniously [5 C].

"Otherwise, help may be needed to keep the course of true love smooth. It may come from a boyhood friend or college chum [J H] or better still, through financial help from an older relative or adviser [K C], the teamwork of a loving, trusting wife [Q H] and a hard-working husband who will go far to find an opportunity [9 D] but is apt to ruin it through sheer obstinacy, which may cause loss of needed friends [8 C] although any of these problems may be overcome, with happiness as the ultimate attainment [9 H]."

Note that this has been told in a somewhat impersonal way, as though the consultant were a mere observer, or even a totally disinterested party, which may be true with some readings. More often, the consultant is eager for a personalized reading. So if the cards prove applicable to such an individual, they should be interpreted accordingly.

In the case just given, the consultant might be a young man planning marriage under circumstances like those described. So the more direct the reading the better. There might even be hints as to the identity of the "friend" (J H) or the "adviser" (K C) or the type of "job" he would travel far to get (9 D).

However, with a woman as consultant, such cards might be interpreted quite differently. The "friend" (J H) could be a former suitor, the "adviser" (K C) might be a lawyer who would represent her in a divorce suit because of "another woman" (Q H), responsible for her husband's long absences from home (9 D).

In going through the pack, at least ten cards should be laid out, as

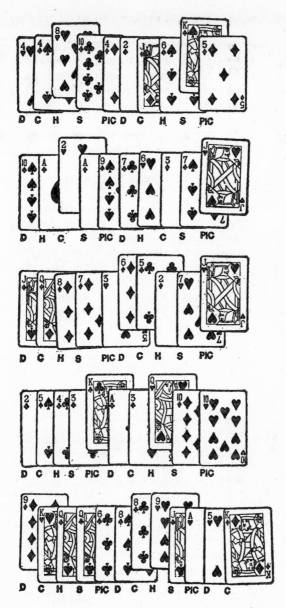

24) Example of how cards are called off and retained for use in the Simplex system.

described. There are twelve in the example given, so it would be satisfactory. If you fall short of ten, turn the pack face down—as it should be at the start—and continue to deal through, calling, "Heart—Spade—Picture—Diamond—Club—Heart—Spade—Picture—" and so on, laying aside any cards that hit, as additions to the row that you have just interpreted.

The reason that you start with a Heart is that in running through the original fifty-two cards in the pack, your final call is sure to be a Club, so in making your second trip, you naturally resume the rotation from that point. If the reading itself seems interrupted or too short, even with more than ten cards on the first run through, it is quite permissible to go through the pack a second time to gain a fuller reading. But a third trip is inadvisable, as it may produce conflicts that would detract from an otherwise well-developed fortune.

It should be specially noted that any face cards have two chances to "hit" and therefore be selected during the deal. They may hit when their suit is named or on the call of "Picture." In the accompanying layout, which shows the cards that were drawn in the sample deal, the K S hit on a call of "Spade" and the Q H on "Heart." In contrast, both the J H and the K C hit on the call of "Picture."

Aces are not counted as picture cards, but simply as spots, hence they are not drawn for interpretation unless their suit is called. In the sample layout, the A C hit on the call of "Picture," but that did not count.

SQUARE OF SEVENTEEN

In basic form, this direct type of reading is concentrated on a card representing the consultant, namely a King or Queen, for man or woman, as the case may be. This card is placed face up in a square of seventeen cards as shown in the accompanying diagram, the other sixteen cards being dealt face up, as well.

The reading proceeds as follows:

Past: Study the cards in the row from upper left to lower right and interpret them according to the Table of Significations, but applied to the consultant's past, and no more.

Present: Study and interpret the cards in the row from upper right to lower left.

Future: Do the same with the cards in the central cross row from left to right, but allow for the next interpretation.

Surprise: This is read straight downward from top to bottom of the layout and may modify the previous readings, either strengthening them or serving as a warning.

However, to give the reading unusual impact, instead of placing a King or Queen in the center, a random card may be dealt there, to establish the nature of the reading. Thus a 7 S as the focal card would make quarrels or disputes the theme to be considered, as the 7 S is the center card in all four rows.

The 5 H, as the central card, would cover matters on which the consultant is undecided; the 10 C would tell how well the consultant's good luck has held, is holding, and will hold. The same would apply to any other focal card that might be dealt.

If the center card does not particularly interest the consultant, he can call for another or even name the type of card that he thinks is most pertinent to a matter of import to himself. Once such a focal card is placed, the pack should be shuffled before dealing the rest.

In the layout on page 256, the 4 D has been dealt as a focal card, indicating disputes or interference in matters involving family or friends, surrounded by other cards as shown. The four rows thus formed would be read in brief as follows:

In the past, you planned many things that failed to materialize as hoped (6 S), because someone close to you (J H) either was left out or wouldn't go along with your ideas (4 D). The result was a complete change of plans or scene (2 S), which eventually turned out well and perhaps for the better (5 D).

In the present, you are enjoying life and planning a good time (8 H) with money and perhaps gambling involved (8 C). Again, you are inclined to disregard your friends and may even now be hurting your own aims (4 D). If such disputes cause you to lose your present doubtful associates (J S), you may be better off, as you are plagued by indecision (5 S) and may really be looking for some form of escape.

In the future, you will meet a kindly, influential man (K H) who may counteract the efforts of a ruthless schemer (K D), and by letting them dispute any issues that arise (4 D) things should work out strongly in your favor (10 H), perhaps far beyond your expectations, with great results from an unexpected source (10 C).

As a surprise, new disputes may cost you friends (9 C) and bring setbacks due to your impetuous actions (3 H), which will bring old issues to the fore (4 D) and confront you with serious obstacles (4 C) that will fortunately prove to be only temporary (9 H), so that all should come your way at last.

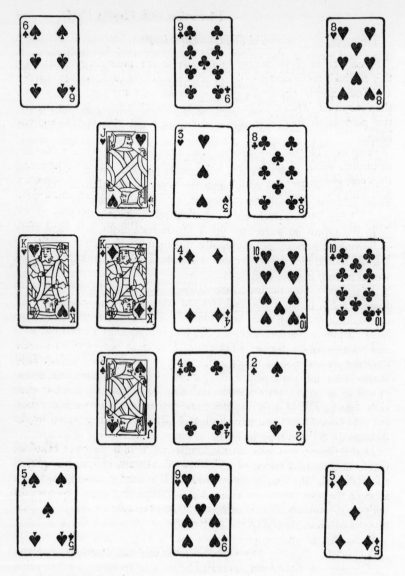

25) Divination with playing cards—fifty-two-card pack. Square of Seventeen: layout and sample reading.

FATEFUL SQUARE

Since chance plays an important part in the preliminary phases of this method, its results should be very gratifying and in fact usually are. You begin by drawing a King or Queen from the pack to represent the consultant. That card is temporarily laid aside face up and the entire pack is shuffled face down, cut, and dealt into two face-down heaps.

From each heap, a random card is drawn face down and the two are discarded, being of no further use. The two heaps are then shuffled together, giving you a pack of forty-nine cards, since you have already laid aside the consultant's card and discarded the two that are unneeded.

Now, from the pack, deal a row of three cards, face down; below that, another row of three; and below that, still another such row, making nine cards in all, represented by letters of the alphabet, in regular order, thus:

A   B   C
D   E   F
G   H   I

That done, you lay the next or tenth card to one side, as a start toward a "surprise." This card, like those in the square, is dealt face down. You then proceed to deal nine more cards on the original rows, in order "A" to "I" just as before, but this time, you skip the surprise. Deal nine more cards on the rows and add one to the surprise, then deal nine, skipping the surprise; finally, deal another nine, again adding one to the surprise.

That will give you nine piles of five cards each, a "surprise heap" of three cards, and an odd card still in hand. Already, chance has played a fateful part, but it is due for still more. The card you now hold is to serve as the selector for a combination of heaps that are to be used in the coming fortune, so you turn it face up and note its suit. You then proceed according to the following formula:

If the selector card is:

A *Spade*:   Gather three heaps diagonally from upper left to lower right (heaps, A, E, I).

A *Club*:   Gather three heaps diagonally from upper right to lower left (heaps C, E, G).

A *Heart*:   Gather three heaps from upper center, downward (heaps B, E, H).

A *Diamond*: Gather the three heaps in the center row, across from left to right (heaps D, E, F).

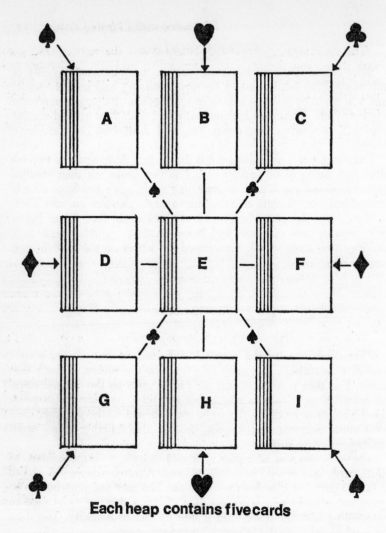

Each heap contains five cards

26) Divination with playing cards—fifty-two-card pack. Fateful Square: card layout.

The six remaining heaps are discarded and the selector card goes with them. You then take the consultant's card, or significator, and add it to the chosen group, inserting it face down among them, giving you sixteen cards in all. These are thoroughly shuffled, cut, and dealt four rows of four cards each, face up; a row from left to right, then right to left, again left to right and finally right to left, so they lie in the following order:

$$
\begin{array}{cccc}
1 & 2 & 3 & 4 \\
8 & 7 & 6 & 5 \\
9 & 10 & 11 & 12 \\
16 & 15 & 14 & 13
\end{array}
$$

This is important, as it represents the order in which the cards are to be read, beginning with Number 1 and ending with Number 16. Each card is interpreted according to the usual table, being linked directly with the two adjacent to it in the order given. Thus 1 links with 2; 2 with 1 and 3; 3 with 2 and 4; 4 with 3 and 5; 5 with 4 and 6; and so on.

When you come to the significator, wherever it happens to lie, special attention should be given to the cards flanking it, as they may represent something of immediate or vital importance to the consultant himself, whereas some of the other indications may only indirectly concern him. Since the reading itself is done in continuous form, Card 1 represents the beginning and Card 16 the finish; hence 1 links only 2 and 15 only with 16. But the over-all reading includes all and you may revert back to any preceding card as you continue.

After concluding the reading of the sixteen cards, the three representing the surprise are turned up and interpreted according to their lights. They serve chiefly to modify the main reading, often providing a ray of hope to an otherwise poor reading, or occasionally furnishing a warning note if the general interpretation sounds too good.

INTERPRETATION OF THE FATEFUL SQUARE

SIGNIFICATOR K H

REPRESENTING A SOMEWHAT AMBITIOUS YOUNG MAN

Watch out for an envious and conniving acquaintance (J D) who may urge you to go after new projects so that he can take over those

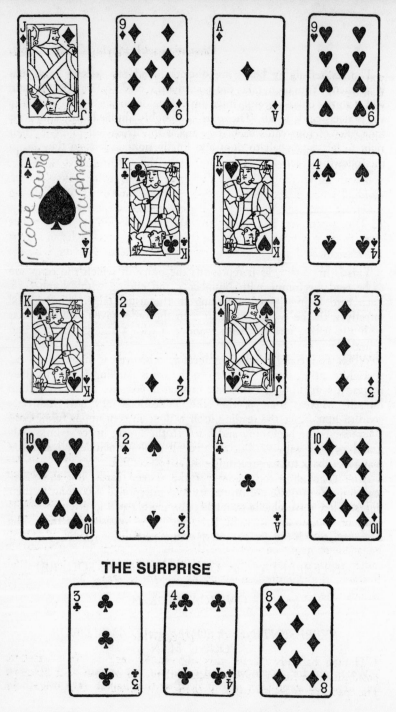

THE SURPRISE

27) The Fateful Square: final layout and sample interpretation.

you already have. Money (9 D) may already be involved, and by waiting for an important message that may concern it (A D) you may be able to dictate terms, as opportunity is sure to come your way (9 H) despite minor misfortunes or petty jealousies from the source already mentioned (4 S). You can depend on two men to help you with such problems (K H and K C) so cultivate their friendship, as you will need it even more if a threatening misfortune (A S) strikes you with all its deadly reality. This may involve an unscrupulous individual who will take advantage of all your difficulties (K S), even upsetting your romantic life and plans pertaining to your marriage (2 D). Again, you will do better to depend on sound advisers rather than trust your business affairs to a fair-weather friend who is a good promiser (J S) but will put his own interests ahead of yours. Disputes and arguments will be further upsetting to your business and home life (3 D), but if you manage to hold things together, all troubles will be forgotten in the light of great and perhaps unexpected good fortune involving money, a long journey, and possibly marriage (10 D). Wealth, fame, and influential friends are potentially yours (A C). They will be needed when serious problems threaten (2 S), but those should be counteracted by luck and ultimate success (10 H).

The Surprise: 4 C, 3 C, 8 D

Here we find a remarkable corroboration of the main interpretation, namely:

Misfortune, failure, and even the insincerity of false friends or associates (4 C) are strongly indicated here, along with the prospects of a second or even a third marriage (3 C), which is confirmed by an indication of extensive travel and a marriage late in life (8 D).

Note: As with all readings that stress business or marital problems, this one should take account of the consultant's present status. With a young, unmarried subject, a simple job might be at stake, or an engagement might be broken, both being interpreted as comparatively minor setbacks. With a married man already established in his own business, the situations indicated by the cards would assume a more serious tone.

MYSTIC PYRAMID

Though basically simple, this cartomantic method offers excellent possibilities for individualistic treatment, as will be seen as it develops. The pack of fifty-two cards is thoroughly shuffled, then, from the top, fifteen cards are dealt face upward, forming rows of 1, 2, 3, 4, 5 cards, respectively (see Fig. 28).

Starting with the top card, the rest are interpreted through an interweaving method that can best be illustrated by the accompanying example, which applies to a woman as questioner:

Travel or marriage later in life (8 D) may involve an ambitious but dangerous man (K S) although luck may nullify any problems (7 C). Note how the single card in the top row is linked to both cards in the second row. Then proceed:

The man involved (K S) may promise domestic happiness, but with family complications (A H) that are sure to be accentuated by the unhappiness of the accompanying card (3 S). Similarly, the good luck already indicated (7 C) must also outlast unhappiness (3 S) because the risk of gambling or false rumor (7 D) is involved. In short, each card gathers import from the two cards linked below it.

In reverting to home affairs (A H), those may be helped by money (10 D) and a man of good intent (K H). Here, we skip the central card (3 S) and consider the gambling factor (7 D), which may be accentuated by reckless action (2 H) that may retard favorable business projects (4 S).

However: The presence of money (10 D), although good in itself, may cause disputes (7 S) that can be offset by perseverance (6 S). The kindly man (K H) should be an excellent partner (6 C) because he has ability in managing money (8 C), provided he is not the one who gambles it! The reckless trend (2 H) is accentuated by the gambling urge (8 C), so it is still a danger, but there is business prosperity (5 D) that may offset it. Any minor problems (4 S) may be nullified by prosperity (5 D) and advice or financial aid from friends (6 C), which strikes the final note.

Final, that is, except for the over-all theme of unhappiness as indicated by the central card (3 S) with omen of misfortune in love or marriage. The fact that it was skipped during the interlocking reading only emphasizes its importance. Wherever there is doubt, the central card may be regarded as a helpful or harmful factor, as the case may be.

This type of reading offers excellent possibilities for intepretation by anyone experienced in cartomancy, as fine points of comparison may be drawn between linked cards, by favoring one link rather than the other. That allows scope for intuition, which skilled card readers regard as their most potent faculty.

28) Divination with playing cards—fifty-two-card pack. The Mystic Pyramid: card layout.

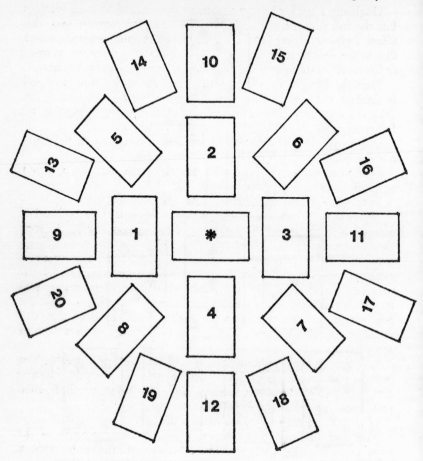

29) Divination with playing cards—fifty-two-card pack. The Wheel of Fortune: card layout.

WHEEL OF FORTUNE

This highly recommended type of reading depends upon the pairing of various cards that have been laid out to represent a Wheel of Fortune. There are twenty-one cards in all, including the central card, which represents the subject of the reading and should therefore be represented by the King or Queen of an appropriate suit.

Originally a pack of thirty-two cards was utilized in such readings, but the full fifty-two are preferable for two good reasons: first, they afford a greater variety with a broader scope of interpretation; second, due to the very form of the wheel, it is difficult to recognize reversed or "inverted" cards, as required with the abridged pack of thirty-two.

Place the King or Queen crosswise, face up on the table, the pack is shuffled, cut, and given a preliminary reading if so desired. Then, from the face-down pack, cards are dealt face up, one by one, in the following order:

One to the left of the center card, one above, one to the right, and one below (1, 2, 3, 4).

Four more cards, one from each corner of the center: upper left, upper right, lower right, lower left (5, 6, 7, 8).

Four more extending left, above, right, and below (9, 10, 11, 12).

Eight more, starting just above the card projecting to the left and filling the spaces in between, running in clockwise fashion, to form an outer wheel (13, 14, 15, 16, 17, 18, 19, 20).

All is then ready for the reading, which begins with the outermost cards and works inward. Note that this is the opposite of many systems, which start from the significator, namely the subject's card, and ascribe important meanings to the cards immediately surrounding it, with the rest lessening in consequence as the reading proceeds. Here, the more remote cards are interpreted first, so that the reading becomes stronger as it proceeds.

Still, there is good initial impact, as the cards are considered in pairs, providing occasional conflict and sometimes double strength. There is a regular formula for these pairings, the cards being matched, interpreted, and then discarded as follows:

15 with 14 ; 13 with 20; 19 with 18; 17 with 16.

Note that this is done in counterclockwise fashion, disposing of the eight cards forming the rim of the wheel. Next, the inner circle is treated in the same manner:

10 with 6; 9 with 5; 12 with 8; 11 with 7.

Here, references may be made to the earlier pairs if their significance is lessened by the new and stronger group of eight. After that the central four are paired:

3 with 2; 1 with 4.

Those, of course, are strongest of all, completing the brief but sharply pointed reading, in terms of the significator. The interpretations are those given in the standard Table of Card Significations (see page 246), but the paired readings cause them to vary from the regular pattern. This becomes quite evident from the following reading, which is taken from the layout shown in the previous diagram.

30) Wheel of Fortune: sample reading.

The man who is the subject of the reading (K C) either will be or has been engaged for a long period (4 H), terminating in a wedding (8 H) of an elaborate or unusual type (pair up 4 H and 8 H).

During the subject's quest for money and adventure (9 D) he rouses the interest and sympathy of a very susceptible and possibly wealthy woman (Q D) who becomes involved quite deeply and perhaps too deeply in his affairs (pair up 9 D and Q D).

At first the subject's wife or bride to be (Q C) is unaware of this, but she receives a sharp and pointed warning of the situation (A S), which threatens her hope of marital bliss (pair up Q C and A S). Note specially the strong significance of the A S in this instance, as it has various interpretations that fit the case.

The situation, whether merely mild or really serious, rapidly goes from bad to worse (10 S) and assumes such psychological proportions that the subject is totally undecided as to what to do about it (5 H) and may even try to run out on the situation (pair up 10 S and 5 H).

That finishes the first set of pairs, bringing the reading to a crux at the very point where it comes closer to the center, the inner circle showing definite developments of indications from the outer. Immediate significations are drawn as follows:

The problem of domestic happiness looms large, perhaps involving other members of the family (A H) and demanding a prompt answer. A surprise solution is offered and accepted, smoothing the situation (10 H) and promising good fortune for all concerned (pair up A H and 10 H).

Naturally, such results hinge on what follows, and, as is to be expected under such rosy but strained circumstances, disputes arise, of the sort that bring real trouble (9 C), which gives rise to false rumors. To make it worse, money may be wasted wildly (7 D) and the whole sticky setup threatened with a total crack-up.

Marriage and romance both are apt to end, with a rift between the subject and his new love as well (6 D) if that has not already come about. New plans will prove futile (6 S) and the subject's only course is to shake off his discouragement and hope for better luck (pair up 6 D and 6 S).

This is strongly corroborated by the next pair of cards. Misfortune through love or marriage (3 S) must definitely be forgotten to regain stability, but unfortunately, the subject is swayed by false hopes and hasty promises (7 H), which may come from sympathizers whose plight is as uncertain as his own (pair up 3 S and 7 H).

Having produced this cliff-hanger, the reading comes right home to the four cards surrounding the significator. It is up to them to provide the final answer, which they do in these terms:

The subject does what he should have done long before, although then the time might not have been ripe for it. He seeks the advice of a generous, sincere friend (J C) whose worth may have been proven during all the problems that the subject has undergone. Whether this restores past ideals or opens new vistas is a tossup. Certainly it does one or the other (2 D) by either furthering romance or interfering with it (pair up J C and 2 D).

Whichever the case, quarrels are sure to arise, involving friends and family (4 D), which are to be expected because of the subject's turbulent career, and therefore may be for the better. That is almost certainly assured by one of the best cards in the pack (9 H), which promises harmony, happiness, and the fulfillment of long-cherished dreams. How much for the better time alone will tell, for even the lucky card (9 H) cannot counteract all that may have gone before (pair up 4 D and 9 H).

This completes the reading according to the Wheel of Fortune. However, a wide range of interpretation is allowable, dependent both on the person whose "fortune" is under scrutiny and the person's own attitude toward the procedure. This sample has been geared to the traditional pattern, wherein the "subject" is a mature person presumably vexed with deep, complex problems, who is seriously consulting the "reader" regarding the probable outcome over an extended period of time.

But today, when such readings may come under the head of "fun and games" rather than a full-fledged "prognostication," it could take a totally different tack. The subject might be a flippant youth who is wondering whether he should drop out of high school just to spite a girl friend who has accepted someone else as her "date" for the senior prom.

Here, the introduction of a feminine rival (Q D as opposed to Q C) could merely mean that the youth's best plan would be to date another girl and thus stir up a tempest in a teapot which would boil away between the night of the prom and graduation day. The whole trivial episode would cover a few months at most, and with the happy ending (9 H) all animosity would be forgotten. The participants would go on to bigger things in life, worthy of another spin on the Wheel of Fortune.

XII. Cheiromancy

Divination from the study of the hand was practiced by Chinese savants as early as 3200 B.C., and during the next few thousand years it spread westward through India and Persia, finally reaching Europe, where many Greek philosophers gave serious consideration to the subject. Among these was Aristotle, who tutored Alexander the Great, around 340 B.C., and may very well have used it to prognosticate his pupil's illustrious future. Mystics and occultists of the Middle Ages added new theories and observations, so that following the invention of printing a comprehensive literature on cheiromancy was developed, offering many findings that have met the test of time and are still highly regarded at present.

In modern times, special emphasis has been placed upon the study of cheirognomy, which has to do with hand shapes and general formations, more than the lines of the palm, although all such factors are considered in cheiromancy as well. The two have long since merged under the popular term of palmistry and have constantly come to corroborate each other, so that traditions of the past are supported by modern scientific study. Hence, instead of limiting this survey to the old-time cheiromancy—or cheirosophy, as it is also termed—it is given a broader treatment, covering all features of the hand in concise order, as traits or prospects rather than fixed, immutable determinants. From these, the reader can form his own cheiromantic forecasts.

THE ART OF CHEIROMANCY
(divination by palm reading)

Palmistry traditionally represents the analysis of personal characteristics or disappointments during life's span. It has many intricacies that

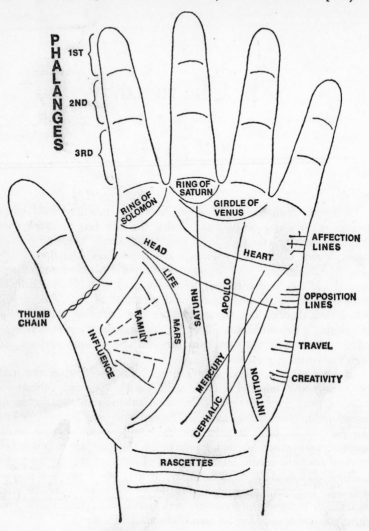

31) General lines of the palm.

depend upon the amount of study that the reader can devote to it. Shapes of the hand, fingers, and thumb; physical consistencies of the hand; lines, marks, and signs, will by degrees and careful study produce a most gratifying knowledge of the lives of each human being. Every-

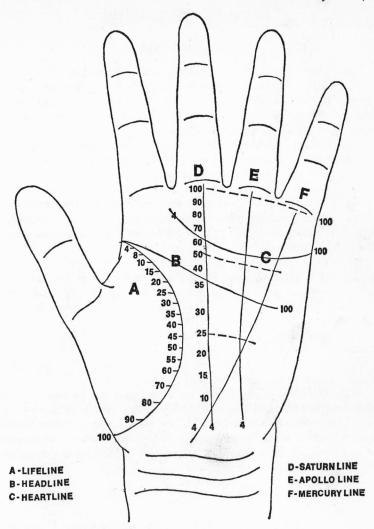

A - LIFELINE
B - HEADLINE
C - HEARTLINE

D - SATURN LINE
E - APOLLO LINE
F - MERCURY LINE

32) Time gauge.

one is so different, so similar, so complex, but compounded into a very identifiable and most interesting you, me, and everybody. And so, as follows, is a simplified version of the Art of Cheiromancy, or Hand Analysis.

SHAPES OF HANDS

(also called types)

Lines and signs are variable according to the hand shape.

SQUARE HAND—Square palm, squared-off fingertips or slightly round. *Practical*, like to be *useful*, helpful to others. Need definite plans and projects to follow. *Orderly*. All predictions of the palm mounts, lines, and signs are modified accordingly.

CONICAL HAND—Whole hand tapers from base to fingertips, giving an oval appearance in shape. Fingertips rounded or oval. *Exuberant, inspirational, receptive*, good company, need to be urged to activate their talents. All predictions must be treated accordingly.

SPATULATE HAND—Over-all appearance of the spatulate is fan-shaped. Palm is either wider at the top or at the base. Fingertips spatulate. *Very active, energetic, original*. Avoid extremes. The spatulate hand increases the evaluation of predictions.

POINTED HAND—So-called psychic hand—*idealistic, intuitive, philosophical*. Narrow, long, and pointed hand. This is the one hand where a very long thumb can detract in great proportion, and there are many such hands. Lines and signs in the palm may ameliorate or expand the qualities.

PHILOSOPHICAL HAND—Knots on both joints of the fingers. Square or conical fingertips. Hands are long, lean, strong. Teachers, philosophers, writers. Many *brilliant minds* have this type hand. *Good students* at any age. *The inquiring mind.*

MIXED HAND—The fingers are mixed and can be any type. If spatulate predominates, the individual possesses more than average energy. The thumb in a mixed hand is the ruling factor. A square thumb adds a practical trend; conic modifies with an artistic bent; the pointed is very idealistic, often intuitive. The length of the thumb determines the degree of will power, reason, and logic. *Adaptable.*

CONSISTENCY OF HANDS

(also called texture)

FLABBY—May be *lazy* and *indifferent*. Strength of mind depends upon the lines and signs in the palm. Often find a *lucrative way of living. Incredible moods* and *temperament*.

SOFT—Listless and limp to the touch. Work is well within their scope. Can be very annoying to other people. Sometimes selfish. Can be very successful, even famous.

FIRM HANDS—Determined. Not easily defeated.

HARD HANDS—Very firm or stiff. Usually opinionated, resolute.

SIZE OF HANDS

(in proportion to the body)

LARGE HANDS—Usually excellent with details.

SMALL HANDS—Should ignore details if possible. Quick perception.

NARROW HANDS—Not usually sociable, not easily adaptable to new surroundings, but can be very successful.

BROAD HANDS—Good mixer. Enjoys work as well as play and relaxation.

FLEXIBILITY

STIFF HANDS—These hands do not bend and their owners are not easily swayed. Dependable.

MEDIUM FLEXIBLE—Considerate and reasonable.

VERY FLEXIBLE—Unconventional, often nonconformists. Talented.

NAILS

SHORT—critical
WIDE—outspoken; *WIDE* and *SHORT*—very critical
NARROW—secretive
FLUTED—nervous
RIDGED (crosswise)—periods of stress or illness
BULBOUS—jealous nature
TILTED OUTWARD—talented
WEDGE (narrow at the base)—too sensitive

FINGERS

(check with illustration of mount areas, thumb, and fingers)

Fingers are named the same as the mount areas beneath them.

First finger, Jupiter—ambition; *second finger, Saturn*—wisdom; *third finger, Apollo*—achievement; *fourth finger, Mercury*—discernment.

LENGTH: Long fingers increase the qualities and *like detail* work. *Short fingers* decrease the evaluation, indicate *impatience. Very long fingers*—exaggeration.

TYPE (SHAPE): Pointed fingers will indicate a desire for *idealism* in ambition, *et al. Conic fingers* will lend *inspiration* to wisdom, *et al. Square fingers* will add *practicality* and *orderliness* to occupation, *et al. Spatulate fingers* will bring *added energy to talent, et al.* FLEXIBILITY—same as thumbs.

JOINTS: Knotted upper joints—good reasoning; *Knotted lower joints*—common sense, practical. *No knots, smooth joints*—can be impulsive.

PECULIARITIES: Crooked fingers—irresponsible. *Thick fingers*—indulgence. *First finger very long*—passion to rule; *second very long*—devoted scholar or philosopher; *third*—the gambler even on personal ability; *fourth*—money means all. *Fingers held apart*—too blunt, careless with money; *Together*—secretive; *Bent back*—talented but a spendthrift.

PHALANGES: Long first phalange—extra strong mentally; *second longest*—practicality, business trends; *third long or fat*—materialistic, sensual.

LEANING: All fingers leaning toward thumb—ambition uppermost; *Leaning toward little finger*—money most important.

PADS: Small pads on first phalanges—great sensitivity. Should be overcome.

Note any difference between left-hand and right-hand fingers.

THUMBS

(character index)
(check with illustration of mount areas and phalanges)

LENGTH OF THUMB—average must reach the middle of the lowest phalange section of the first finger. If in proportion to the hand, success and happiness will result from work and personal effort. *Short thumbs* reach below this mark and are called *small*. They predict greater effort and a need for co-operation from other people. Reaching beyond this mark they are called *long thumbs* and predict a strong mentality, good will power. All this, provided there are good lines to corroborate. In a bad hand with wavy or broken, badly marked lines, no good will ever materialize.

THUMB SHAPE (*types*) including tips and nails: *SQUARE*—practical worker; *CONIC*—amenable similar to hand type; *POINTED* —idealistic, may be too impulsive; *SPATULATE*—clever, talented, not strong on patience; *CLUBBED*—uncontrollable temper; *FLAT*—good manager; *PADDED*—sensitive.

FLEXIBILITY—stiff thumbs—stubborn, at least very determined; *PLIABLE*—reasonable, good mental balance; *BENT BACK*—adaptable, spender; *VERY SUPPLE*—talent should be developed. Will go to extremes. Reckless spender.

JOINT: KNOTTY JOINT—analytical; *SMOOTH*—impulsive; *PECULIARITIES—BROAD THUMBS*—temperamental, violent; *SLENDER*—considerate, patient; *WAISTED*—sympathetic, love for all creatures, good understanding.

PHALANGES—If first and second are equal—good mental balance; *If first is longer*—will power supersedes reason; *If second longer*—reason and logic are stronger.

THUMB ANGLE—Set close to the first finger—cautious; *SET VERY LOW*—impulsive, adaptable; *AVERAGE*—lies in between, on the lower half of the palm—balanced judgment.

Note any difference between thumbs.

AREAS OF THE MOUNTS
(check these qualities by the illustrations of mount areas)

The mounts are fleshy elevations on the palm. Hold the palm outstretched at eye level to ascertain which mounts are high or low. Compare both hands. Note which are more important. If the right hand does not show the mounts to be of equal appearance, the talents would not be fully developed. For left-handed people, the reverse is in order.

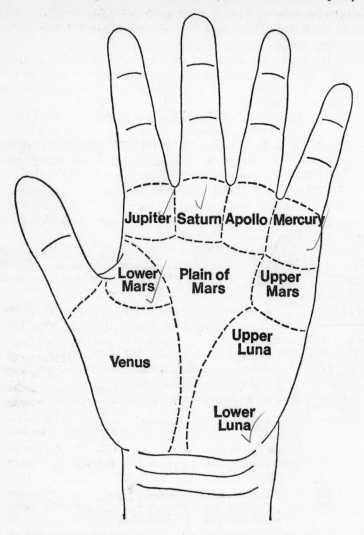

33) The areas of the mounts.

High mounts—the evaluation of the qualities becomes stronger.
Low mounts—evaluation weaker.
Absent—no evaluation.
Marked with small lines or signs—evaluate according to the signs and/or lines.

Two or more mounts, high—incorporate the strength or weakness of the two mounts and either increase or decrease the importance of the signs on those mounts.

MOUNT COMBINATIONS

Note the mounts that are most prominent, then combine their meanings. Weigh the importance of the fingers and thumb. Determine the type of the hand, then add the interpretation of the signs accordingly to form a fuller analysis of the palms.

THE MOUNTS OF THE PALM
(the areas of the palm)

The palm is divided into nine areas. They are the key to our natural abilities and emotional traits. Each area is called a mount, which sounds as though there is a point or hump in each section. This is not the case. It has been a traditional term to designate the different qualifications of each area. Naming them, in order around the palm, they are as follows: the mount (area) of Jupiter, under the first finger; Saturn, under the second finger; Apollo, under the third; Mercury, under the fourth; Upper Mars, under Mercury, on the percussion side of the palm; Luna, occupying the rest of the percussion side of the palm; Venus, between the root of the thumb to the encircling line called the line of life and extending from the wrist to about three fourths of the distance upward within the line of life; the rest of this area is called Lower Mars; the center of all these areas is called the Plain of Mars. The higher or the more space that is developed, the more important are the traits attributed to that area. They are a fleshy elevation filling the entire area, or they can be off center. Each location has a variation of the meaning of the area and its relation to the entire analysis of the palm. The Plain of Mars is the plain or hollow center of the palm.

If the mount area is so high or spread out that it appears to unbalance the rest of the palm, the qualities represented by that mount must be kept under control. Lacking height, look for the center or apex of the whorl formation. Overlapping mounts partake of both areas.

THE INTERPRETATION OF
THE MOUNT AREAS

MOUNT OF JUPITER

The mount area of Jupiter normally represents ambition and social prestige. If the development is closer to the side of the palm, family pride is the chief ambition; closer to the head line, leadership, a desire for authority. Here, arrogance would have to be subdued. Placed nearer Saturn, scholarly attributes. If the area is very high or large, conceit. Generally, idealism is the keynote for Jupiter. Fanaticism, exaggeration, and lack of dignity cannot be tolerated by a balanced Jupiterian (sometimes called Jovian). One vertical line—success. Two lines—more than one ambition. A cross—a happy marriage. A star—fame. Too many lines—too many interests. The grille—very unfavorable, the reverse of all the good qualities of Jupiter. Absence of the mount—superstitious, vain, boastful, lack of respect.

MOUNT OF SATURN

This mount area is seldom highly developed. Usually it partakes of either or both Jupiter and Apollo. Saturn in itself is the epitome of sobriety. Love of solitude, cautiousness, and mental reserve are characteristics. Developed close to the heart line—the qualities magnify. Toward Jupiter—very serious viewpoint about life. Toward Apollo—genuine interest in the arts; sentiment becomes important. Very active Saturnians, those with spatulate fingers, have ability for sturdy occupations such as mining or agriculture. Absence of the mount—indifference, periods of morbidness, often antisocial, a realist with little care for anyone. A single small vertical line—luck in spite of self. Two small lines—unusual success, a philosophical mind. Crossline—too much interference; Saturnian must have solitude. Delicate, fine lines—mental problems. A cross—suicidal tendencies, prone to accidents. A star—health problems. A square—danger from fire. A grille—unscrupulous, entanglements with the law.

MOUNT OF APOLLO

This mount area represents the talent for and appreciation of the arts. It stands for brilliance in achievement in any field of endeavor. Developed toward Saturn—a serious aspect is uppermost. Toward Mercury—a practical business mind is added to the talents; shrewdness in all deals. One vertical line—fame or fortune, perhaps both. Two lines—may

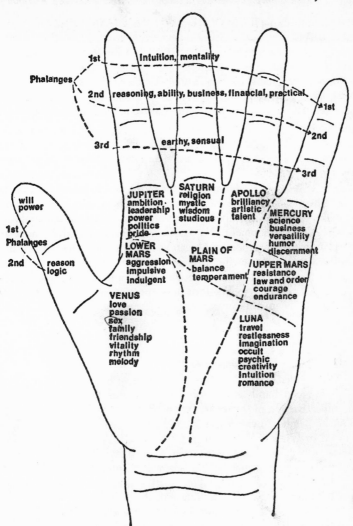

Phalanges

1st   Intuition, mentality

2nd   reasoning, ability, business, financial, practical

1st

3rd   earthy, sensual

2nd

3rd

will power

1st Phalanges

2nd   reason logic

JUPITER
ambition
leadership
power
politics
pride

SATURN
religion
mystic
wisdom
studious

APOLLO
brilliancy
artistic
talent

MERCURY
science
business
versatility
humor
discernment

LOWER MARS
aggression
impulsive
indulgent

PLAIN OF MARS
balance
temperament

UPPER MARS
resistance
law and order
courage
endurance

VENUS
love
passion
sex
family
friendship
vitality
rhythm
melody

LUNA
travel
restlessness
imagination
occult
psychic
creativity
intuition
romance

34) The areas of the mount and their qualities, and the phalanges of the fingers and thumb and their qualities.

have two good talents. Several lines, usually crossed by one or more lines but not a grille—too many talents, causing a diversion of interest. All Apollonians are versatile and enchanting. Overdeveloped mounts—

fantastic natures inclined to overrate their ability. Absence—nonintellectual, despise culture in every aspect, reckless, but sometimes one of this class has a tremendous acumen for high finance with great possibilities for success. A star promises great fortune. Cross—if no line of Apollo, poor judgment in speculation. A cross with the line of Apollo—success after long and arduous work. A circle—fame. A grille—exaggerated valuation of personal talent. Horizontal lines—many obstacles to overcome.

MOUNT OF MERCURY

The mount area of Mercury represents hope. Normally it adds gaiety and cheerfulness to the clear-thinking, practical, managerial faculties that make this area so important. Fortunately, many classes of people can have this development. Top-bracket business executives, men and women in every profession and business niche, the underrated but magnificently capable housewife, all must possess some degree of the qualities of the mount of Mercury, otherwise they could not be successful.

Developed toward Apollo—love and appreciation for everything artistic; love of beautiful surroundings. Toward the percussion—a touch of humor. Toward the base of the finger—business before pleasure. Toward Upper Mars—an indomitable spirit, willing to fight for a cause. Very dependable under stress. Absence of the mount—lacking all business ability; an utterly purposeless life.

Overdeveloped—swindlers and criminals may have this driving force, though in good hands it furnishes the stimulus for inventive minds. Also indicative of a high-pressure salesman.

The horizontal lines on this area are the marriage lines, which are discussed in Lines of Affection in Chapter XII. A single vertical line—promise of wealth, interest in scientific achievements. Two or three lines—varied interests that have a business possibility or that materially aid in the building of a career. Four vertical lines are called the medical stigmata. There may be a crossline with them. This is a very old term; nevertheless, many a nurse and doctor has these lines. More than four lines—very loquacious, also careless about money. A cross—a born diplomat, one who says the right thing at the right time; in a scheming hand—deceit. A grille—severe punishment or death due to malpractice or violation of the law. Square—great business foresight.

MOUNT OF LUNA

The mount area of Luna represents imagination, intuition, creative ability, and motivation. It is a large area so it must be examined carefully to determine the exact location of the apex or precise spot of development. Luna has varied physical forms. It can bulge in spots or all over. It can be thin and almost flat. There may be few lines or many. It may have the color of a lot of blood or a little. All of these things have a meaning. When developed toward Upper Mars—the practical dreamer able to apply imaginative ideas to everyday needs. If the entire percussion bulges—need for physical activity combined with some creative project. Near the wrist—sensuality, sometimes just imaginative. Toward Venus—romantic, emotional. Toward the Plain of Mars—aggressiveness to further one's ability. All of these types are intensified if the mount shows a reddish color. A bluish color—sadness, even melancholia enters the imagination, such as the gloomy poet or composer. Pale color—may possess any one of the qualifications for the specific type, but indifference would be evident unless pressure were exerted. Absence of any development—the poseur, the imitator, usually satisfied with their place in life, no matter what it happens to be

Lines on the area of Luna are very important because they are directional. Every talent will be corroborated on this area. Inventors, artists, writers, actors, musicians, builders, designers, in fact, every imaginative, creative talent is represented with a Lunarian mark or development. In excess, this talent becomes fanciful or foolish. If the imagination is too strong without a well-balanced intelligence, lunacy may result, or at least a very confused and erratic mind. The horizontal lines show many interests. Lines that extend to the areas of Jupiter, Saturn, Apollo, or Mercury automatically assume the names of those respective mounts and are explained under the major lines. The short lines starting on the percussion are lines of change often called travel lines, and are so interpreted as journeys. In a creative hand these lines can be considered as many interests. Slanting lines pertain to the same creative ideas.

Many fine lines—nervous tension.

Oblique lines—more important interests concerned with travel.

A cross—dreamy nature, superstitious, such as many theatrical people.

A large cross—wild imagination. A grille—inconstancy, fickleness, neurotic nature. Islands—fear and possible danger from water. Star—conflicting translations, i.e., meritorious achievement by risking life or fortune; serious accident or death on a perilous expedition. Triangle—unusual talents, brilliant success. Square—escape from dangers of water and sky.

MOUNT OF VENUS

The mount area of Venus represents love, sympathy, passion, and vitality. A well-centered, moderately cushioned area partakes of all qualities. The top section is the area of the mount of Lower Mars. A low, flat area—cool, calculating, dispassionate unless Lower Luna is very accentuated. In that case perverted ideas may rule the subject. If Venus is developed toward Lower Mars—antagonistic nature. Near the wrist—affectionate, sensual. Near Luna—self-indulgent. Near the thumb base —very emotional. Excessively cushioned—dynamic in love and friendship. If the area is hard, very muscular—resentful, will not tolerate interference.

Curved lines parallel to the line of life (not the line of Mars, which is described elsewhere in this book)—friends or relatives influential to happiness. Diagonal or horizontal lines that touch the life line—interferences. A grille—passionate nature. Many very small fine lines in crisscross effect—the constant worrier. A large cross—happy love and marriage.

MOUNT OF LOWER MARS

This area is really part of the Venus area since it lies within the line of life, filling the upper section of the enclosure. It is termed "lower" because it lies below the head line, as opposed to Upper Mars, which lies above the normal head line, on the percussion side of the palm. It represents the will to fight for a cause, for family, for country, or for personal reputation or aim. This can be mental activity or it can be physical, such as men in the armed forces. In a woman's hand it is aggressiveness for self and family. Overdeveloped—an abusive temperament. Hollow—fearful, reticent.

A star—death of a loved one. A grille—too sensitive. A square—quick thinker, very poised.

MOUNT OF UPPER MARS

This area, located between Mercury and Luna on the percussion side of the palm, represents endurance, bravery, fortitude, and resistance. This is a passive form as opposed to the activity of Lower Mars, but it takes both for balance. Higher or stronger toward Mercury—nothing can defeat this person in business or profession, very persistent. Toward the center of the palm, the Plain of Mars—guard against overaggressiveness. Toward Luna—takes advantage of imaginative inspirational qualities, such as an attorney who can sway a jury by his choice of words. Toward the percussion—physical reserve. Overdeveloped—cruelty. Absent—morbid, always on the defensive.

A single vertical line—bravery in face of death. Many parallel lines—brutality. A cross—quarrelsome. Short horizontal lines—obstacles or enemies. Long horizontal lines—lawsuits or participation in the legal profession. Triangle—honors in warfare. Circle—wounds.

LINES OF OPPOSITION

The lines on Upper Mars are also called the lines of opposition. They are the short horizontal lines that run straight across the area parallel to the line of heart. If any line is longer and reaches another area, it takes on the characteristics of the other area. If, for instance, one line curves up to the area of Apollo, it is then considered as a line of Apollo and its interpretation falls under that nomenclature in this book.

If a long line from Upper Mars touches a major line, the Mars line then becomes an influence line and registers as a hindrance or deterrent force against the major line. If it touches the line of Mercury, it threatens a health problem that would interfere with business. Cutting the Apollo line—financial problems connected with a profession.

THE PLAIN OF MARS

This is the area in the center of the palm. The two directive influences controlling it are Upper and Lower Mars. A high plain—good control of emotions, especially under argumentative or combat circumstances. A flat plain—great restraint as a result of a negative attitude toward everything. A hollow plain—fearful, nervous, need for co-operation from friends or family.

SIGNS AND SMALL MARKINGS

All signs have variations in shape and size. They may also be incomplete but must be interpreted in relation to their placement on mount areas or lines. Their basic interpretations are as follows:

BARS—opposition, hindrance that will be overcome.

CIRCLES—defects, sometimes physical except on the line and mount area of Apollo, where it predicts brilliant success through the subject's own talent.

CROSSES—obstacles, adverse prognostications. One exception is on the Jupiter area under the first finger, where the cross foretells happiness by marriage, love affair, or achievement. *BATTLE CROSS*—traditionally predicts war service. *MYSTIC CROSS*—dedication to cult, family, business, or whatever is expedient. Especial interest in the occult, psychic and mystic.

DOTS—physical or mental hindrances. Large dots—prolonged illness.

GRILLES—a mass of crossed or recrossed lines—adverse complications.

ISLANDS—show physical weakness that vary according to location.

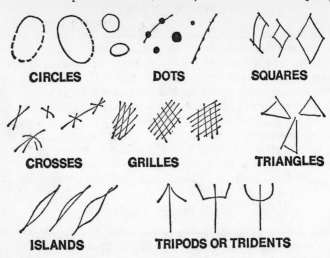

35) Signs and small markings of the palm.

MEDICAL STIGMATA—four or more vertical lines on the Mercury area under the little finger—scientific aptitude such as required in the professions of medicine, nursing, chemistry. Sometimes visible in the hands of talented comedians.

SQUARES—avert danger, shock, losses, illness *provided* the square surrounds or touches the particular threatening sign.

STARS—unlucky most everywhere except on the area of Apollo under the third finger, where it means fame almost because of luck. On the heel of the palm toward the outside—great imaginative ability applied to the arts or sciences, such as writers, teachers, logicians; on fingertips, too, stars are good luck; under first finger—honors.

TRIPOD or TRIDENT—a sign of luck and brilliant career.

TRIANGLES—are always lucky. Often indicative of very special ability. Quick perception, tremendous ingenuity.

THE LIFE LINE
Health, vigor, strength, longevity

STARTING POINTS, BEGINNING OF THE LIFE LINE

A—*Normal beginning,* joined to head line—a constructive planner,

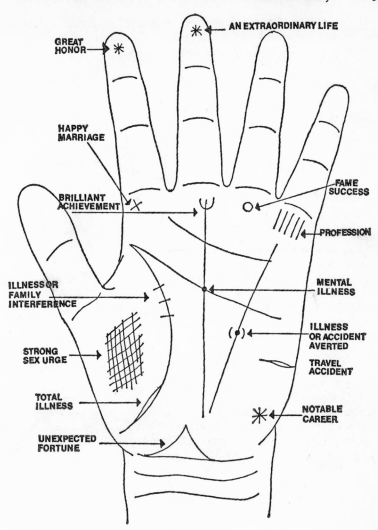

GREAT HONOR

AN EXTRAORDINARY LIFE

HAPPY MARRIAGE

BRILLIANT ACHIEVEMENT

FAME SUCCESS

PROFESSION

ILLNESS OR FAMILY INTERFERENCE

MENTAL ILLNESS

STRONG SEX URGE

ILLNESS OR ACCIDENT AVERTED

TOTAL ILLNESS

TRAVEL ACCIDENT

UNEXPECTED FORTUNE

NOTABLE CAREER

36) Random sign divination.

one who proceeds with cautious study. Joined to head line with netted lines—need to consider every step before acting on any venture. Joined solidly for a short distance—timidity especially during early years.

B—*Starting high under the first finger* (Jupiterian)—great ambition, lofty ideals, sometimes ruthless. Leadership.

C—*Separated from the head line*—impulsive, energetic, independent. Widely separated—reckless, too hasty in making decisions that culminate in faulty conclusions or disappointment.

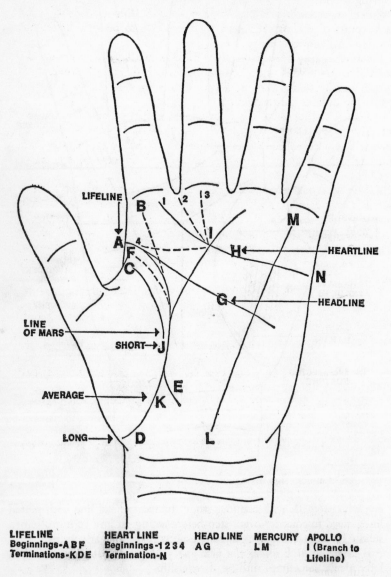

37) The life line.

Forked beginning—if, for example, the dotted lines of A and B are solid, this formation is called a fork indicating a gifted ability to help others. Good understanding such as in doctors, lawyers, benefactors, a loving parent.

Branches—ascending branches from the life line—periods of good luck, spurts of enthusiasm, often a change due to personal effort but possibly involving another person.

I—An ascending branch that cuts through the head line G and the heart line H—honors and good fortune for brilliant achievement. A branch ending under the first finger—tremendous desire for power or leadership in some particular way.

A branch ending under the second finger—often a desire for solitude, intensive study, or just unsocial if the head line is short or drooping toward the lower outside part of the palm. The owner of any such line formation usually needs the companionship or co-operation of another person to succeed.

A branch toward the little finger—professional or business success, but if it crosses solid lines of fate like Saturn or Apollo (lines from base of palm to second and third finger areas), there will be interference.

A branch to the lower base of the palm (Luna)—desire for travel, continuous change, or, in a neurotic hand, it refers to lasciviousness, alcoholism, dope addiction, or any relative forms of escape from reality.

A branch to the middle outside area of the palm (Upper Mars)—noticeable physical strength, sacrificial nature, devotion to service, family, and country.

TERMINATIONS OF THE LIFE LINE

A long line ending near the wrist (D)—vitality can extend well past age seventy if other main lines are clear and long.

A short line—lessening of physical reserve or a change, often a weak constitution.

Forked (E)—decrease of vitality.

Tasseled, ending with many little lines—complete dissipation of energy and vitality.

APPEARANCE OF THE LIFE LINE

Clear, solid, unbroken—good vitality.

Chained—uncertain physical weakness.

Broken—periods of health problems or a change.

Color and *Pale lines*—indecision, shyness; *Very dark*—forceful, revengeful, sometimes bad temper; *Blue*—health warning; *Black*—extremely forceful but often secretive.

Deep lines—intensive.
Wavy lines—Lack of decision, health problems.
Split line—illness; in both hands—illness or period of change.
Double life line—extraordinary physical resistance.
Triple life line—great ability, passion, lust, deceptive.

SIGNS AND SPECIAL MARKINGS ON THE LIFE LINE

Cross—illness or danger.
Grille or small mesh of lines—maladjustment.
Circle—brilliant home life or love life period will follow hardships.
Dot—temporary obstacle.
Island—serious physical weakness, illness.
Lines—horizontal short lines or bars—nervous strain.
Star—shock.
Triangle—fortunate period for love or marriage, eloquence.
Square—protection from a predicted danger, obstacle, or illness within or near the square.

THE HEAD LINE
Mentality, degree of intelligence, and application

STARTING POINT OF THE HEAD LINE

A—*Normal beginning, joined to the life line, just touching it and halfway between thumb and forefinger*—cautious. If the line is long—good mental power, very capable, sensitive under strain.

B—*Separated slightly from life line*—likes to think and act independently of others, spirited.

C—*Separated widely*—impatient, reckless, very independent.

D—*High, under first finger*—very ambitious, often egotistical, talented.

E—*Inside the life line*—irritable, easily worried by other people.

BRANCHES

D—*Ascending branches to Jupiter area under the first finger*—ambition that leads to success if applied.

J—*Strong branch to Saturn area under second finger*—intensive fervor toward serious study in a particular field such as religion, philosophy, or science.

G—*A branch to Apollo under third finger*—great chance for success.

H—*A branch to Mercury under fourth finger*—good sign of pros-

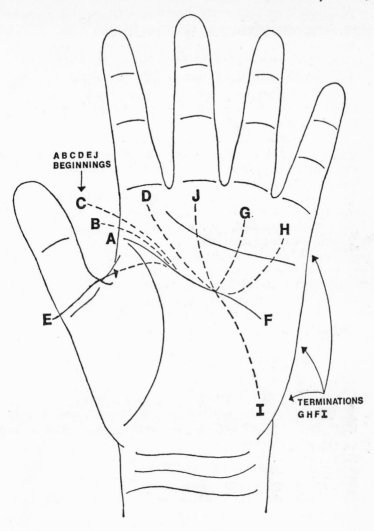

38) Head line.

perity, business acumen, or application to science, trade, or a profession.

I—*A branch to Luna, lower right area of the palm*—imagination in a creative hand; in a weak hand—mental or physical problems.

Many small branches—easily distracted, inclination toward nervousness, poor concentration.

TERMINATIONS OF THE HEAD LINE

F—A long line ending on the Mercury area below little finger—very good ability in management. Heart rules mentality.

About the middle of the palm—unusual memory in early years. Frivolous, desirous of wealth without effort.

Very short—little intelligence, irresponsible.

Long straight line extending to edge of palm—secretive, selfish, ambitious for self-aggrandizement. Very capable in your own field of endeavor or occupation.

Forked—imaginative, artful. The larger the fork the greater the desires for good or evil. Usually some degree of artistic ability.

Triple fork—a practical, brilliant mind.

Tasseled—confused mentality.

Head and heart line as one single line crossing the palm—the most cool and calculating mentality dedicated to self. Egotistical even if noncommunicative. This line is known as the simian line.

I—Dropping down on Luna area, lower heel edge of palm, as a solid line—imaginative, creative in a good palm; in a weak palm—aberrations.

APPEARANCE OF THE HEAD LINE

Clear, solid, unbroken—good mentality.

Chained—poor mental stability, uneven temperament.

Broken—periods of unhappiness due to health or occupation. Squares or small parallel lines beneath the breaks offer some security or modification of the problems.

Deep lines—intensity.

Wavy lines—unable to meet responsibilities.

Split line—period of mental depression.

Double head line—unexpected good luck, sometimes two interests.

Color—Red—aggressive, determined; very red—need control of temper.

SIGNS AND SPECIAL MARKINGS OF THE HEAD LINE

Islands—mental disorder or periods of ill luck.

Cross—disappointment or warning of an accident; will spurn advice.

Dots—warning of danger to health.

Star—warning of danger or shock.

Rebekah -N- David! ♡

Triangle—unusual intelligence.
Square—preservation or protection during a dangerous period.

THE HEART LINE
The emotional and physical strength dependent upon the heart itself

A—*Normal beginning of the heart line*—on the base of the first finger called the area of Jupiter, then dropping down and proceeding in a straight line to the end of the palm called the percussion (or batting edge of the hand)—clear and straight, it signifies steadfast love, devotion, and great affection, sympathy.

C—*From the middle of the Jupiter area*—emotions and sympathy may be given as a matter of sacrificial love.

D—*Starting between the first and second fingers*—a very practical form of love that combines sympathy with emotion, sensual, tolerant.

E—*Starting under the second finger, Saturn*—love rules by passion and sex alone; *closer to third finger*—lack of passion.

Forks at the beginning—partake of the areas they touch, such as leadership, home protection, and devotion or the vagaries of Saturn, melding wisdom with all the adversities of indiscretion.

Joined to the head line at the beginning—an envious disposition.

Joined to the head and life lines at the beginning—an unreasonable disposition that could end in disaster, very extreme, due for disappointments.

Close to head line—calculating, head rules heart.

Closer to fingers—emotional, affectionate.

BRANCHES

Small—fun loving, flirtatious. *Downward branches*—disappointment in love affairs.

TERMINATIONS OF THE HEART LINE

Normal line terminates at the percussion of the hand (B), good emotional balance if the line starts in the Jupiter area under first finger, loyal.

Curled up or backward under little finger area—complexity of love affairs involving money.

Forked end—marital status threatened.

Tasseled end—too many sexual alliances.

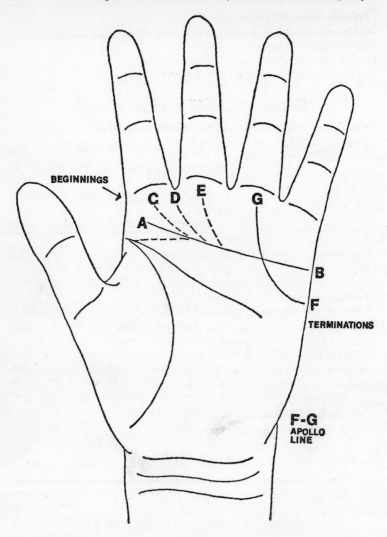

39) Heart line.

APPEARANCE OF THE HEART LINE

Clear, solid, unbroken—good physical and emotional constitution. Devoted, sympathetic, and loving nature.

Chained—fickle, unfaithful in love.
Broken—inconstant, subject to disappointment in love.
Wavy—indecisive in choice of love.
Double—a great love, all consuming.
Triple—irrational in affections, often very talented.

SIGNS AND SPECIAL MARKINGS

Cross—interference in love and marital affairs usually due to finances.
Circle—separation from a loved one.
Dots—obstacles with loved ones.
Island—misunderstanding leading toward separation. If there is an island on the life line, check with your physician.
Star—physical shock that can affect the emotional system.
Triangle—very lucky liaison in love or marriage.
Square—protection.

THE LINE OF SATURN
Commonly called the fate line.
It represents the pattern of living.

Absence of the line of Saturn does not mean failure or lack of success. It means that a pattern of living can be established by choice of the individual actually without the direction or help of anyone else. *Line of Sun or Mercury can act as a fate line.* Sometimes a Saturn line will appear in a palm after a career has been launched.

STARTING POINTS OF THE LINE OF SATURN

A—*Starting from the life line*—self-reliance in searching for a career. Moral support from family or friend is helpful but not necessary. Marriage is indicated at such a starting point—a career and success in itself.

B—*Beginning inside the life line*—the subject either receives or needs parental assistance or guidance by way of financial help toward an education or career in business or a profession.

C—*Starting from the base of the palm near the wrist lines*—a line of luck whereby the subject follows a pattern of living or career with little resistance or effort.

C+—*Starting on the lines of the wrist*—obstacles must be overcome before success can be achieved.

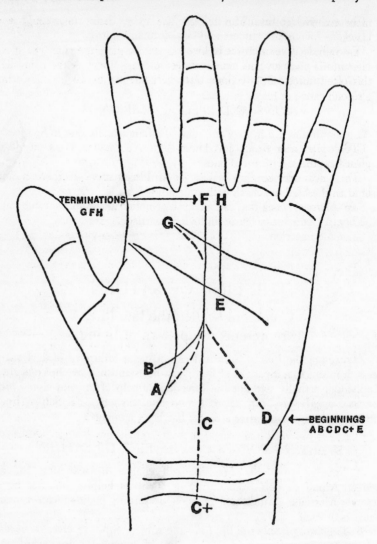

40) Line of Saturn.

D—*From Luna area, lower outside of palm*—imagination and restlessness play a strong part in the formation of the future of the subject. With a good head line and a prominent Luna area nothing will hinder the way to a desired goal for success. The lower the line, the more creative ability. The higher, the more desire to expand and travel.

E—*Starting from the head line*—a career or marriage can take place later in life and can have equal success and happiness. A short line like this often accompanies a long Saturn line right beside it, indicating a second career or major interest.

BRANCHES

To Jupiter area under first finger—family assistance, good marriage, great happiness.

To Apollo area under third finger—a second interest or occupation of artistic nature and commercially feasible.

To Mercury area under little finger—usually good communicative ability in a business or profession. Good sense of humor.

To the heart line—disappointment in either environment or love. Look for other associations.

To the head line—a dual interest or hobby, but put buisness first.

To the life line—need for a strong family alliance.

TERMINATIONS OF THE LINE OF SATURN

On Saturn area under second finger—always a need to understand human relations. Early responsibilities may continue many years.

For a man, success should be made through his own efforts. *For a woman*, this termination signifies a marital tie or a life of shelter or protection.

On Jupiter area under the first finger—ambitions that must be satisfied in a profession or business, security, and a good home.

Close to the head line—career or environment may change. Obstinacy must be avoided.

Close to or on the heart line—sometimes a new interest must be chosen to avoid emotional distress or jealousy.

Forked—more than one talent.

APPEARANCE OF THE SATURN LINE

Clear, solid, unbroken—excellent chances for success.

Chained—moody, often due to frustration.

Broken—periods of temporary change, uncertainty.

Color—Very dark—avoid outbursts of temper; *Dark and deep*—danger of overwork can end in nervous disability.

Wavy—need assistance to follow normal undertakings.

Frayed—nervous condition that can interfere with work.

Split—uncertainty about obligations.

Double—rare but important; duplicity in a bad palm; two interests in a good palm.

SIGNS AND SPECIAL MARKINGS
ON THE SATURN LINE

Cross—period of bad luck, financial problems.

Circle—a crisis.

Dot—a crisis involving health.

Island—career affected by a temporary misunderstanding, money troubles.

Lines, short cross lines—interference.

Star—unlucky time, physical hardship.

Triangle—trickery, occult involvement.

Squares—near or around a bad sign mean protection from harm.

THE LINE OF APOLLO
Line of luck, brilliance, success

This is a second fate line that follows the same interpretation as the line of Saturn except that the stress lies and depends directly upon talent and a brilliant personality. *Starting points* are identical to the line of Saturn. *One variation,* often seen in the palms of successful people, starts about halfway down the edge of the hand on the area of Upper Mars. Wealth and outstanding achievement are predicted on this line (see illustration of heart line. F-G is this Apollo line).

Termination of the Apollo line is under the third finger (Apollo mount area). *Ending at the heart line*—marriage may end the career of a woman. For a man, a change in career.

A cross line joining lines of Saturn and Apollo—partnership.

Branch touching heart line—love affair. *If it crosses the heart line*—a broken romance.

Star—brilliant success. Career depends upon particular talents.

Absence of the line—career must be charted by the subject alone.

THE LINE OF MERCURY

Also known as
Line of liver, health, hepatica.

Represents a third alternative fate line

STARTING POINTS OF THE LINE OF MERCURY

A—*From the wrist, above the wrist lines* (see illustration of the life line; L-M is the Mercury line)—this is the normal starting point. It signifies health and success if it is in good form. Independent by nature so tends to overdo work or pleasure resulting in physical depletion.

B—*From the life line*—ailments in the digestive system.

C—*From Luna*—restlessness. Desire for constant change. Good commercial enterprise.

Absence of Mercury line—lucky sign. Good appetites, usually a strong constitution. Should select a career without restrictions or defined channels dictated by other people. Excellent discernment. Usually good business acumen.

D—*From the middle of the palm*—a period to begin an interest in an enterprise.

E—Branches—*to Apollo area under third finger*—clever and talented.

F—*To Saturn area under second finger*—unusual philosophical trend applicable to daily work or business.

Many branches—too many interests.

TERMINATIONS OF THE MERCURY LINE

A long solid line ending under the little finger, Mercury area—want quick results and compensation in hard cash. Need to conserve physical energy (A-G).

Ending at the head line (H) or the heart line (I)—general activity may lessen or stop, depending upon health or occupation.

APPEARANCE OF THE MERCURY LINE

Clear, solid, unbroken—great urge for prosperity.

Chained—psychotic problems, depressive periods.

Broken—business may be good, but physical or psychic complications may concur to cause interrupted periods of losses. *Broken overlaps*—recuperation from losses. Check both hands. If the future hand shows improvement, follow; otherwise forget it.

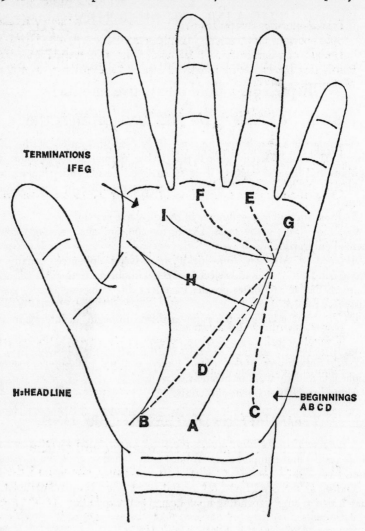

41) Line of Mercury.

Color, red or yellow—possible fever spells or bilious attacks.

Faint lines—little discernment.

Wavy—unpredictable, envious, unable to cope with business relations.

Frayed—nervous complications.

Split—obvious indecision and helplessness.

Double—the author herself has two, yes, three occupations with a fourth that has monetary compensation, so there is surety in a double Mercury line.

SIGNS AND SPECIAL MARKINGS ON THE MERCURY LINE

Breaks are like fragments of lines that mar the strength of the Mercury line. Parallel lines or squares are protective measures that save the subject from loss or embarrassment.

Cross—illness that may be checked by a similar line on the line of life.

Grille—always a complication of circumstances.

Circle—if an actual circle, consult a physician.

Dot—a temporary illness that also needs a physician's opinion.

Island—these are very serious signs and need the competence of a qualified physician.

Lines—horizontal short lines are hindrances of any number of physical reasons.

Star—extraordinary achievement.

Triangle, on the line of Mercury and on the area of Mercury under the little finger—great genius.

Square—always a protection against adverse circumstances.

THE CEPHALIC LINE
Also called the via lascivia, the milky line

The cephalic line is parallel to the Mercury line toward the percussion side of the palm. This line indicates a *physical reserve* that can act when the Mercury line shows a weakness. *When exactly parallel* it foretells a *craving for sensual pleasures* and *greed for wealth* (see illustration of the general lines of the palm).

Joined to life line—extraordinary interest in vice and immorality.

From Saturn (fate) line—two equal interests, talents, or occupations.

Branches, to Apollo area under third finger—wealth and luxury.

APPEARANCE OF THE CEPHALIC LINE

Wavy or curved toward edge of palm—excessive waste of money.

Broken—periods of loss or embarrassment.

Chained—unmoral.
Island—Illness.
Star—loss of wealth due to excessive living.

THE LINE OF INTUITION
Also called the line of Luna, line of the moon

The line of intuition is crescent-shaped (see illustration of the general lines of the palm) and indicates *psychic tendencies*.

STARTING POINT

On Luna area—near percussion following a crescent shape and terminating also near the percussion on Upper Mars or Mercury area under the little finger.

TERMINATION

On Upper Mars area—hypnotic powers. *On Mercury area under little finger*—good communicative psychic ability with possible commercial value.
Branches—restless nature.

APPEARANCE OF THE INTUITION LINE

Clear, solid, unbroken—talent for the occult: if in both palms—mediumistic ability. Definite presentiments.
Broken—nervous temperament bordering on the irrational, poor intuition.
Reversed crescent—wrong impressions.

SIGNS

Island—somnambulism.
Star—a dreamer with some rare psychic bent. Combined with a head line dropping down on the Luna area—various possible forms of insanity or mental unbalance.

THE LINE OF MARS

The line of Mars is parallel to the line of life, just inside it (see illustration of the general lines of the palm). It represents an extra gift of physical reserve.

APPEARANCE OF THE LINE OF MARS

Clear, solid, unbroken—great physical strength especially under stress or illness. Sometimes too aggressive.

Short, broken—periods of added vigor when needed; brave heart.

Very long line—very active life such as the police or military. Possible change of surroundings.

BRANCH

To Luna area—given to brutality; unusual appetite.

Star—little control of physical strength.

If the line is only in the left hand (subjective)—very imaginative. Sometimes psychic trends.

LINES OF INFLUENCE

Also called rays of influence

These are lines that fan out from the area within the life line (see illustration of the general lines of the palm). They cross the life line, ending in various parts of the palm. They indicate family or friends close to the subject.

TERMINATIONS OF THE INFLUENCE LINES

On the mount area of Jupiter under first finger—ambition reached through family or friends, for better or worse.

To affection lines on Mercury area under little finger—marital disappointment, separation, or divorce.

To the Saturn line under the second finger—love affair or marriage.

To the Apollo line—career dependent upon family or friends.

To the mount area of Luna—an escape line starting from within the life line to the area of Luna—a tremendous desire to escape from responsibilities or by some obsession that is overwhelming, no matter what.

SIGNS

Frays, signs, breaks—these are variations of the magnified probabilities involving any of the terrible but irresistible chances.

The escape line—established by the author in a previous publication, extends from the area of Venus to Luna. This is in reality a line of escape from problems pertaining to self or otherwise leading to drugs, perversion, or destruction.

LINES OF AFFECTION
Also called the lines of union or lines of marriage

Little short lines on the percussion side of the area of Mercury under the little finger refer to and indicate affairs of the heart, marriage, and the complications thereof (see illustration of the general lines of the palm). They are numerous, such as three or more. They imply a sexual relationship, consummated or not, but registered in the mind of the subject. *The longest line* usually represents the love most important to the subject regardless of law.

APPEARANCE OF THE LINES

Clear, long—happy marriage; confirm with a cross line on life line. *A longer line extending to area of Apollo under third finger*—brilliant marriage.

Broken—separation or more serious incompatibility. *If a line overlaps*—reconciliation may work.

Curved up at end—love, sex, no marriage in sight.

Curved down—disappointment in love affair, will end finally.

Forked at the percussion—separation desired by the subject.

Forked to the end of the line—the mate desires the separation.

Somewhere about this time these signs must be corroborated by signs on the life line to the fate lines by a break, cross, or cross line showing a change at the same time.

Line closest to the heart line—early love or marriage.

Line close to little finger—possible marriage late in life.

Absence of the affection lines—marriage can happen, though it may not be the ultimate event of the subject's life, so it might not register on the lines of the palm.

Two parallel lines close together on the percussion of Mercury area —the so-called mother-in-law line. Could also represent a sister or brother without interference in the family life.

SIGNS AND OTHER LINES

Island—always the unfaithful, intrigue; two or more islands—more affairs.

Star—hopelessly immoral.

Short vertical lines—predict children when the little line touches the horizontal line. *Dark lines*—boys; *light lines*—girls.

LINES OF OPPOSITION

These are horizontal lines on the area of the mount of Upper Mars on the percussion side of the palm (see illustration of the general lines of the palm). They refer to financial or personal complications that become a feud or a legal matter.

APPEARANCE OF THE LINES

Clear, long, extending to the Venus area within the life line—complications that revert to the family. Serious.

Short line—petty friction.

Extended line reaching to Apollo or Saturn line or mount area—serious problems dealing with law and justice. This can mean a wife married to an attorney or judge with whom she has no legal problem, but the actual relationship does exist and register in the subject's palm.

Cutting the heart line—sexual love will suffer.

Reaching to and curling back on the area of Apollo—a wonderful career in spite of marital alliance.

LINES OF TRAVEL

These are horizontal lines starting from the percussion edge toward the heel of the hand (see illustration of the general lines of the palm).

Slanting lines in this Luna area also signify a desire to travel; if deep and clear—travel in foreign countries.

Clear, solid lines are a prediction of a restless urge that will take the subject to other places.

Small crisscross lines will mar the possibilities. *Mal de mer* could enter into the probabilities and change plans.

Very long lines that proceed across the palm toward the fingers become fate lines and should be checked under the proper classification of fate lines, Saturn, Apollo, or Mercury.

SIGNS

Island—a warning of danger while traveling.

Star—it must touch one of these lines to predict misfortune, death.

Square—as always a protective measure against danger or ill-luck.

CREATIVITY

These are short horizontal lines starting from the percussion edge of the lower part of the heel of the hand (see illustration of the general lines of the palm). They predict creative talent such as that of writers, composers, inventors.

Slanting lines reaching upward and across this Luna area will increase the interest and strengthen the talent.

A star on this area promises success.

SPECIAL LINES

THUMB CHAIN

This is a chain formation that lies at the base of the thumb separating it from the Venus area (see illustration of the lines of the palm).

Clear, well defined—arguments will cause many misunderstandings.

Light tracing formation—diplomacy and gentleness will be the key to good understanding with family, friends, and associates.

THE RASCETTES

These are the lines that cross the wrist horizontally. Traditionally they predict the span of life. Usually three lines, each one signifying thirty years. *Chained formation*—a life of struggle. *A triangle in the middle*—unexpected wealth or gain (see illustration of the lines of the palm).

THE FAMILY LINES

These are lightly traced lines that parallel the line of Mars on the Venus area enclosed by the life line. The ones on the left hand will be relatives or immediate family who will help the subject. On the right hand (objective) the lines pertain to people who will form the nucleus of later years.

THE ESCAPE LINE

This line is not often registered on the palm, but it is very important. It is a line that starts on lower Venus area inside the life line crossing horizontally to the lower Luna area. It predicts the desire to escape from reality and responsibility so the subject will turn to drink, wandering, drugs, or vice.

THE GIRDLE OF VENUS

This line is a crescent (arc) that stretches from a point near or between the first and second fingers to another between the third and fourth (see illustration of the lines of the palm).

Clear, solid, unbroken—subject will be able to control sexual tendencies and devote self to artistic efforts.

Chained—unpredictable sexual actions.

Broken—sensuality will border on hysteria.

Pale—nervous spells will dominate.

Deep—cutting through fate lines, sex will tend to injure career.

Double lines—sexual tendencies will be difficult to control.

Triple lines—sex deviations will be main interest.

SIGNS

Cross—will help to lessen the problems.

Islands—physical abnormalities.

Star—extreme excesses will mar success and happiness.

THE RING OF SOLOMON

This is a curved line that starts near or between the first and second fingers, then curves down around the Jupiter area beneath the first finger to the side of the hand (see illustration of the lines of the palm).

Clear, solid—should take an active interest in the occult, psychic.

Broken, partial—anything mysterious will enhance and take hold. Many professional people have this partial formation, such as magicians, mystery writers, readers of the mystic.

THE RING OF SATURN

This is an arc like a ring at the base of the second finger (Saturn) (see illustration of the lines of the palm).

Clear, solid—changeable moods will hinder success or even happiness.

Broken—spasmodic moodiness will hinder ambition, if any.

Star—hatred and jealousy will lead to incarceration or confinement unless someone stronger willed can intervene.

THE QUADRANGLE

This is the distance between the heart and head lines, A, B, C, D, in the illustration. This foretells the power of the emotions versus mentality.

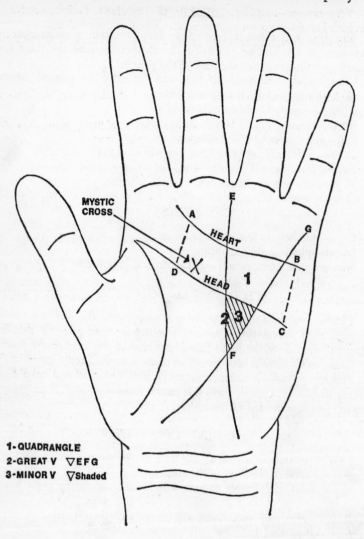

1 - QUADRANGLE
2 - GREAT V ▽EFG
3 - MINOR V ▽Shaded

42) The quadrangle.

Very wide space between—the subject will not have control of emotions, hence dominating and willful, very independent.

Average wide—broad-minded, tolerant, understanding.

Very narrow—mentality will rule the emotions. Selfish, fearful. If in both hands—exaggeration will cause difficulties. Penurious.

Normal—thoughtfulness and good judgment will turn to prosperity.

THE GREAT TRIANGLE

Basically formed by the life, head, and Mercury lines. E, F, G, in the illustration.

Plainly visible (one side is always open)—a lucky sign. A strong constitution and mentality will produce a good living.

THE MYSTIC CROSS

This is a cross often found within the area of the quadrangle. The mysterious and occult should be of great interest.

To form a complete, personalized divinatory reading, simply go through the following charts, checking each feature of the hands and palms as listed.

Then, by checking those against the traits and indications—as also given in the preceding pages—you can write down a running column of individual trends and prospects relating to the person whose hand is under analysis.

These, in turn, can be checked for highlights, particularly points of similarity, that corroborate one another, and any points of a conflicting or contradictory nature. These can be marked with a red pencil for one type, a blue for the other, thus giving an added dimension to the reading.

New charts can be prepared by copying or duplicating the original charts that follow, so that you can give special divinatory readings for anyone who is interested. From these draw your own conclusions where personal prognostications are concerned.

CHART FOR HAND ANALYSIS

Rule: Left hand predicts natural inclinations and abilities. Right hand indicates what has been achieved or changed. Take each category on the chart, refer to the text in the book. Decide which description applies to the hands you are analyzing, then put a check mark after each quality that you have selected. Upon completion of the chart you can make your analysis either orally or written.

Left-handed people must read the right hand first for abilities, the left for achievement or change.

THE HAND OVER-ALL

SHAPE OF THE HANDS. Square . . . conical . . . spatulate . . . pointed . . . philosophical . . . mixed . . . (page 272).

CONSISTENCY. Flabby . . . soft . . . firm . . . hard . . .

SIZE. Large . . . small . . . narrow . . . broad . . .

FLEXIBILITY. Stiff . . . medium flexible . . . very flexible . . .

NAILS. Short . . . wide . . . wide and short . . . narrow . . . fluted . . . ridged . . . bulbous . . . tilted outward . . .

Note any difference between left and right hands.

FINGERS

SHAPE OF THE FINGERS. Pointed . . . conic . . . square . . . spatulate mixed . . . (page 274).

LENGTH. Long . . . short . . . very long . . .

FLEXIBILITY. Stiff . . . pliable . . . very supple . . .

JOINTS. Knotted upper . . . knotted lower . . . smooth . . .

PECULIARITIES. Crooked . . . thick . . . first finger very long . . . second . . . third . . . fourth . . .

FINGERS HELD APART . . . *TOGETHER* . . .

THE LINES (abbreviations: L.H., left hand; R.H., right hand)

PHALANGES. Long first phalange . . . second . . . third, long or fat . . .

LEANING. Toward thumb . . . toward little finger . . .

PADS . . .

Note any difference between left and right hands.

THUMBS (page 274)

LENGTH. Average . . . short . . . long . . .

SHAPE. Square . . . conic . . . pointed . . . spatulate . . . also check next two qualities. Flat tip . . . pad . . .

FLEXIBILITY. Stiff . . . pliable . . . very pliable . . .

JOINT. Knotty . . . smooth . . .

PECULIARITIES. Broad . . . slender . . . waisted . . .

PHALANGES. First and second equal . . . first longer . . . second longer . . .

Compare both thumbs. Note any difference.

MOUNTS (areas)

Read carefully the information about mounts (page 275). Use the illustration of the AREAS OF THE MOUNTS (Diagram 33) to as-

certain the qualities of each. Decide which mounts are most important
in the hands you are analyzing, then list them separately under:
Left hand . . . .
Right hand . . . .
There should be at least three important mounts in each hand.

SIGNS ON THE MOUNT AREAS (page 283)

List the signs or special markings on each mount.
Left hand . . . .
Right hand . . . .

THE LINES (abbreviations: L.H., left hand; R.H., right hand)
LIFE LINE STARTING POINT—L.H. Normal . . . under first
finger . . . separated from head line . . . forked . . .
R.H. Normal . . . under first finger . . . separated from head line . . .
forked . . .
BRANCHES—L.H. Ascending through head and heart lines . . .
ending under second finger . . . ending under third finger . . . fourth
finger . . . ending on lower heel of the palm . . .
R.H. Ascending through head and heart lines . . . ending under second finger . . . third finger . . . fourth finger . . . ending on lower
heel of the palm . . .
TERMINATIONS—L.H. Ending near wrist . . . short line . . .
forked . . . tasseled . . .
R.H. Ending near wrist . . . short line . . . forked . . . tasseled . . .
APPEARANCE—L.H. Clear . . . chained . . . broken . . . deep
. . . wavy . . . split . . . double . . . triple . . .
R.H. Clear . . . chained . . . broken . . . deep . . . wavy . . . split
. . . double . . . triple . . .
SIGNS AND SPECIAL MARKINGS—Read the text and study
the illustrations of the signs. Look at the palms carefully to find ade-
quate signs that correspond. List them:
L.H. . . . .
R.H. . . . .
TIME—Study the illustration of time (page 271). Compare the lines
and signs on the palms to gauge the time of events and happenings.

Glossary of Methods of Divination

AEROMANCY: Divination from atmospheric conditions ranging from halos around the sun or moon to the unexpected appearance of heavenly bodies such as the comet of 44 B.C., which presaged the death of Julius Caesar, and that of A.D. 1066, which preceded the Norman Conquest of England. Mirages have also been responsible for omens of this type, as were the famous "Bowmen of Mons," huge spectral figures seen by British soldiers during World War I, which encouraged them to hold off the attacks of superior German forces, a phenomenon still not fully explained by natural means.

ALECTRYOMANCY or ALECTOROMANCY: See Chapter I.

ALEUROMANCY: Divination by predictions written on slips of paper and baked in cakes that are chosen at random by interested persons, like Chinese fortune cookies. This has also survived in the custom of baking a coin or ring in a large cake, which is then divided among guests, one of whom is lucky and finds the gift.

ALOMANCY or HALOMANCY: Use of salt in various divinations, probably dating from its ancient use as an offering to pagan gods, because of its scarcity and necessity. From that developed other rites in which salt played a significant part; hence any careless waste of such a precious substance was sure to rouse the wrath of the presiding deities This has survived in the modern superstition that spilling salt brings bad luck.

ALPHITOMANCY: Determining an accused person's innocence by having him swallow a piece of a specially baked barley loaf, with choking or other ill-effects marking him as guilty. In the year 1053, Earl Godwin of Wessex, England, collapsed while taking this test to support a false oath, and died a few days later. This case has frequently been cited as a strong argument in favor of alphitomancy as a divinatory process.

AMNIOMANCY: A term applied to traditional predictions made regarding a child that is born with a membranous caul over its head.

ANTHROPOMANCY: A form of divination used by ancient Egyptians and Greeks, involving human sacrifice and the dissection of bodies. It continued intermittently through the period of the Roman Empire and was probably revived by notorious practitioners of black arts during the Middle Ages.

ANTINOPOMANCY: Similar to anthropomancy but somewhat more gruesome, as children were among the principal victims.

APANTOMANCY: Divination from omens depending on observations of chance objects, meeting certain types of animals, or other unusual occurrences. In ancient times such events were frequently interpreted by oracles, and their importance persisted through the Middle Ages, even up to modern times. From them have stemmed countless superstitions that many people still believe may bring them good or bad luck, though the interpretations may vary in different localities.

ARITHMANCY or ARITHMOMANCY: Fortunetelling by numbers. See Chapter III.

ARMOMANCY: A long-forgotten mode of divining suitable candidates for sacrificial rites by inspecting them physically. Any modern survival of such practices is probably computerized rather than divinatory.

ASPIDOMANCY: A primitive form of divination in which an entranced sorcerer, seated in a magic circle, becomes inspired by the devil and upon awakening recounts the predictions revealed to him from that source.

ASTRAGALOMANCY or ASTRAGYROMANCY: Divination with dice, ranging from crude bones with primitive markings to cubes bearing spots, letters, or cabalistic symbols, all interpreted by the bone caster.

ASTROMANCY: The ancient forerunner of astrology, as developed in Babylon and later carried to Greece, ascribing heavenly thrones to gods as represented by the sun, moon, and planets. From their movements, wise men divined the purposes of such deities, taking into account the phases of the moon, eclipses, the proximity of planets to the brighter fixed stars, and other phenomena, including the positions of constellations other than those forming the signs of the zodiac. As examples, the new moon rising in a cloudy sky presaged victory in a coming battle, while, if it failed to rise at an anticipated time, it became an omen of defeat. With the advance of astrology as a science, the casting of horoscopes and other exact calculations supplanted the old traditions and astromancy dwindled in importance. Its systems are largely obsolete, but its lore has survived as modern superstitions, such as expecting bad luck if you look at the moon over your left shoulder, or making a quick wish when you see a shooting star.

AUSTROMANCY: Divining the future by a study of winds. Where weather forecasts are concerned, this is a solid science in its own right. As to foretelling the fate of individuals or nations, it is less certain but still worthy of consideration. Human affairs are often related to weather conditions.

AXINOMANCY: Primarily used as a mode of finding a guilty person, this consisted of heating an ax head, setting it upright, placing a marble on it, and turning it slowly until the marble rolled in someone's direction. Treasure can presumably be uncovered by the same procedure. Another way is to suspend a hand ax or hatchet from a string attached to its handle, start it twirling and see to whom it points when it stops. A third and perhaps the best method is to drive the ax blade into the top of a post and let it waver there, while a group dances around the post. When the ax finally falls, its handle is supposed to point to the culprit if he is still around. If he has gone, it will point to the direction that he took.

BELOMANCY: Dating from the time of ancient Babylon, this type of divination depended on tossing arrows to determine the direction a person was to take. Later, the arrows were handled like divining rods and the famous historian Herodotus (450 B.C.) tells how Scythian soothsayers spread bundles of such rods upon the ground and interpreted each in turn. In still another form of belomancy, arrows bearing various inscriptions were drawn at random, so their advice could be followed. In its simplest form, three arrows were used to answer any direct question; one for "Yes," another for "No," and the third a blank, which meant to mix them and try again.

BIBLIOMANCY: A traditional divination in which anyone can be his own consultant by simply opening a book at random, pointing to a paragraph, reading it, and following its advice by his own interpretation. Originally, religious books were used and still are, but later, consultants swung to the classics—Homer, Vergil, and eventually Shakespeare. In recent years, all inspirational books have filled the purpose, and now all sorts of publications may suggest the course to follow.

BOTANOMANCY: The ancient magi ascribed mystic properties to various plants and herbs, some of which were later used for purposes of divination. The practice of botanomancy, as this is termed, includes inscribing questions on branches of brier or vervain, which were burned with due ceremony so that answers could be revealed by the seer.

CAPNOMANCY: Early wise men, observing the smoke from sacrificial fires, noted that if it rose straight, clear weather was in order, hence they pronounced it as a good omen; while if it hung low, a storm threatened, so they called it a bad omen. Such was the origin of capnomancy, which up until modern times was still practiced by the European peasantry, who lighted bonfires on special occasions and let the direction of the smoke decide whether the harvests would be good or bad. The indoor version of this divinatory game was to throw various substances upon a hearth fire and study the resulting smoke or fumes, interpreting them according to stipulated rules.

CARTOMANCY: Divination by traditional tarots or modern playing cards. See Chapters VIII and X.

CATOPTROMANCY or CATOXTROMANCY: Divination with the aid of a magic mirror. This originated in Persia and spread throughout the ancient world. Two techniques were used: In one, the mirror was suspended in a pool of water; in the other, it was turned to catch the light of the moon. Either way, it showed mysterious reflections revealing future events. This practice increased through the years, reaching its peak during the Middle Ages with such remarkable results that it is highly probable that concave mirrors were used to reflect distorted images or other scenes. However, simple magic mirrors are still used, their surface being painted a glossy black, and some persons who gaze into their depths claim to see visions there.

CATTABOMANCY: Use of brazen vessels for special forms of divination.

CAUSIMOMANCY: A form of divination in which articles are thrown into a fire. If any fail to burn when they should, it is regarded as a good omen.

CEPHALOMANCY: A weird and long-obsolete rite of boiling a donkey's head for divinatory purposes.

CEROMANCY: A time-honored divination performed by melting pure wax in a brass bowl and pouring it slowly into another bowl filled with water, so that it forms various shapes, which are duly interpreted by the diviner. Special listings were made of those, so that ceromancy became a widespread art, which fortunately has survived in the form of tasseomancy, as described in Chapter V.

CHALCOMANCY: Divination by striking bowls of copper or brass. Such tones were given definite interpretations at the ancient Oracle of Dodona.

CHAOMANCY: A medley of ancient divinations based on atmospheric conditions in general, some of which survive as modern superstitions.

CHARTOMANCY: Divination by writing or interpreting inscriptions, sometimes of mysterious origin. Predictions written in invisible ink, which appears when papers are heated, come in this general category. So do greeting cards.

CHEIROMANCY or CHIROMANCY: Divination from the palm and hand. See Chapter XII.

CHRESMOMANCY: Divination from the utterances of a person in a frenzy. This dates back to the famous Greek Oracle of Delphi.

CHRYSTALLOMANCY or CRYSTALOMANCY: Generally known as "crystal gazing," this consists of divining future events by interpreting signs or scenes visualized in a crystal ball. Dating from remote antiquity, it is more popular than ever today and may be regarded as a higher development of catoptromancy, as visions from a crystal ball are often clearer and more realistic than those seen in a magic mirror.

CLEIDOMANCY or CLIDOMANCY: A very mysterious form of divination in which a key is suspended by a thread several inches in length, which in turn is wrapped about a person's finger, so that the dangling key can rotate, swing back and forth or become immobile. Upon questions being asked, mentally or verbally, the answers are interpreted according to the actions of the key. From this has developed a popular modern device termed the "exploratory pendulum," which consists of a ball hanging from a string, which should revolve for "Yes" and swing for "No"—or vice versa, according to tests with individual operators. The pendulum is also supposed to swing in the correct direction when looking for a lost article or missing person in the actual locality or when held above a map.

In earlier forms of cleidomancy, more elaborate measures were used, one favorite method being to open a Bible at a certain Psalm or at the first page of a specific gospel. A large key was inserted there, with its loop extending up from the pages, and the book was firmly tied with string to hold the key in place. The loop of the key is then hung upon the third finger of a girl's left hand and either she or a diviner recites scriptural quotations according to an established formula. In another variant, the key is held in place by two persons, each pressing a forefinger against an opposite edge. Either way, names of persons are finally called off, and if one happens to be guilty of some theft or other crime, the key is supposed to turn at mention of his name.

CLEROMANCY: An ancient mode of casting lots, with pebbles, beans, or other objects of different shapes, colors, or markings. As a variation, slips of paper were used, each bearing a different symbol, which persons picked at random for appropriate interpretation.

COSCINOMANCY: A forerunner of cleidomancy, in which a sieve or strainer is clipped between the spread blades of a pair of shears, or large scissors. The handles of the shears are then pressed in opposite directions by two different persons, using their respective thumbs or fingers until the sieve begins to turn. For sure results, the operator should pronounce the words *Dies, Mies, Jeschet, Benedoefet, Dowima, Enitemaus.* That will promptly bring a demon to his aid.

CRITHOMANCY or CRITOMANCY: Opinions vary regarding this mode of divination. All agree that it involves corn or other grain used in sacrificial rites, but the procedure may range from forming patterns with the kernels, or the flour ground from them, to a study of the dough used for baking cakes, or the actual cakes themselves.

CROMNIOMANCY: Onions figure in this long-range divinatory process. Names or other significant items are written on different onions, which are planted with due ceremony. Careful check is kept of each, and the first onion that sprouts will represent the person or thing chiefly concerned. A good way to predict next year's election or the winner of a pennant race.

CYCLOMANCY: Divination depending upon a revolving device. Dating from time immemorial, this has its modern counterparts in the "jury wheel," from which listed names are drawn to determine the members of a jury panel; and the so-called "wheel of fortune," seen at county fairs, which stops on prize-winning numbers. In both cases, the decision of the wheel is automatically fulfilled, so it is not surprising that many people believe that questions concerning their future can be answered by a similar contrivance. Spinning arrows may be used instead of revolving wheels for telling fortunes; and, on the lighter side, cyclomancy has survived in various parlor games, such as "spin the bottle."

DACTYLOMANCY: Broadly, this covers divinations utilizing finger rings, but that should exclude cases where such rings are used chiefly as adjuncts to some cabalistic ritual, as in necromancy. Greek and Roman rings supposedly produced divinatory results when inscribed with words suited to their times. By the Middle Ages, the names of the Three Wise Men—Caspar, Melchior, and Balthasar—were popular as inscriptions. Later, the custom was applied to wedding rings, which had the words "Love and Obey" engraved on the inside, but such a positive prediction could be nullified if the bride crossed her fingers. Gems, too, had power when set in rings, but they promised a vast variety of benefits, ranging from invisibility to immunity from snakebite, so only a few were specifically associated with divination.

Of those, the turquoise was outstanding, and a popular procedure was to attach a turquoise ring to a string and dangle it within a goblet, where it would begin to swing and tell the hour by clicking against the sides of the glass, or even spell out words, if letters of the alphabet were recited in order until the final clink. Since the diviner holds the string between his thumb and forefinger, this is practically a form of cleidomancy, with a ring being used instead of a key, hence almost any type of ring will do unless the diviner finds that it takes one set with a turquoise to put him in the proper mood. There was also an ancient form of dactylomancy practiced with rings composed of different metals, which were placed on certain fingers according to planetary conditions then prevailing; hence it might more properly be termed a form of astromancy.

DAPHNOMANCY: An ancient Greek divination in which questions of great moment were answered in varying degrees of "Yes" or "No" by throwing laurel leaves on a fire. The louder the leaves crackled, the better the omen; the more profound the silence, the worse. Since the laurel had to be plucked from a grove sacred to Apollo and tossed on an equally sacred fire, it is doubtful that the process would work now, even if it did back then.

DEMONOMANCY: Divination through questions put to demons and the answers that they give. To do this, demons must first be evoked. This should not be difficult, if we accept the figures of medieval authorities, who claimed that exactly 1,758,064,176 lesser devils are constantly at large and ready to appear in some strange shape or form at anyone's mere wish. The problem is how to recognize demons when they do appear; and even then, how to know if their answers are correct, as they delight in deceiving those who summon them.

EROMANCY: An Oriental form of divination in which a person covers his head with a cloth and mutters questions above a vase of water. Any stirring of the surface is regarded as a good omen.

FELIDOMANCY: Divination involving the behavior or actions of a cat, ranging from changes in weather to unexpected visitors, or other occurrences. Dating from the Middle Ages, many of these have survived as popular superstitions.

FLOROMANCY: Any interpretation of future prospects through the study of flowers or plants, including their colors, petals, time of planting, and where planted. Many omens concerning the gathering of flowers at Midsummer's Eve have survived to modern times; and the "good luck" commonly attributed to the finding of a four-leafed clover falls in this category.

GASTROMANCY: Purported divination through mysterious voices

that are actually produced by ventriloquism, as the term itself means "stomach speaker" indicating that such deception was recognized in ancient times. Presumably, the voices came from trees, rivers, deep in the ground, or wherever else the diviner pointed. Modern spirit mediums have improved on this by going into pretended trances or working in complete darkness to convey the impression that the voices come from another world.

GELOMANCY: Predictions gained by translating hysterical laughter into tangible terms. Probably a carry-over from the ancient oracles, where persons inhaled natural gas from volcanic fissures and babbled incoherent utterances which gifted listeners interpreted as prophecies that determined the fate of nations. A useful device for political conventions.

GEOMANCY: This runs the gamut from tracing mystic figures in the sand to throwing stones on the ground and studying the patterns that they form. Such figures have been classed as signs of the zodiac, with the stones representing positions of the planets, thus linking geomancy with astromancy, but those may be regarded as exceptional cases. Geomancy's contribution to divination is probably more random in nature, forming the basis of the mystic oracle. See Chapter II.

GYROMANCY: Originally performed by persons moving around a circle marked with letters or symbols, until they became dizzy and stumbled, thus spelling out words or enabling a diviner to intepret the symbols. From this, according to some authorities, developed wild, whirling dances by fanatics who uttered prophecies after collapsing in a state of complete exhaustion. Rolling down the side of a hill can produce a similar state of ecstasy for those who care to try it.

HIEROMANCY: Divination through various forms of sacrifice, or preparation for such, especially when performed by adepts in accordance with accepted rituals.

HIPPOMANCY: Observation of the gait of horses during ceremonial processions, as a means of divination. Now outmoded, but some modern prognosticators apply similar systems at race tracks.

HYDROMANCY: This relates to forms of divination with water, which naturally figures in other types of predictions involving various objects, which are therefore listed under separate heads. In some cases, however, water plays such an important part that they must be regarded as hydromancy despite the presence of those other factors.

One method is to study the depths of a placid pool, noting any images or symbols that appear therein, interpreting them as seems most fit. This is similar to using a magic mirror (as with catoptromancy) or gazing into a crystal ball (as with chrystallomancy) but on a large scale. However, if results are slow, another type of hydromancy may be used; that of dropping three stones into the pool and noting any figures or other effects caused by the ripples. For best results, the first stone should be round, the second triangular, the third square. Diviners who used this method generally referred to special lists that told the proper interpretations to be given to various types of ripples.

Another time-honored method was to invoke any evil spirit that dwelled in the neighborhood of a pool or stream. This demanded knowledge of cabalistic ceremonies, with all the danger accompanying such work, putting it into the realm of demonomancy. However, it still depended on hydromancy to a marked degree, since the demon's mode of answering questions was by inscribing words on the surface of the water. Often, these were visible to the seer alone, and they had to be read quickly while they lasted, as they were invariably written backward, to prove that they were the devil's work.

Methods of hydromancy that were both simpler and safer included casting offerings, such as bread, into a pool. If they remained there, it was a good omen; if they drifted ashore before they sank, it boded ill. This may account for the still popular custom of throwing coins into a fountain for good luck, as they are sure to sink and stay there. Where names of persons are involved, the old way of picking one through hydromancy was to write each name on a separate stone and toss them all in a pool. Later, the stones were fished out and if all the names were washed off, or nearly so, with the exception of one, that name represented the person to whom the question pertained. A modern combination of these methods, which is simpler, easier and more convenient, is the Floating Slip. See Chapter I.

ICHTHYOMANCY: Divination by the examination of fish offered for a sacrifice. This can be extended to include the actions of living fish, which have many traditional interpretations, some still popular with present-day fishermen.

IDOLOMANCY: Use of idols or images for purposes of divination. The answers may come through dreams, by drawing lots, or anything else that believers may attribute to the power of such images. Some ancient oracles belonged in this category, and pagan priests often spoke from within hollow statues to give direct replies to questions regarding the future. In many cases, idolomancy has been closely identified with demonomancy, in as much as the idols simply represent the demons who are supposed to inhabit them when properly invoked.

KLEIDOMANCY: The same as cleidomancy.

LAMPADOMANCY: Use of lighted lamps for divinatory purposes, according to the appearance or duration of their flames. The ancient Egyptians held a "Feast of Lamps," at which many rites were performed, including divination; and its modern counterpart in India is held in honor of the goddess of prosperity, Lakshmi, on the new moon of the month of Kartik, which begins about the middle of our October. During the Diwali, as this festival is termed, lighted lamps are set on floats that are sent downriver or out to sea; and the longer they remain alight, the better the omen.

LECANOMANCY: A method of recognizing good or bad omens by dropping various gems in water.

LIBANOMANCY or LIVANOMANCY: Forms of divination involving the burning of incense and the smoke arising from it.

LITHOMANCY: Divination by means of stones of unusual origin or appearance, such as meteorites, which inspire the diviner with visions, or issue sounds that he alone can hear and interpret as words. Foretelling the future by observing the colors of precious stones (as with lecanomancy) is often included under the general head of lithomancy.

LOGARITHMANCY: A mathematical method of divination performed with the aid of logarithms. Now supplanted by modern computers.

LYCHNOMANCY: Divination from the flames of three identical candles set in a triangle. These are lighted and their flames are interpreted as follows: If wavering back and forth, a change of circumstance. If twisting, spiral fashion, beware of secret plotters. Rising and falling flames, real danger. One flame brighter than the others, good fortune. A sputtering flame, disappointment soon due. A bright point at the tip of a wick, increasing success, but short-lived if the point fades. For a candle to extinguish itself, severe loss or tragedy for the consultant or others involved in that particular divination.

MACHAROMANCY: Use of swords, daggers, and knives as instruments of divination. Presumably of ancient origin.

MARGARITOMANCY: A singular procedure requiring a charmed pearl that is placed in a pot and covered with a lid. Names of persons suspected of theft or some other crime are then recited, and at the right name the pearl leaps up and strikes the pot lid. Choice of a pearl for this curious rite may stem from the fact that it is the only gem created by a living organism and might thereby become imbued with life as if to escape the oyster shell in which it was originally imprisoned. Whatever its origin, some form of deception must have been introduced to make it work.

METEOROMANCY: A special branch of astromancy dealing with omens that pertain to shooting stars. Ancient Roman augurs included thunder, lightning, eclipses, and other heavenly phenomena in such divinations.

METOPOMANCY: Predicting a person's future by certain lines on his forehead. A restricted phase of the broader subject of metoposcopy.

MOLYBDOMANCY: Dropping hot lead on a flat surface to divine the future by interpreting the shapes that result. Hot lead may also be dropped in water and conclusions drawn from the hissing sounds.

MYOMANCY: An ancient form of divination based upon the activities or sudden appearance of rats or mice, as well as the sounds they made. All sorts of prognostications could be made, ranging from wars to famine and pestilence, by comparing various occasions involving the behavior of such rodents. Many omens resulted regarding rats and mice, persisting through the centuries and forming the basis for various modern superstitions.

NECROMANCY: The raising of the spirits of the dead for divinatory purposes. The biblical account of the Witch of Endor is a good example of its practice in ancient times, and it rose to formidable proportions during the Middle Ages, including all forms of divination along with sorcery and witchcraft under the general head of Black Art. Today, however, the term is applied chiefly in its original sense.

NEPHELOMANCY: A study of the clouds and their various formations, as a means of divining future events.

OCULOMANCY: Divination dependent upon a study of a person's eyes. Akin to hypnotism in a primitive form.

OINOMANCY: The art of divination through a study of wines, including their color, their appearance, and their taste. This dates from ancient Greece and Rome, when wine was poured as a libation to the gods, in hope that they would ensure a prosperous future. Drinking to someone's health is a modern survival of such customs.

OMPHALOMANCY: Contemplation of one's own navel as a mystical procedure that promises divinatory results. Often recommended in connection with yoga exercises.

ONEIROMANCY or ONIROMANCY: The interpretation of dreams to divine the future. A vast subject in itself, ranging from consulting the time-honored references found in various "dream dictionaries" to the modern symbolism endorsed by psychoanalysts. One special phase is that of "dreaming true," in which coming events unfold in the dreamer's mind with such exactitude that the dream can later be corroborated by an actual occurrence.

ONOMANCY or ONOMATOMANCY: Use of names and the letters composing them to divine the future of persons, places, or things. Sometimes the naming of a person or place has been prophetic in itself, and from that has stemmed the practice of giving children impressive or significant names in hope that they will live up to them. Naming a child after a wealthy relative is a still better way of forecasting a prosperous future; one that may really pay off.

ONYCHOMANCY: Divination by studying the reflection of bright sunlight upon a person's fingernails and noting any symbols—real or imaginary—that may appear there. These are interpreted in accordance with established rules, as with crystal gazing or teacup reading.

ONYOMANCY: A specialized phase of onychomancy whereby a person's future is gauged by the appearance of the fingernails themselves. This has become a part of cheiromancy and is detailed under that head.

OOMANCY or OVOMANCY: Methods of divination utilizing eggs, some dating back to antiquity. One modern survival consists of dropping whites of eggs in water and noting the shapes or markings thus obtained. The custom of coloring eggs, so popular today, also stems from ancient traditions.

OPHIOMANCY: Recognition of serpents as agents in divination. Dating from the Garden of Eden, this was found in Egypt, Greece, Rome, and among the Aztecs of Mexico.

ORNITHOMANCY: Pertaining strictly to birds, this form of divination depended on their flight, songs, and feeding habits. It was practiced extensively in ancient Rome, one theory being that the birds, being high in the heavens, might be aware of the intentions of the gods who dwelled there, and even act as their messengers. The fact that changes in weather and seasons could also be foretold by watching birds caused them to be credited with divinatory powers of their own.

PEGOMANCY: A form of hydromancy, or divination by water, applicable chiefly to springs and fountains. A change in color could be an omen, such as a spring turning reddish to symbolize the approach of war. Shapes formed by the swirl of a spring or the play of a fountain were also given appropriate interpretations.

PESSOMANCY or PSEPHOMANCY: Use of pebbles in divination, one ancient form being to draw different types from a large heap. The same system can be used with colored marbles, giving each type a special intepretation and drawing one from a bag.

PHYLLORHODOMANCY: Clapping rose leaves against the side of the hand and noting the sounds that they make. This trifling pastime was used for divination by the ancient Greeks.

PODOMANCY: Study of the feet as a form of divination. This applies specifically to the soles, which can be interpreted in terms of lines and mounts, exactly as in cheiromancy or palmistry, but to a greatly limited degree. This mode of divination is of great antiquity in the Orient, particularly among the Chinese.

PSYCHOMANCY: Here, divination depends upon human reactions or emotions and therefore covers a wide range. Broadly, it can be defined as "psychic perception" attained through the astral counterparts of the five physical senses, thus including such factors as clairvoyance, precognition, automatic writing, and coherent messages obtained from an Ouija Board. Since these are often mistaken for spirit communications, psychomancy is sometimes linked with necromancy, or the evoking of the dead.

PYROMANCY: This covers a wide range of fire omens. If a sacrificial fire kindled slowly or uncertainly, the prospect was bad indeed. If smoky or crackly, it still augured ill. A bright, strong flame, growing rapidly and evenly, was the best of signs. With ordinary fires, omens were obtained by throwing substances such as powdered peas or pitch upon the flames; the more rapidly these were consumed, the better. In northern climes, where winter nights were long, these traditions carried on through the Middle Ages and were common to every hearth and home. Sudden sparks from knotty logs, colored flames from burning driftwood, curious shapes caused by flames or smoke, all were accepted as omens, good or bad.

RHABDOMANCY: Use of a wand is found in the earliest forms of magical ritual, hence it not only became an important adjunct in many types of divination, but served that purpose in its own right. Held in the hand of a true mystic, a wand might dip in the manner of an arrow, or turn in the fashion of a wheel, hence its use as a final convincer increased with the years. From this developed the divinatory process of rhabdomancy, utilizing a forked stick, held by the Y-shaped branches, one in each hand, so the stem could serve as a pointer in uncovering hidden treasure, lost objects, or missing persons. The tendency of the rod to dip made it especially popular in locating mines or other minerals, but its use in that field gradually waned. Instead, the forked rod became the property of modern dowsers, a group of hardheaded, down-to-earth practitioners who use it chiefly to find springs or underground streams. However, their efforts are not confined to "water witching," as critics of the process still term it. Some of the older claims have been revived and demonstrated with sufficient success to gain the art a degree of scientific notice under the head of radiesthesia, which is being studied as a form of ESP, thus supplanting much of the superstition that was found in old-time rhabdomancy.

RHAPSODOMANCY: A form of bibliomancy in which books of poetry are used instead of sacred writings or classical works. The consultant opens the book at random and divines the future from the first verse that catches his eye.

SCAPULOMANCY or SPEALOMANCY: Divination from the markings on the shoulder bone of an animal, particularly a sheep.

SCARPOMANCY: A modern method of reading character from a study of a person's old shoes.

SCIOMANCY: Primitive lore abounds with omens pertaining to shadows, their size, shape, and changing appearance. It was believed that danger or death could follow an attack on a person's shadow, which was often identified with the soul. From this developed sciomancy, or the art of divination through shadows, which could supposedly be called back from the dead and questioned as to future events. This represented an early form of necromancy.

SCYPHOMANCY: Dating from ancient Egypt, drinking cups were used in divination, the early form being to fill the cup to the brim, pour out a libation to the god invoked, and look for the answer in the cup. Later methods consisted of dropping small particles of tinsel in a cup of water and noting the shapes they took, this being an early mode of modern teacup reading.

SELENOMANCY: A specialized form of divination involving the various aspects, phases, and appearances of the moon.

SIDEROMANCY: An old rite of dropping straws upon red-hot iron and divining the future by studying the peculiar shapes they take.

SPLANCHOMANCY: A form of anthropomancy practiced by the ancient Etruscans, involving predictions gained from a study of the entrails of sacrificial victims.

SPODOMANCY: An ancient mode of divination through an examination of ashes, particularly those remaining from a sacrificial fire.

STAREOMANCY: A somewhat general term, covering divinations by the ancient elements of fire, earth, air, and water.

STICHOMANCY or STOICHOMANCY: Another form of bibliomancy, utilizing a random passage from a book for divining the future.

SYCHOMANCY: This consisted of writing names or messages on leaves of a fig tree and letting them dry out. If they dried slowly, it would bode well for whoever or whatever was mentioned; if rapidly, a bad omen. This ancient form of augury can be tested with leaves from sycamores or other trees. There is a modern version involving ivy leaves, which are placed in water for five days and then examined. If still fresh and green, good health should attend the person named thereon, but a spotted, darkened leaf denotes illness or misfortune in proportion to the number of such sinister marks.

TASSEOMANCY: Divination by tea leaves or coffee grounds. See Chapter V.

TEPHRAMANCY or TEPHROMANCY: Akin to spodomancy, this is another mode of divination from the ashes of a sacrificial fire.

THEOMANCY: Divination through direct appeal, usually with special formula, to oracles that were supposed to be divinely inspired.

THERIOMANCY: Assorted omens drawn from the actions or appearance of various beasts. Such sayings as, "A barking dog never bites" might be traced back to that source.

TIROMANCY or TYROMANCY: A curious form of divination based upon observation of the coagulation of cheese and its results.

TRANSATAUMANCY: Divination based on something seen or heard accidentally. Even trifling mistakes were accepted as omens by the ancient Romans, and even today many people are apt to attribute their good fortune to chance occurrence or coincidence.

XYLOMANCY: Interpreting the forms or appearance of fallen tree branches or other wood seen on the ground; also the positions of logs burning in a fire. If one falls suddenly, a surprise is due.

ZOOMANCY: Portents involving imaginary animals that people claim to have seen, such as a salamander, resembling a lizard, sporting in a fire; or a sea serpent riding the ocean waves.

INDEX